1492

Ojibwe

Potawatomi

Iroquois

Wampanoag

Delaware

Powhatan

Shawnee

Cherokee

Chickasaw

Muskogee

Our Star-Spangled Story
Curriculum Package

Designed for children in grades 1-4, *Our Star-Spangled Story* is a one year U.S. history course. It features simple lessons with easy-to-follow instructions, full-color photographs and illustrations, and engaging supplemental activities. The full curriculum package includes:

- *Our Star-Spangled Story Part 1*
- *Our Star-Spangled Story Part 2*
- *Star-Spangled Rhythms and Rhymes*
- *A Star-Spangled Timeline*
- *My Star-Spangled Student Workbook*
- *Our Star-Spangled Story Answer Key and Literature Guide*

Our Star-Spangled Story has a total of ninety lessons for use over one school year (thirty units of three lessons each). All of the instructions for how to use the material are included in Part 1 and Part 2, so you do not need a separate teacher's manual. The daily instructions are easy to follow. *My Star-Spangled Student Workbook* is the only consumable book. You may purchase additional copies if you have more than one child using the curriculum.

We recommend eight works of literature to read along with the lessons in *Our Star-Spangled Story*. Each book gives your child a richer perspective on a certain time period. The student has three to five weeks to read each book. The first four books go with Part 1, and the next four books go with Part 2.

For more information, visit notgrass.com or call 1-800-211-8793.

Our Star-Spangled Story
Part 1

We dedicate *Our Star-Spangled Story* to our husband and father, Ray Notgrass. He is the walking family encyclopedia for history and just about everything else. He loves his country and helps his fellow Americans live well and to the glory of God. He read us books and told us stories and inspired our whole family to love history. We love you.

Charlene, Bethany, and Mary Evelyn

Our Star-Spangled Story Part 1
Charlene Notgrass, Bethany Poore, and Mary Evelyn McCurdy

ISBN 978-1-60999-124-1

Cover Photo Credits: Field: ArtMari / Shutterstock.com; People (left to right): William Ladd Taylor / Library of Congress; Frederick W. Greenough / Library of Congress; John George Brown / Library of Congress; Edwin Forbes / Library of Congress; Bowdoin College Museum of Art
Authors Photo: Gregory Poore

Previous Page: Portrait of Edith Wharton by Edward Harrison May (American, 1869)

Unless otherwise noted, Scripture quotations taken from the
New American Standard Bible, Copyright © 1960, 1962, 1963, 1971, 1972, 1973, 1975, 1977, 1995 by the Lockman Foundation. Used by permission.

Cover design by Mary Evelyn McCurdy.
Interior design by Charlene Notgrass and Mary Evelyn McCurdy.

Printed in the United States of America.

Notgrass History • 975 Roaring River Road • Gainesboro, TN 38562
1-800-211-8793 • notgrass.com

Table of Contents for Part 1

Acoma girls collecting water, New Mexico

i

Gateway to Freedom International Memorial to the Underground Railroad, Detroit, Michigan

Sod House in Custer County, Nebraska, 1886

Dear Student

Welcome to *Our Star-Spangled Story*. American history is not something sitting closed up in a box or in a book, far away and long ago. American history is a story, and you're in it! God is writing history every single day. He made you to be a part of it.

People have done a lot of living in this place called America:

- People built houses and planted crops.
- People explored places that weren't on any map.
- People sacrificed for what they believed to be right.
- People worshipped God and shared Jesus with others who didn't know Him.
- People enjoyed happy dinners around their kitchen tables with their families.
- People gathered for celebrations.
- People comforted each other when they lost someone they loved.
- People moved to new places to find better homes for their families.

American history is a big story of people living their lives, facing problems, finding solutions, and working hard. American history is a lot of little stories, funny stories, scary stories, stories of singing and dancing, stories of disagreement, and stories of working together.

American history is about people. We hope you enjoy meeting people from American history in this book. We hope you learn from their stories. We still have a great deal of work to do in our country: victories to celebrate, problems to overcome, people to help, and faith to share. We pray you will bring glory to God in your own part of the story of American history.

Charlene Notgrass, Bethany Poore, and Mary Evelyn McCurdy

Dear Parent

Thank you for choosing *Our Star-Spangled Story* to help you explore American history with your child!

We present this curriculum to honor the Lord and His work in history. We are privileged to have the opportunity to show your family what American history is really about: people living their lives here in this place we call America. We pray your family will grow and learn through the journey we present in these pages. We hope you make memories as you read, discover, create, sing, laugh, dance, and connect with each other.

We at Notgrass History believe that you are in charge of your child's education. You know the needs, abilities, strengths, weaknesses, and interests of your own child. You also know the bigger picture of the needs and commitments of your family.

We design our curriculum to be a tool to make learning rich, meaningful, simple, and fun. Curriculum should not be a burdensome taskmaster. The next few pages will give you some suggestions, but you get to decide how to use this curriculum in a way that works best for your family!

Don't worry about dates and details. Don't worry about making sure you remember everything. Unlock a creaky old door, step into the past, meet people just like your family, and hear what they have to say. Enjoy the journey of a rich story that you and your family are part of writing every day.

Charlene Notgrass, Bethany Poore, and Mary Evelyn McCurdy

How to Use
Our Star-Spangled Story

Our Star-Spangled Story is a one-year American history course designed for students in grades one through four. The curriculum has thirty chronological units of three lessons each. We recommend completing one unit most weeks. If your school year has thirty-six weeks, this allows you six weeks of flexibility.

In addition to history, this curriculum incorporates literature, music, creative writing, geography, and art. It also brings up many concepts that you can use for conversation to deepen your child's Christian worldview. Each lesson ends with a Bible verse.

We wrote the lessons in a narrative style and richly illustrated them with color photographs and maps. We designed every part of the curriculum to help your student connect with history in a personal way. Part 1 and Part 2, the main lesson texts, include all of the instructions for what to do each week and each day.

How to Use *Our Star-Spangled Story Part 1 and Part 2*

Part 1 is the lesson book for the first semester. It has forty-five lessons that cover life in America from before Europeans came through the late 1800s. Part 2, for the second semester, has forty-five lessons that cover from the late 1800s through modern times.

Parents can read lessons aloud or students can read lessons by themselves. We encourage you to enjoy looking closely at the photos and illustrations. Talking about them is a great way to learn.

At the end of each lesson is a blue box with activity ideas. Don't look at these as a checklist that you must complete. Look at these as ideas to choose from to enhance your study. Let your student's grade, age, abilities, needs, and interests be your guide as you select activities. The activities should challenge your student, but he or she should also feel competent and successful.

The Lesson Activities at the end of each lesson include some or all of the following:

- Instructions for what to do with *Star-Spangled Rhythms and Rhymes, A Star-Spangled Timeline, My Star-Spangled Student Workbook,* and the literature.

- Many locations mentioned in the lessons are shown on the "All Around the USA Map" at the back of the book. We note these so that you and your student can find them on the map if you wish.

- Three review questions highlight key facts and concepts from the lesson and help your student think critically about what he or she learned. We recommend using these as oral discussion questions. You may also occasionally want your student to answer the questions in writing.

- The Hands-On History Ideas provide inspiration for pretending, playing, and building. Don't view these as assignments, but as ideas and encouragement for your child to have fun, use his or her imagination, and be creative. We also include one project for each unit. We discuss these below.

Unit Projects

Each unit includes a project idea connected with one of the lessons. Projects include arts and crafts, recipes, and games. You will find the instructions on the last page or pages of each unit. We recommend reading the instructions and gathering the supplies early each week. You can complete the project on the day it is assigned or on another day that is convenient. You might also wish to make the project an activity for your entire family to enjoy together.

Parental Supervision Required

Please review each project and discuss with your child what he or she may do alone and what he or she needs your supervision to do. The projects include the use of scissors, the oven, and the stove. Some children may be allergic to recipe ingredients or craft supplies. Notgrass History cannot accept responsibility for the safety of your child in completing these activities. Thank you for being a conscientious parent who takes responsibility for your child's safety.

Like all components of *Our Star-Spangled Story*, the unit projects are optional. We offer them as extra learning experiences. You, the parent, are the best one to decide if you are able to schedule time to complete them.

How to Use *Star-Spangled Rhythms and Rhymes*

Star-Spangled Rhythms and Rhymes is a collection of 60 songs, poems, and dances enjoyed throughout American history. The book includes an MP3 CD of all the selections. Each selection goes along with a particular lesson in the curriculum. The Lesson Activities at the end of two lessons in each unit will guide you to the appropriate selection.

How to Use *A Star-Spangled Timeline*

A Star-Spangled Timeline provides an easy way to review material in the lessons. Students can get a better sense of what was happening during each particular era. At the end of each unit, we tell you what pages to look at in the timeline.

How to Use *My Star-Spangled Student Workbook*

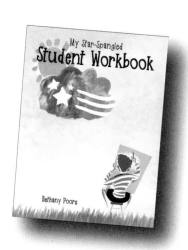

My Star-Spangled Student Workbook has one activity page for each lesson. Each week, students have a coloring page, a drawing or writing activity, and a unit review.

Coloring: Our favorite medium for coloring is quality colored pencils such as Prismacolor®. These provide rich color and the ability to color in detail.

Drawing or Writing: We suggest that you have your student complete a combination of drawing and writing activities throughout the curriculum. The grade, age, ability, and interests of your child should determine whether he or she does more drawing or more writing and the level of work you expect.

For example, a fourth grader should generally write a longer composition than a first grader. A first grader might not include as much detail in a drawing as a fourth grader.

As the parent and teacher, you know if your student is learning, making personal connections with history, and meeting appropriate challenges. We suggest that you have your student talk about their drawings and writing. This is a great opportunity to discuss your student's thoughts on what he or she is learning. You may wish to address any grammatical or spelling corrections.

Unit Review: The Unit Review page always follows the final lesson of the unit. These are intended to be a simple review of the key points covered in the unit. It is not necessary to test your student over *Our Star-Spangled Story*, but if you feel your student would benefit from testing, you can use the Unit Review as a weekly test. If you feel your student needs more challenging assessment, you can use the review questions included with each lesson as an oral quiz.

My Star-Spangled Student Workbook is the only consumable book in this curriculum. If you are using the curriculum with more than one child, you can purchase additional copies of the *Student Workbook*.

How to Use *Our Star-Spangled Story Answer Key and Literature Guide*

This booklet for parents contains answers for the lesson review questions in the text and for the *Student Workbook* activities. It also includes a guide and discussion questions for the literature titles.

How to Use the Literature

We chose eight literature titles to complement the lessons in *Our Star-Spangled Story*. All of the titles are in print and available from Notgrass History and other sources.

You can read them aloud with your student, which is a fun and memorable way to spend time together. You can have your child read the books on his or her own. Or you might do a combination depending on what else you are doing as a family.

We give you three to five weeks in which to read each book. Each book coincides with the historical context of the lessons you study during that period. You may wish to read them slowly, one chapter each day. Or your student may like to read an entire book in one sitting! If reading the literature adds too much pressure to your homeschool schedule, feel free to skip some or all of them. Each book adds a rich perspective to a certain period in American history, but you don't have to read the literature to understand the lessons.

These are the literature titles we recommend:

- *Benjamin West and His Cat Grimalkin* by Marguerite Henry (Units 1-4)
- *Toliver's Secret* by Esther Wood Brady (Units 5-9)
- *Freedom Crossing* by Margaret Goff Clark (Units 10-12)
- *Farmer Boy* by Laura Ingalls Wilder (Units 13-15)
- *Mountain Born* by Elizabeth Yates (Units 16-18)
- *Emily's Runaway Imagination* by Beverly Cleary (Units 19-22)
- *The Year of Miss Agnes* by Kirkpatrick Hill (Units 23-26)
- *Katy* by Mary Evelyn Notgrass (Units 27-30)

We chose these books with careful consideration. Some of the books have minor elements or dialogue that we want you to be aware of in advance. You can find our notes in *Our Star-Spangled Story Answer Key and Literature Guide.* You are the best one to decide what your child is ready to read or hear.

How Much Time Will Each Lesson Require?

Each lesson takes about ten to fifteen minutes to read straight through. Beyond that, the amount of time you invest will depend on the additional activities you choose. You can usually complete the lesson and all the activities except "Hands-On History" in under an hour. The time needed for "Hands-On History" varies depending on what activities you choose and from one student to another. You can use *Our Star-Spangled Story* three days per week, or spread the lessons and activities over all five days of your school week. The curriculum has a total of ninety lessons divided into thirty units.

What Supplies Will My Student Need?

Students will need a pencil and colored pencils. Unit projects will require additional supplies. You can access a complete supply list on our website (notgrass.com/osss). The individual unit project instruction pages also list these materials.

How Many Activities Should My Student Complete?

You know best what your student is capable of accomplishing. We include a variety of activities in each lesson so that the curriculum is flexible.

A parent may require a fourth grader who is academically gifted to read the daily lessons and complete every activity at the end of each lesson independently. On the other hand, the parent of a first grader with learning challenges may decide to read aloud each lesson and pick and choose from the activities.

The variety of activities makes it easy for your student to have a positive, rich, engaging, unique learning experience. You should not feel pressure to complete every assignment.

How Can I Make My Homeschool Experience Easier?

As you look ahead to your school year or evaluate midway, consider how you might make your student's education less complicated and richer by using *Our Star-Spangled Story* as a large part of his or her learning for the year.

Our Star-Spangled Story is much more than history. You can also use this curriculum as all or part of your geography, literature, creative writing, music, art, and handwriting practice. You may find that eliminating busywork in an entirely separate subject and incorporating that subject into this study makes for a less stressful, more engaging, more memorable school year!

How Can I Help My Struggling Student?

For students who struggle with reading or writing, feel free to make adjustments to help them be successful and not become frustrated. You or an older sibling can read the lessons and literature aloud. Struggling students might also benefit from reading aloud to you.

You can easily alter, shorten, or orally complete the writing activities and review questions. You can also eliminate them if you feel your student is not ready. We designed *Our Star-Spangled Story* to be flexible to meet the needs of individual families and students.

How Can I Use *Our Star-Spangled Story* with Multiple Ages?

While we designed *Our Star-Spangled Story* especially for first through fourth graders, other ages can certainly benefit. Younger siblings can listen in on the lessons and literature, look at the pictures, and take part in the hands-on history ideas. Students older than fourth grade who have learning challenges or a particular learning style might benefit from this format for learning history.

If you have more than one child in grades one through four, you may enjoy reading the lessons aloud together. Afterward, you can also enjoy many of the activities together. You can assign each child different activities, depending on his or her age and skill level.

Sample Walk-Through of Unit 5

You can easily complete *Our Star-Spangled Story* in three days per week. For example, when teaching Unit 5, you can do everything for Lesson 13 on Monday, everything for Lesson 14 on Wednesday, and everything for Lesson 15 on Friday.

However, if you want to spend less time each day and spread the lessons over a five-day week, here is an example of how you can do that with Unit 5.

Bruce and Jennifer Smith have three children. Sam is in fourth grade, Lily is in second grade, and Allen is four years old.

Monday: Jennifer and all three children gather on the couch. Jennifer opens to Unit 5 and reads aloud Lesson 13, "A Midnight Ride with Paul Revere." Jennifer, Sam, and Lily discuss the review questions at the end of the lesson. They all listen to "War Song" while they read along in *Star-Spangled Rhythms and Rhymes*. They listen to "War Song" a second time and sing along. Sam and Lily each color the picture for Lesson 13 in their own copy of *My Star-Spangled Student Workbook*.

Tuesday: Jennifer, Lily, and Allen work together to make the Unit 5 project, "Revere and Son Shop Window." Sam works alongside them making one of his own.

Wednesday: Jennifer and all three children gather on the couch to read Lesson 14, "Thirteen Colonies and Independence." Jennifer, Sam, and Lily discuss the review questions at the end of the lesson. They all sing along with "Yankee Doodle" from *Star-Spangled Rhythms and Rhymes*.

Sam completes the Lesson 14 writing activity in his workbook. Lily completes the Lesson 14 drawing activity in her workbook. Later that day, all three children pretend they are carrying messages to troops inspired by the "Hands-On History" idea.

Thursday: Jennifer and all three children gather on the couch to read Lesson 15, "James Madison and the Constitution." Jennifer, Sam, and Lily discuss the review questions at the end of the lesson. Sam and Lily complete the Lesson 15 / Unit 5 Review page in *My Star-Spangled Student Workbook*. Later that day, all three children build with blocks inspired by the "Hands-On History" idea.

Friday: Jennifer and her children enjoy singing along again with "War Song" and "Yankee Doodle" from *Star-Spangled Rhythms and Rhymes*. They look at a section of *A Star-Spangled Timeline* as instructed at the end of Lesson 15. After supper Bruce reads the first three chapters of *Toliver's Secret* with the whole family.

Encouragement for the Journey

Remember that God designed your family and the daily responsibilities you carry. A homeschooling mother who has one child can complete more activities in *Our Star-Spangled Story* than a homeschooling mother who has seven children and an elderly grandparent living in her home. God will use the efforts of both of these mothers.

God does not expect you to do more than you can do. Be kind to yourself. He knows exactly what you and your children need this year. We encourage you to pray about your family's experience using *Our Star-Spangled Story*. Let it be a tool to help you have a wonderful learning experience with your children.

Remember that out of all the parents in the world to whom God could have given your children, He chose you. He is the one who put your family together. He knows what He is doing. Trust in His choice. God created you. He created your children.

Relax and remember that this is the day that the Lord has made. Rejoice and be glad in it (Psalm 118:24)!

We are here to help you. If you have questions or simply need some encouragement, send us an email (help@notgrass.com) or give us a call (1-800-211-8793).

Unit 1

An Acoma Puebloan Woman

1

The First People
Come to
America

The story of how the first people came to America starts long ago at the beginning of time. The story begins when God made Adam and Eve. Adam and Eve became husband and wife. One day Eve gave birth to the first baby ever born. Adam and Eve later had other children.

Adam, Eve, and their children were the first family in the world. Every person who has ever lived is a descendant of Adam and Eve.

The Great Flood

Adam and Eve's descendants grew up. They married and had children. Their children grew up, married, and had children, one generation after another. Soon there were many people. Sadly, Adam and Eve's descendants became so wicked that God was sorry He had made people at all. God decided to send a flood to destroy them.

God saw one righteous man. His name was Noah. God told Noah to build an ark so that he, his family, and pairs of all kinds of animals could be safe during the flood. When the flood ended and the ground dried up, Noah and his family stepped out of the ark.

Soon Noah's sons and their wives began to have children. Their children grew up and had children, one generation after another. Soon there were many people again. Everyone spoke the same language.

The Tower of Babel

A few generations after the flood, Noah's descendants decided to build a city and a tower out of bricks. They wanted the tower to reach into heaven. God was not pleased about what they were doing. He forced them to stop. The tower became known as the Tower of Babel because of what God did to make them stop building. He made them sound like they were babbling to one another.

The Bible says:

Therefore its name was called Babel, because there the Lord confused the language of the whole earth, and from there the Lord scattered them abroad over the face of the whole earth.
Genesis 11:9

Statue of Noah in Cologne Cathedral in Germany

Eastern Hemisphere

Europe

Tower of Babel

Asia

Africa

Indian Ocean

Australia

Antarctica

Western Hemisphere

North America

Atlantic Ocean

Pacific Ocean

South America

Antarctica

From Babel to America

God shaped the earth like a giant ball. The Eastern Hemisphere is on one side and the Western Hemisphere is on the other. The continents of Africa, Europe, Asia, and Australia are in the Eastern Hemisphere. North America and South America are in the Western Hemisphere. Antarctica is at the bottom of the world in both hemispheres.

The Tower of Babel was in the Eastern Hemisphere. It was probably in what is now the country of Iraq in Asia. When the descendants of Noah's sons and their wives spread out from there, they moved into Asia, Africa, and Europe. They could walk, ride on camels or donkeys, or ride in carts to get to those places. Getting to Australia and to North and South America was harder.

Sometime after people left the Tower of Babel, some of Noah's descendants went to Australia. Some came to North and South America. It may have happened soon after Babel. It may have happened many years later. No one knows for sure.

Did They Come by Land?

The wide Pacific Ocean lies between North America and Asia, but far up in the cold North these two continents are close together. The Chukchi Peninsula is at the far eastern side of Asia. The Seward Peninsula is at the far western side of North America. The Bering Strait separates these two peninsulas. They are only fifty miles apart. Find the Bering Strait and the Chukchi and Seward Peninsulas on the map on page 8.

The Bering Strait is cold and icy now, but some people believe it was once much warmer. Some historians think that a land bridge connected the Chukchi and Seward Peninsulas. They call it the Bering Land Bridge or Beringia.

Those who believe the land bridge theory think that people came across Beringia from Asia. According to this theory, some went east across what is now Canada; some went south into what is now the United States; and others went farther south into Mexico and South America and to the islands surrounding North and South America.

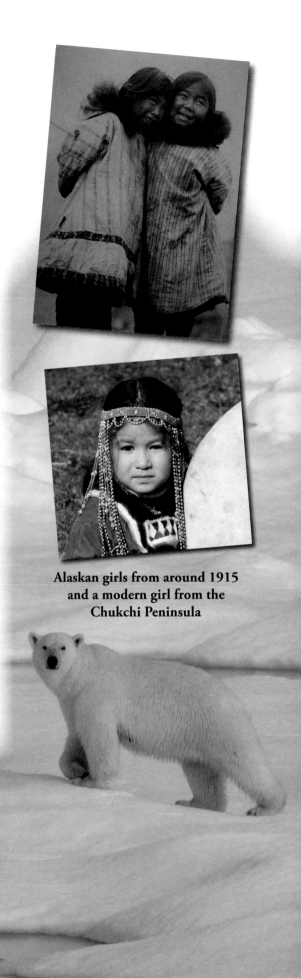

Alaskan girls from around 1915 and a modern girl from the Chukchi Peninsula

Maybe people came to North and South America on boats. Perhaps some came by land, and others came by boat. No one knows for sure.

People of the Western Hemisphere

The people who came to the Western Hemisphere lived in family groups, tribes, and nations scattered across North and South America. Each group had its own style of clothing. Groups built different kinds of houses. They created different kinds of games, music, and art. They taught their traditions to their children and grandchildren from generation to generation.

Modern descendants of the native people of the United States

6

Vikings Sail West

Just before the year 900, Vikings from Norway sailed to Iceland and settled there. Almost one hundred years later, another Viking, Erik the Red, sailed west from Iceland into the Western Hemisphere. He discovered the largest island in the world. He named the island Greenland. Erik brought other Vikings to Greenland where they built two settlements.

Shortly before 1000, Erik's son Leif Eriksson went back to Norway. While he was there he learned about Jesus. The king of Norway told him to go to Greenland and teach the Greenlanders about Jesus.

While Leif was on his way to Greenland, the wind blew his ship to North America. A few Vikings later moved to North America for a short time. They lived in Newfoundland on the east coast of Canada. They called this place Vinland. Though the Vikings met some of the people already living in North America, they didn't stay long. Find Norway, Iceland, Greenland, and Newfoundland on the map on page 8.

Statue of Leif Eriksson in Iceland

Viking Ship

A Look at the World from Above the North Pole

Eastern Hemisphere

Asia

Europe

Africa

Norway

Arctic Ocean

Iceland

Greenland

Chukchi Peninsula

Newfoundland

Bering Strait

Seward Peninsula

North America

Western Hemisphere

On the Other Side of the World

Even if people never crossed a land bridge across the Bering Strait, the people who lived on the Chukchi and Seward Peninsulas likely visited one another by boat. They probably sold things to one another. Perhaps a few people from other places in Europe came to North America by ship like the Vikings did.

However, for many centuries very few people living in the Eastern Hemisphere knew about the lands or people in the Western Hemisphere. Few in the West knew about the people in the East.

The Bible says:

> . . . and He made from one man
> every nation of mankind
> to live on all the face of the earth,
> having determined
> their appointed times
> and the boundaries
> of their habitation . . . .
> Acts 17:26

Lesson Activities

- Look at the America in 1492 map on the inside front cover of this book.

- Rhythms and Rhymes: Enjoy "Coyote Song" on page 1.

- Student Workbook: Complete the Lesson 1 page.

- Literature for Units 1-4: *Benjamin West and His Cat Grimalkin*

Review Questions

- Who are the two people from whom everyone in the world is descended?

- What are two ideas about how people reached North America and South America?

- What are some reasons people want to move to new places?

Hands-On History Ideas

- Pretend that you are moving away from the Tower of Babel. How far will you travel? What will you look for in a new home? What do you need to take with you?

- Use building blocks to build Noah's Ark or a Viking ship (see page 7).

At Home
in
Acoma Pueblo

Vikings sailed between Norway, Iceland, Greenland, and North America around 900-1000. During the same time period, ancestors of the modern Puebloan people lived in what we now call the Four Corners region of the United States. This is where the states of Utah, Colorado, Arizona, and New Mexico come together. Historians once called their ancestors the Anasazi. Their descendants today prefer to call them the Ancestral Puebloan.

Chaco Canyon, A Puebloan Gathering Place

The Ancestral Puebloan people were farmers. For many years small groups lived on scattered farms and in small villages. By 1250 most had moved to large villages. They lived in apartment buildings made of stone, wood, and adobe. Adobe is a hard building material made of clay, water, and pieces of plants.

Between the years 850 and 1250, the Ancestral Puebloan people built a city in Chaco Canyon in northwest New Mexico. They cut sandstone into blocks and used the blocks to build large buildings. Some buildings were four or five stories tall. The grandest building in Chaco Canyon was Pueblo Bonito. It had over six hundred rooms and took many years to build.

Fajada Butte in Chaco Canyon, New Mexico

Puebloan Ruins in Chaco Canyon, New Mexico

Roads connected the buildings of Chaco Canyon to more than 150 other "Great Houses" nearby. The Ancestral Puebloan and other native people used these roads to travel to Chaco Canyon. Some came to buy and sell pottery, copper bells, seashells, turquoise, and even beautiful macaws. Some objects they bought and sold came from as far away as Mexico, the Gulf of Mexico, and what is now California.

The Ancestral Puebloan people came together to share knowledge, traditions, and ceremonies. They may have used the Great Houses at Chaco Canyon as hotels.

Cliff Villages

At places such as Mesa Verde in Colorado and Bandelier in New Mexico, the Ancestral Puebloan people built villages of cliff dwellings.

Macaws

11

Cliff Palace at Mesa Verde, Colorado

At Mesa Verde, villages are on ledges on the sides of cliffs. At Bandelier, the Ancestral Puebloan people built rock, wood, and adobe rooms at the bottom of a cliff. They also carved other rooms into the cliff. They used ladders to reach them.

On Top of Acoma Rock

At some point, the Ancestral Puebloan people left their older villages. They built new villages in what are now Arizona, New Mexico, and Texas. Around 1150 a Puebloan group moved into the desert that is west of what is now Albuquerque, New Mexico. They built a village on top of Acoma Rock. The village had about five hundred square and rectangular homes. Like other Pueblo villages, these homes were connected to each other like apartments.

Bandelier, New Mexico

Acoma Buildings

Acoma Pueblo on Top of Acoma Rock

The homes on top of Acoma Rock were three to four stories tall. The Acoma Puebloan people built firepits in first-floor rooms. They lined them with flat stones. The first floor had no doors. People climbed ladders to enter the buildings through holes in roofs.

As their ancestors had done, the Acoma Puebloan people built special rooms called kivas. They used kivas for ceremonies and for spending time together.

Modern Kiva Ladder

From their 350-foot high mesa, the Acoma Puebloan people could see far into the distance. To the northeast, they could see beautiful Enchanted Mesa. On top of Acoma Rock, the people were safe from enemies.

Enchanted Mesa

In the Valley Below

God filled the soil of the valley below Acoma Rock with minerals that plants need to grow. Like their ancestors, the people of Acoma Pueblo grew corn, squash, and beans. They raised five kinds of corn and nine kinds of beans. They grew gourds, which they used to store food and to carry water. They raised crops of cotton. They built lookout towers and took turns watching over their fields. They cut firewood in the valley.

God sends rain to the valley. He has placed springs there. The river called Rio San Jose is close by. The Acoma Puebloan people built dams and canals to bring water from the springs and river to their fields.

Acoma Puebloan people around 1900

13

Puebloan pottery

The Puebloan people did not use metal. Their main farm tools were digging sticks and hoes made from stone, bone, and wood. They hauled dirt in baskets. The men of the pueblo worked together to raise their crops.

For hundreds of years, the Puebloan people kept turkeys. Those who lived in Acoma Pueblo kept large flocks and herded them like sheep. They raised turkeys mainly for their feathers, which they used to make blankets.

The Acoma Puebloan people and Puebloan people from other villages walked across the valley to trade with each other. They also traded with tribes who lived as nomads.

Life on the Mesa

Men living in Acoma Pueblo made tools, weapons, baskets, and blankets. They hunted animals and dressed their skins. Women in Acoma Pueblo cared for their children and cooked meals. They ground corn to make meal, made bread from the meal, and baked it in outdoor ovens.

The Acoma Puebloan people built cisterns on top of the mesa to catch rainwater. They took baths in large pottery tubs in their houses.

Acoma girls gather water.

Acoma Pottery

Like other Puebloan people, the residents of Acoma made beautiful pottery. Puebloan potters gathered clay and minerals from the earth around them. They formed the clay into long ropes and coiled it into the shapes they wanted. They smoothed it with gourds and coated it with a mixture of clay and water. They polished it, decorated it, and fired it outdoors beside a fire to harden the clay. The Puebloan people made miniature pots. Children may have made these for toys while they were learning to make pottery.

Though their lives have changed, the Acoma Puebloan people have lived on Acoma Rock for more than 850 years. It is perhaps the oldest town in America where families have lived one generation after another.

The Lord God wants us to be soft and moldable like clay in His hands. The prophet Isaiah prayed:

> But now, O Lord,
> You are our Father,
> We are the clay,
> and You our potter;
> And all of us
> are the work of Your hand.
> Isaiah 64:8

Lesson Activities

- All Around the USA map (at the end of this book following the Credits): Find Acoma.

- Student Workbook: Complete the Lesson 2 page.

- Literature for Units 1-4: *Benjamin West and His Cat Grimalkin*

Review Questions

- What building materials did the Puebloan people use?

- Why do you think the Acoma Puebloan people wanted to build their village on top of Acoma Rock?

- What are three things that are different about the life of the Puebloan people compared to your life?

Hands-On History Ideas

- See the Unit 1 Project instructions on page 22.

Columbus, Cabot, and Coronado in America

Dominico Colombo was a wool weaver in Genoa, Italy, when his wife Susanna gave birth to their firstborn son, Cristoforo. In America we translate his son's name into English and call him Christopher Columbus.

Columbus was born in 1451, about five hundred years after Leif Eriksson sailed to North America. He was born three hundred years after the Acoma Puebloan people built on top of Acoma Rock.

Genoa was a port city on the Mediterranean Sea. Ships and sailors from many lands came to Genoa. Christopher grew up listening to stories of their adventures. Dominico taught his son how to weave wool. Christopher also studied mapmaking and sailing.

Christopher Columbus became a sailor when he was fourteen years old. He made many voyages in the Mediterranean Sea. In his twenties, he worked as a mapmaker.

Lighthouse in Genoa, Italy

In the 1400s, many Europeans bought and sold spices from far away China and the Indies. The Indies included India, Southeast Asia, and the islands of Indonesia. Europeans used the spices for cooking, for preserving food, and for making medicine. Getting these spices was difficult because they came from far away. Europeans had to travel across land for many miles.

Spices for Sale in Genoa, Italy

Christopher Columbus wondered if a ship could sail west across the Atlantic Ocean and end up in China and the Indies. He tried for many years to convince King Ferdinand and Queen Isabella of Spain to pay for a voyage so he could find out. Finally, in April of 1492, they agreed. Columbus gathered food, fresh water, and other supplies for his crew of eighty-seven men.

On August 3, 1492, Columbus and his crew set sail from Palos, Spain, on three ships named the *Niña*, the *Pinta*, and the *Santa Maria*. They prayed and sang hymns each morning. They worshiped God again each evening. The crew kept time with a sandglass. They worked for four-hour shifts. The sailors spent much time adjusting the sails. The crew ate one hot meal each day.

Italian stamp celebrates the 500th anniversary of Columbus' voyage.

Supplies in the hold of a replica of the *Santa Maria* in Palos, Spain

On October 12, 1492, Columbus and his men saw land. Columbus believed he had arrived in the Indies. In reality, the land he and his men saw was one of the Bahama Islands in the Caribbean Sea. Because he believed he was in the Indies, he called the people living there Indians. Columbus claimed the region for Spain. He and his crew explored islands in the area until January of 1493. After he returned home, news of his voyage spread to European cities.

The Italian stamp at right shows the routes that Columbus took from Spain to the Caribbean Islands and back to Spain.

This Italian stamp shows the route of Columbus' first voyage.

John Cabot in North America

While the Italian Christopher Columbus was making plans to search for the Indies, another Italian had the same idea. His name was John Cabot.

Cabot and his family moved to London, England, in the late 1400s. News of Columbus' first voyage to the Caribbean reached London by 1496. That same year, England's King Henry VII gave Cabot and his three sons permission to explore "to all parts, countries, and seas of the East, of the West, and of the North." King Henry did not want Cabot to go south to the places Columbus had claimed for Spain.

In May of 1497, Cabot and a crew of about twenty sailors left Bristol, England, on the ship *Matthew*. They landed in North America thirty-five days later. Cabot claimed the land for England. They did not meet any native people. When Cabot returned to London, he was a hero. People called him "the Great Admiral."

Cabot Tower in Bristol, England, honors the voyage of John Cabot.

Missionaries, Settlers, and Conquistadors

Christopher Columbus made three more voyages to what came to be called the New World. On his second voyage in 1493, he brought at least seventeen ships and well over one thousand men. Some came to settle on islands in the Caribbean Sea. Some came to bring Christianity to the islanders. Their first settlement was on the island of Hispaniola, which is the home of Haiti and the Dominican Republic today.

Many of the Spanish caused great pain and suffering for people living in the Caribbean Islands. They killed some of the islanders in battles. They enslaved some islanders. Other islanders died of diseases they caught from the Spanish.

The Spanish moved on to other islands. They began to conquer native people in Central and South America. A few genuinely worked to share the gospel with native people, but many worked to conquer them. The Spanish conquerors were called conquistadors.

The Spanish began to explore North America. Some of the first people of North America who met the Spanish were those living in Florida. Juan Ponce de Leon was born into a noble family in Spain. He became a Spanish official in the Caribbean. He explored Florida in 1513.

Beginning in 1539, Hernando de Soto led hundreds of soldiers into Florida. De Soto was a Spanish explorer and conquistador. He and his men explored all the way to the Mississippi River. They met members of many different native tribes. In some places, the Spanish and native people met peacefully. At other places, they fought battles against each other.

Ponce de Leon

Hernando de Soto

Native people of Florida left behind this shell carving, bead necklace, and pot.

19

Coronado Expedition

Francisco Vázquez de Coronado was born into a noble family in Spain about 1510. When Coronado was 25 years old, he traveled to New Spain. This was the area that is now southern and central Mexico. Coronado traveled with Antonio de Mendoza, who was moving there to become governor of New Spain.

De Mendoza heard rumors about a great empire in what is now the Southwestern United States. He heard about Seven Cities of Gold. He wanted to conquer the empire and claim it for Spain.

Mendoza chose Coronado to lead an expedition to find the Cities of Gold. From 1540 to 1542, Coronado led soldiers, enslaved persons, and Mexican natives into what is now the Southwestern United States.

Landscape in the area Coronado explored

Routes of the De Soto and Coronado Expeditions

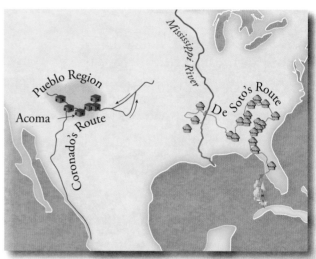

"Coronado's March" by Frederic Remington

Coronado and his men explored a large area. Some explorers went as far as what is now Kansas. They met many native peoples. Some saw the Grand Canyon. Some stopped at Acoma Pueblo.

While Coronado was in Kansas, De Soto's men were a few hundred miles south in what are now Arkansas, Louisiana, and Texas.

Coronado returned to New Spain two years after he began. He did not find a great empire or Seven Cities of Gold because they did not exist.

God loves all the people of the world. In Matthew 28:19, Jesus told His followers to "go and make disciples of all the nations." The native people of the New World needed the gospel of Jesus Christ. Some Europeans loved them and shared the gospel with them. Others acted shamefully. Each of us has the choice each day to do right or to do wrong. As the Bible teaches us in Psalms:

Depart from evil and do good;
Seek peace and pursue it.
Psalm 34:14

Lesson Activities

- Rhythms and Rhymes: Enjoy "Green Grow the Rushes, Oh!" on pages 2-3.
- Timeline: Look at pages 2 and 3.
- Literature for Units 1-4: *Benjamin West and His Cat Grimalkin*

Review Questions

- What did Columbus think he would find if he sailed west across the Atlantic Ocean?
- How do you think native people felt when the Spanish arrived in their homeland?
- Why do you think people wanted to explore in the New World?

Unit Review

- Student Workbook: Complete the Lesson 3 / Unit 1 Review page.

Hands-On History Ideas

- Pretend you are an explorer leading an expedition to the New World. You might want to start by loading supplies on your "ship," which could be a couch or bed.
- Use building blocks to create the imaginary "Seven Cities of Gold."

Unit 1 Project
Puebloan Pottery

Supplies

- flour
- salt
- water
- parchment or waxed paper
- baking sheet and oven, optional
- white craft paint
- paintbrush
- black marker

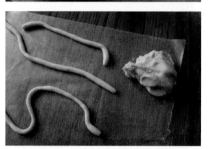

Directions

1. Mix 2 cups flour and 1 cup salt. Fill a 1-cup measure with hot tap water. Slowly stir it into the mixture.

2. Use your hands to knead (press, squeeze, fold, and flip) the clay. If clay is sticky, add flour one spoonful at a time. Clay should be soft and smooth.

3. Place clay on a piece of parchment paper or waxed paper. Knead for a few minutes, until clay is smooth. You will have enough clay for several pottery pieces.

4. Pinch off a ball of clay about the size of a golf ball. Roll into a long rope. Repeat to make several ropes.

5. Make a coil base.

6. Coil the ropes around the base and up, pinching as you go to make the coils stick together.

7. Pinch gently to smooth and shape pottery into desired shape.

8. Let your pottery dry. You can let it air dry, which will take several days. With adult help, you can place the pottery on a baking sheet and bake in a 200-degree oven until hard. (Length of time depends on the thickness of your pottery's sides. Ours required about five hours. Use oven-safe parchment paper if you plan to bake the pottery.)

9. Once dry and hard, paint the pottery with white craft paint. Let dry.

10. Use a black marker to draw Puebloan-style designs on the pottery. See examples on page 14.

Unit 2

The Brewster Family at Plymouth

Young Wrestling Brewster waved to the people he loved on the shore. His parents, William and Mary, and his brother Love stood on the ship's deck with him. They all swayed back and forth with the ship as it sailed away from the Netherlands. Together they sailed into the unknown. Wrestling felt strange leaving his other brother and two sisters behind, but they would join the family soon. The Brewster family and the others with them were bound for North America in the New World. The year was 1620.

Replica of the *Mayflower*

The Separatists in the Netherlands

Wrestling Brewster was born in the Netherlands between 1611 and 1614. (The country of the Netherlands is also called Holland. The people of the country are called Dutch.) Wrestling's family had moved to the Netherlands from England. They and other Separatists were searching for a place where they could worship God as they believed they should. They had different beliefs from the Church of England, England's official church. Many English people were unfriendly toward them. Wrestling's father William had spent time in prison because of his beliefs. The other Separatists respected Wrestling's father. William Brewster served as the leading elder in their church.

King James I

In the Netherlands, William Brewster taught the English language to earn money. He later worked with another Separatist to print books about their faith. Some of the books criticized King James I of England. The English government did not want the books to be sold in England. People smuggled the books into England and sold them secretly. The English government took away the Separatists' printing equipment to keep them from printing more books.

25

Windmill in the Netherlands

While living in the Netherlands, Separatist parents tried to encourage their children to continue speaking English. This was hard because people in the Netherlands speak Dutch. Some of the Separatist children made friends with Dutch boys and girls who led them away from God.

The Separatists wanted to protect the souls of their children. They wanted them to stay faithful to God. They also wanted to share their faith with people in other parts of the world. Some of the Separatists decided to travel across the Atlantic Ocean to a new English colony. The Separatists are now better known as Pilgrims.

What is a colony?

Europeans had heard amazing stories about the New World ever since European explorers first traveled there. The explorers told of rich land. The New World had vast forests that were full of animals. The rivers and coastal waters were full of fish. Huge areas of land seemed to be open and unused. Countries in Europe wanted to gain from this rich, new land.

During this time in history, many countries established colonies in faraway places. The kings of Europe granted permission for some groups to establish colonies in America. The country that started the colony controlled the government of the colony. The country hoped to make money from their new settlements. The settlers who established the colonies were called "colonists." Colonies often started as a small fort or town. Soon colonists built other towns nearby. Colonists turned much of the surrounding land into farms.

Replica of an English colonial ship

England, France, the Netherlands, Portugal, Spain, and Sweden all established colonies in what we now call America. The country of England had the most success. The kings of England gave many groups permission to settle in the land they had claimed in the New World. The Pilgrims were one of these groups.

The Pilgrims in Plymouth

Young Wrestling Brewster traveled with around one hundred other passengers. They endured nine long weeks at sea on board the ship *Mayflower*. Many of the men, women, and children became seasick as the waves tossed their little boat up and down on the endless ocean. One young Pilgrim died on the voyage. Another young Pilgrim was born.

Finally, on November 11, 1620, they reached the coast of North America. The weary Pilgrims fell on their knees and thanked God for bringing them safely to their new home. While they were still on the ship, the men wrote a document called the Mayflower Compact. This document established the rules for their new settlement of Plymouth.

William Brewster holds an open Bible as the Pilgrims set sail.

Life was hard in the New World at first. Many Pilgrims became sick. About half of the Pilgrims died the first winter. At times only six or seven adults were healthy enough to take care of all the rest. William Brewster stayed healthy. William Bradford, the governor of Plymouth, wrote about how Brewster and Miles Standish cared for the sick. Bradford wrote that they were tender-hearted and compassionate. They brought in wood to build fires to keep the sick people warm. They prepared their food and made their beds. Brewster said they did all these things willingly and cheerfully. These actions showed the true love they had for their neighbors.

As spring approached, William Brewster spoke to the group of Pilgrims. Everyone was sad. So many people they loved were dead. Brewster tried to encourage them. He told them:

> Thankful to Almighty God should we be that our case is not worse, that so many of our number yet live . . . . And in even our heaviest trials has not the Divine Providence been with us? Did not His providential hand open for us the way through every difficulty? . . . Generations to come shall look back to this hour, to these scenes of agonizing trial, . . . and say, "Here was our beginning as a people. These were our fathers. Through their trials we inherit our blessings. Their faith is our faith; their hope our hope; their God our God." . . . Let us go hence, then, to work with our might, that which we have to do.

Recreated Pilgrim homes

Thankful to Almighty God

The Pilgrims became friends with Squanto, a native of the Patuxet tribe, who lived nearby. Squanto had been to England and had learned to speak English. He helped the Pilgrims learn how to survive in their new home. The Pilgrims also befriended Chief Massasoit of the Wampanoag tribe. The next year the Pilgrims' crops grew well. The Pilgrims invited several Wampanoag to join them in a harvest feast. At the feast, the Pilgrims thanked God for seeing them through their first year in the New World. They thanked Him for their good harvest. Their feast was the beginning of our traditional Thanksgiving holiday.

Wrestling Brewster grew up in this settlement that the Pilgrims called Plymouth. The community grew in number. More Separatists left the Netherlands and joined the Pilgrims in the New World. Wrestling's father William was "beloved and honored among the people." He lovingly guided them in the teachings of the Bible.

Now may the God of hope
fill you with all
joy and peace in believing,
so that you will abound in hope
by the power of the Holy Spirit.
Romans 15:13

Lesson Activities

- All Around the USA map: Find Plymouth.

- Rhythms and Rhymes: Enjoy "Providence and the Pilgrim" on pages 4-5.

- Student Workbook: Complete the Lesson 4 page.

- Literature for Units 1-4: *Benjamin West and His Cat Grimalkin*

Review Questions

- What is a colony?

- Why did the Pilgrims give thanks at their harvest feast?

- What do you think would be hard about living in Plymouth the first year?

Hands-On History Ideas

- See the Unit 2 Project instructions on pages 43-44.

Pieter Claesen Wyckoff
Indentured Servant in
New Netherland

Pieter Claesen rocked with the motion of the waves. Would he ever reach New Netherland? One storm after another had pounded against the ship for weeks on end. One of Pieter's fellow passengers gave birth to a baby on the journey. The family named the baby Storm. This entry from the ship's log describes one day at sea for the weary travelers:

In the morning, the wind changed to the west. It blew so hard that . . . we could not carry a single sail . . . . There blew a violent gale from the northwest and we then drifted east with a very rough sea. The waves rose to such an awful height that the waves and the sky seemed one . . . it lasted the entire night.

The journey had been much longer than Pieter and the other passengers expected. Surely the journey would be worth it. They had all heard such wonderful things about New Netherland, the land that would soon be their home.

Ships arrive in New Netherland.

Many of the passengers on the ship were indentured servants. An indentured servant was bound to serve his or her master for a set period of time. The servants usually served between four and seven years. Some people decided to become an indentured servant because they were poor. They wanted to settle in the New World but didn't have enough money to do so on their own. After their time of service was over, the master provided the servant with supplies to establish a farm.

Dutch Settlers in America

In 1609, several years before Pieter came to America, Henry Hudson explored the area that became New Netherland. Hudson was searching for a way to reach Asia through North America by ship. He explored a river that was later named the Hudson River in his honor.

Hudson did not find the route to Asia he hoped to find, but he did find the island of Manhattan. Manhattan Island was covered with thick forests. The Dutch bought the island from the native people who lived there. Now Pieter Claesen, a young teenager traveling alone, was among the Dutch immigrants who were settling the new Dutch colony. The year was 1637. Other Dutch colonists chose to settle in areas that later became New Jersey and Delaware.

Henry Hudson meets native people in America.

Dutch settlers in New Netherland

Pieter Claesen in America

When Pieter Claesen reached America, he became an indentured servant on a one-million-acre farm in New Netherland. After he worked there for six years, he became free to start his own farm. He married another Dutch immigrant. They moved close to the settlement of New Amsterdam on Manhattan Island. They were part of a tiny community of about fifteen settlers. (Today over 1,500,000 people live on Manhattan Island!) Pieter and his wife built a one-room house with a dirt floor. They had eleven children.

In 1664 the English took control of Dutch settlements in North America, including New Netherland. They renamed the New Netherland colony New York. New Amsterdam became New York City.

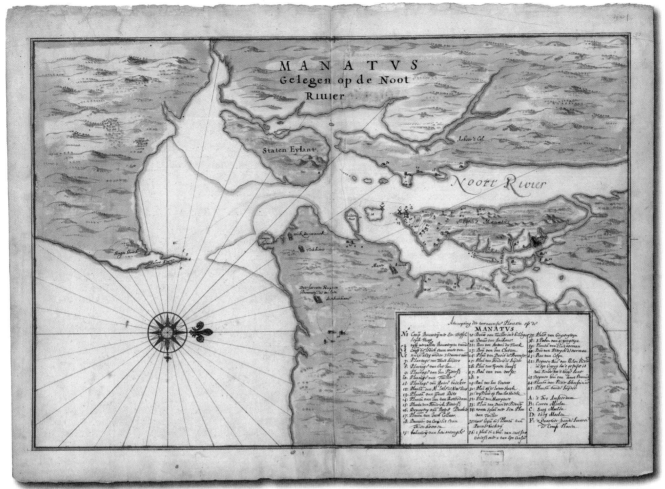

Dutch map of New Netherland from the 1600s

At this time in history, many Dutch people used their father's first name as their own last name. When the English took control of the area, they said each Dutchman must choose a last name that would pass on from one generation to the next. Pieter Claesen chose the last name Wyckoff.

Pieter Claesen Wyckoff prospered as a farmer. He became one of the wealthiest men in the area. He served as a judge. Wyckoff also helped to establish the Flatlands Dutch Reformed Church.

Many generations of the Wyckoff family lived in the house Pieter Wyckoff built. Sadly, in the 1700s, the Wyckoff family bought enslaved persons. They continued to own slaves for many years. During the 1800s, the family freed their slaves. They hired their former slaves to work on the farm as paid laborers.

33

Wyckoff House

The Wyckoff House

Descendants of Pieter Claesen Wyckoff lived in the house he built until 1901. Different family members built additions onto the house. The original first room is still a part of it. After the family sold the house, no one took care of it for a long time. A later owner gave the historic house to New York City. People worked for many years to restore the home. It opened as a museum in 1982.

The land around the Wyckoff farm has changed a great deal. Today only a little more than an acre of the original farm remains with the house. Modern buildings crowd the Wyckoff land on all sides. A McDonald's restaurant stands nearby. A junk yard and a car wash are across the street. The Wyckoff house is the oldest building in New York City.

In 2012 a powerful hurricane hit New York City and surrounding areas. The storm knocked down four trees on the Wyckoff land. The trees came close to falling on the house, but the house survived and stood strong. It has stood strong for well over 350 years.

Manhattan Island before
the arrival of the Dutch

Manhattan Island today

The Flatlands Dutch Reformed Church that Pieter Wyckoff helped to establish still meets. The original building no longer stands, but the congregation has one of the oldest histories of any church in the country. The congregation is small, but each week they reach out to hundreds of people in the community.

Today visitors to the Pieter Wyckoff house learn about a man who came to America a young indentured servant and grew up to make a big impact in his corner of the world.

Instruct those who are rich
in this present world
not to be conceited
or to fix their hope
on the uncertainty of riches,
but on God, who richly supplies us
with all things to enjoy.
Instruct them to do good,
to be rich in good works,
to be generous and ready to share,
storing up for themselves the
treasure of a good foundation
for the future,
so that they may take hold
of that which is life indeed.
1 Timothy 6:17-19

Lesson Activities

- All Around the USA map: Find New York City and the Hudson River.

- Student Workbook: Complete the Lesson 5 page.

- Literature for Units 1-4: *Benjamin West and His Cat Grimalkin*

Review Questions

- How did indentured servants get help after their time of service was over?

- How has the area around the Wyckoff house changed since it was built?

- Do you think it is important for people to preserve the Wyckoff house as a museum? Why?

Hands-On History Ideas

- Pretend that you are opening a museum. What will your museum be about? It could be a toy museum, a kitchen museum, a history museum, or something else. Set up one room of your house as a museum.

- Use building blocks to build the Wyckoff house as shown on page 34.

John Eliot, Missionary to the "Praying Indians"

On the last Sunday in October of 1646, John Eliot prayed for God's blessings. John Eliot was a minister. On that day John Eliot would preach for the first time in the village of Nonantum. He would tell the native villagers about God.

Eliot told the villagers at Nonantum ahead of time that he was coming. He and three other settlers walked five miles to the village. Waban and other villagers came to welcome them. Waban was a leader in Nonantum.

The Nonantum villagers and the Englishmen walked into Waban's wigwam. They found many people waiting to listen. John Eliot preached to them in Algonquian, their native language.

Modern replicas of temporary homes, called wigwams

John Eliot taught the villagers that God made the world. He told them about Adam and Eve and their sin in the Garden of Eden. He told them about Jesus, the Savior of the world.

Eliot had prepared for this day for many months. He had invited a native person who spoke English and Algonquian to live with his family, but we do not know the man's name. This man taught Eliot the Algonquian language. Eliot taught the man how to write.

John Eliot asked the people of the village if they understood what he had told them. Many voices answered that they did understand. He asked if they had any questions. They did. The people in Waban's wigwam wanted to know:

How can we know Jesus Christ?

Can God or Jesus Christ understand our prayers if we pray in our own language?

Was there ever a time when the Englishmen did not know about God?

Some of the foods that the native people in the area ate are pictured here. They also made clothing from deer skin.

John Eliot answered their questions. This first meeting lasted three hours. The people told Eliot that they were not tired and they asked him to come again.

More Visits to Nonantum

John Eliot and his friends went back to Nonantum two weeks later. They found more people waiting in Waban's wigwam. This time Eliot had special lessons for the children. He gave them apples and cakes. The children were happy to listen and learn what he taught them.

Again, John Eliot preached a sermon in the Algonquian language. He said that he had come to bring them good news from God. An elderly man asked if he was too old to become a Christian. Eliot and his friends told him that a good father is always glad to welcome home a son who is sorry for what he has done wrong.

For the first time, one of the Englishmen said a prayer in Algonquian. One man began to cry. When John Eliot talked to him after the prayer, he cried even more. This man and other people took the message into their hearts.

In late November, John Eliot preached at Nonantum a third time. Later that day, Waban taught his fellow villagers lessons Eliot had taught. Waban started waking up during the night to pray to God. The elderly man, who had wondered if he was too old to become a Christian, decided to follow God. His six sons decided to follow God, too.

When John Eliot came to Nonantum for a fourth meeting in December, the people of the village asked him if the English people would teach all of their children.

Who Was John Eliot?

John Eliot was born in Essex County, England, in 1604. His parents taught him to respect God, to pray, and to study the Bible. When he was fourteen years old, he went to Jesus College at Cambridge University.

After college, John taught school in a village in Essex. The school's headmaster was Thomas Hooker. John lived with Thomas Hooker's family. John Eliot wrote this about the Hooker family:

When I came to this blessed family, I then saw . . . the power of godliness . . . .

Puritans Found the Massachusetts Bay Colony

Thomas Hooker and John Eliot were Puritans. Puritans did not believe that the Church of England was pure. The Church of England persecuted Puritans. In 1630 seven hundred Puritans came to America. Their leader was John Winthrop. These Puritans founded the Massachusetts Bay colony. John Winthrop encouraged the colonists with these words:

For we must consider that we shall be as a city upon a hill. The eyes of all people are upon us.

1630 · GOVERNOR WINTHROP AT SALEM
BRINGING THE CHARTER OF THE BAY COLONY TO MASSACHUSETTS

The Massachusetts Bay colony later became Boston. John Eliot came to America in 1631. He settled near Boston in the new town of Roxbury. John Eliot's fiancée Hannah Mumford sailed to America a short time later. Their wedding was the first wedding in Roxbury. John soon became the Puritan minister of First Church in Roxbury.

Thomas Hooker came to America in 1633. He later founded the colony of Connecticut.

"Praying Indian" Villages

The colony of Massachusetts Bay later set aside land for a village. In this village, called Natick, native people who believed in Jesus could live together. They built homes, a bridge, and a meetinghouse. They used the meetinghouse for a school and a church. They built an apartment inside for John Eliot to use when he came there to preach.

People began to call these believers "Praying Indians." In a few years, Massachusetts had fourteen "Praying Indian" villages. Because of his deep devotion to native people, John Eliot became known as the "Apostle to the Indians." A group called the "Praying Indians of Natick and Ponkapoag" still exists in Massachusetts.

Natick Woods

First Book Printed in America

The writers of the Old Testament wrote in the Hebrew language. John Eliot helped to translate the book of Psalms from Hebrew into English. It was the first book printed in America. It was called *The Whole Booke of Psalmes*. People later called it the *Bay Psalm Book*.

The First Bible in America

John Eliot believed that the "Praying Indians" needed a Bible in their own language. He kept busy working with the Roxbury church and with the native people who had become Christians. When he could find time, he and a small number of "Praying Indians" translated the Bible into Algonquian. The Algonquian Bible was the first complete Bible printed in North America.

Page from *The Whole Booke of Psalmes*

Page from the Algonquian Bible

Site of the "Praying Indians" church in Natick

Tomb of native minister Daniel Takawambpait beside the church

John Eliot continued to minister to his church in Roxbury. He also preached to native people every other week until he was in his eighties.

John Eliot wrote: "Prayer and pains through faith in Christ Jesus will do anything." In Philippians the apostle Paul wrote:

I can do all things
through Him who strengthens me.
Philippians 4:13

Lesson Activities

- All Around the USA map: Find Boston and Natick.

- Timeline: Look at pages 4-5.

- Rhythms and Rhymes: Enjoy "Psalm 1" on page 6.

- Literature for Units 1-4: *Benjamin West and His Cat Grimalkin*.

Review Questions

- How did John Eliot learn to speak Algonquian?

- How would you answer the question, "How can we know Jesus Christ?"

- How does it help people to have the Bible in their own language?

Unit Review

- Student Workbook: Complete the Lesson 6 / Unit 2 Review page.

Hands-On History Ideas

- Pretend that you are a missionary to a people that has never heard about Jesus before. How will you tell them about God and Jesus? How will you show them what it means to be a Christian?

- Use building blocks to build a wigwam as shown on page 36.

Unit 2 Project
Origami Mayflower

Supplies

- 1 piece brown construction paper
- 1 piece blue construction paper
- 3 popsicle sticks
- white paper
- white glue
- marker
- blue crayon

Directions

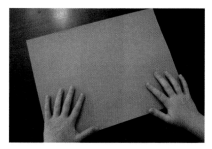

1. Lay paper flat.

2. Fold in half left to right.

3. Fold in half bottom to top.

4. Open last fold, turn paper.

5. Fold top corners down.

6. Fold front bottom flap up.

7. Turn over. Fold corners down.

8. Fold bottom flap up. Tuck corners around to back.

9. Bring bottom points of triangle together.

10. Lay down diamond with open end facing you.

11. Fold front bottom flap up.

continued

12. Crease.

13. Turn over and fold bottom flap up. Crease.

14. Bring bottom points of triangle together . . .

15. . . . to form a diamond.

16. Gently tug top points.

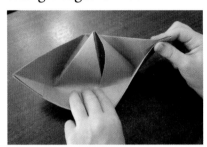

17. Ease out points.

18. Crease along bottom.

19. Ease open.

20. Glue in popsicle sticks.

21. Cut sails from white paper. Glue onto popsicle sticks. Draw waves and write words on blue paper. Sail your boat on the ocean!

Unit 3

Conrad Weiser
German Peacemaker

John Weiser and thousands of other Germans were discouraged. Wars in the 1600s had caused great suffering. A famine in 1710 made life worse. Weiser's wife Anna Magdalena died that spring. Their son Conrad was twelve years old. Years later Conrad Weiser wrote this about his mother:

She was much beloved by her neighbors and feared God. Her motto was: "Jesus Christ, I live for you, I die for you, thine am I in life and death."

John Weiser heard that Great Britain's Queen Anne was willing to help refugees get land in America. Less than a month after his wife died, John Weiser sold his house, fields, meadows, vineyard, and garden to his oldest daughter and her husband. He and his eight youngest children set out for England. They arrived at the beginning of September.

Thousands of Germans crowded into London. Chiefs of the Mohawk tribe were visiting there. The Mohawk felt sorry for the German refugees. They offered to give them some of their land in the New York colony. Queen Anne arranged for ships to take refugees to America. The nine Weisers set sail with about 3,000 other Germans.

Queen Anne

Iroquois Village

Tee Yee Neen Ho Ga Row was one of the Mohawk who visited London in 1710. He was a Christian preacher.

John Weiser married again soon after his family arrived in America. His new wife was an unkind stepmother. Conrad Weiser later wrote this about that time:

> I frequently did not know where to turn, and learned to pray to God and His word became my most agreeable reading.

Conrad Weiser and the Six Nations

Three years after the Weisers arrived in America, Mohawk chief Quaynant asked John Weiser if Conrad could come to live with the Mohawk. John Weiser agreed. Conrad went to live in Quaynant's village in November of 1713. He stayed eight months.

Some native nations joined together to help each other. The Mohawk nation was part of one of these groups. Their group had three different names. Each name described one characteristic of the group. In 1722 people began calling the group the Six Nations when the sixth nation joined. They were the Cayuga, Mohawk, Oneida, Onondaga, Seneca, and Tuscarora tribes.

Mohawk Chief Joseph Brant

Tuscarora Corn Husk Doll

Oneida Ceremonial Collar

47

Iroquois hunter in snowshoes

The tribes all spoke the Iroquois language, so people called them the Iroquois Confederacy or simply Iroquois.

The tribes lived in longhouses, so people called them the Haudenosaunee Confederacy. Haudenosaunee means "people of the longhouse."

While living with the Mohawk, Conrad learned Iroquois customs and the Iroquois language. The Mohawk made Conrad a permanent member of their tribe.

Iroquois Longhouse

Trouble for German Settlers

Life was not as easy in America as the Weisers had hoped. They worked as indentured servants for the first few years. While Conrad was living with the Mohawk, the Weisers and about 150 other German families moved to the Schoharie Valley, on the land the Mohawk had given them. Many Mohawk lived nearby. When Conrad returned to his father in the summer, he helped the Mohawk and the settlers communicate with each other.

Oneida Chief Daniel Bread

The governor of New York did not believe the Germans should be living in Schoharie. He sold their land to merchants. Some of the German settlers bought land back from the merchants and stayed at Schoharie. Others built a road and also canoes. They used these to move to Pennsylvania.

William Penn had founded Pennsylvania in 1682. It was America's twelfth English colony. Penn was a Quaker. He called the Pennsylvania colony a "Holy Experiment." He made plans for a city he called Philadelphia. The word means "brotherly love."

When Conrad Weiser was 24 years old, he married Ann Eve Feck. They had fourteen children. The couple remained at Schoharie until 1729, when they also moved to Pennsylvania. Conrad worked as a farmer and he also tanned leather.

Schoharie Valley

Conrad Weiser, "Indian Agent"

When Europeans began coming to North America to trade and to settle, some men, like Conrad Weiser, became experts in native languages and customs. Traders and settlers hired these experts to help them in their relationships with native nations. They called them "Indian agents."

Beaded belts called wampum were important to the Six Nations. Wampum was like a history book. Wampum bead designs told about past battles, treaties, and events. Conrad Weiser understood how the Six Nations used wampum. This knowledge helped him in his work as a peacekeeper.

Shikellamy

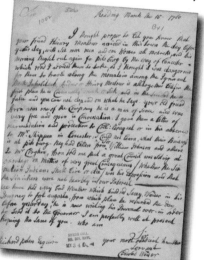

Letter in Conrad Weiser's handwriting

Iroquois trade with Europeans.

the Wampum

Conrad Weiser and Shikellamy

Conrad Weiser met Shikellamy in Pennsylvania. Shikellamy was a leader in the Oneida tribe, which was part of Iroquois Confederacy. The two men became friends. In 1731 Shikellamy went to Philadelphia to meet with leaders of the Pennsylvania colony. He invited Weiser to go with him.

Leaders of the Pennsylvania colony and of the Six Nations trusted both Conrad Weiser and Shikellamy. Weiser used his knowledge of the Iroquois language and customs to help the colonists and native people make many treaties.

Conrad Weiser and Shikellamy traveled often between Philadelphia and the Six Nations capital in Onondaga. Their friendship grew.

Until the end of his life, Conrad Weiser helped native people and European settlers live in peace. He also helped the Six Nations live in peace with other native nations.

Faith and Ministry

Conrad Weiser was a devout believer in Jesus Christ. He was a teacher and a minister in the Lutheran Church. Conrad and Ann's daughter Anna Maria married Henry Muhlenberg. Muhlenberg was an early leader of the Lutheran Church in America. Many people in the Iroquois Confederacy believed in Jesus.

Home on the Conrad Weiser Homestead
in Berks County, Pennsylvania

Near the end of Shikellamy's life, he became part of the Moravian Church. A Moravian minister was with him when he died.

Conrad Weiser died in 1760. Among his possessions were an English Bible, three German Bibles, a book of sermons, a German prayer book, two hymn books, a framed map of Pennsylvania, and two "Indian blankets."

When native people and European settlers met at a conference in 1761, Seneca George of the Seneca nation said:

> We . . . and our cousins are at a great loss and sit in darkness . . . by the death of Conrad Weiser, as since his death we cannot so well understand one another.

Keeping peace is important to Jesus. In the Sermon on the Mount, He said:

> Blessed are the peacemakers, for they shall be called sons of God.
> Matthew 5:9

Lesson Activities

- All Around the USA map: Find Philadelphia, Iroquois Confederacy, Onondaga, Berks County, and Schoharie Valley.

- Rhythms and Rhymes: Enjoy "Ho Ho Watanay" on page 7.

- Student Workbook: Complete the Lesson 7 page.

- Literature for Units 1-4: *Benjamin West and His Cat Grimalkin*

Review Questions

- How did the Mohawk offer to help German refugees in London?

- Why do you think Conrad Weiser did a good job as an "Indian agent"?

- Why did many German settlers move from New York to Pennsylvania?

Hands-On History Ideas

- Pretend that you are invited to live with the Mohawk. You get a chance to learn their language and way of life. What can you also teach them about your way of life?

- Create a wampum belt design with building blocks.

Serving Others in the Georgia Colony

James Oglethorpe visited England's prisons with a broken heart. He saw prisoners who were hungry, sick, and miserable. Many prisoners hadn't hurt anyone or stolen anything. Many people were in prison simply because they owed money to someone else. Whole families were stuck inside stinking, dirty, dangerous prisons. They had no way to escape. James Oglethorpe wanted change in England's prisons.

Oglethorpe's broken heart came from the loss of his friend Robert Castell. The government had thrown Castell in prison because he owed money to another person. Prisoners in that day had to pay for a decent room and food. Robert Castell didn't have money for that. Prison keepers placed him in a room with another prisoner who was dangerously sick. Robert Castell also became sick and died.

Oglethorpe convinced the government of England to make prisons better. Those changes helped one problem. There was still another problem. Poor people in England had very few ways to help their families. Most poor people stayed poor. Their children grew up to be poor, too. Many poor families ended up in prison for debt. James Oglethorpe dreamed of a better life for England's poor. What if England established a colony in America to help poor people begin a new life?

English Prison

A New Colony

England's King George II listened to James Oglethorpe present his idea. The king granted him permission to start a new colony in 1732. The colony was named Georgia in honor of King George II. It was Britain's thirteenth colony in America. The king chose twenty-one men to serve as trustees to lead the new colony, including James Oglethorpe. The trustees wanted to help people. They received no pay for their work.

The trustees interviewed people to select Georgia's first English settlers. They looked for people who had skills like carpentry, baking, farming, and store-keeping. Each family received supplies and boat passage to America. In the colony, each family received a piece of land.

James Oglethorpe

The trustees wrote the laws for the new colony. They expected the settlers to build houses, take care of their land, and help the colony as a whole. The trustees did not want Georgia to become another place where the rich could get richer and the poor would get poorer. People who had enough money could buy a farm in Georgia, but they could not have slaves. When Georgia began, slavery was against the law.

James Oglethorpe traveled with the first 114 men, women, and children who left England to settle Georgia. They sailed in November of 1732 and arrived in South Carolina two months later. While the settlers waited in South Carolina, Oglethorpe and a band of soldiers traveled to Georgia. They looked for a good place to establish the colony's first town.

St. Simons Island, Georgia

53

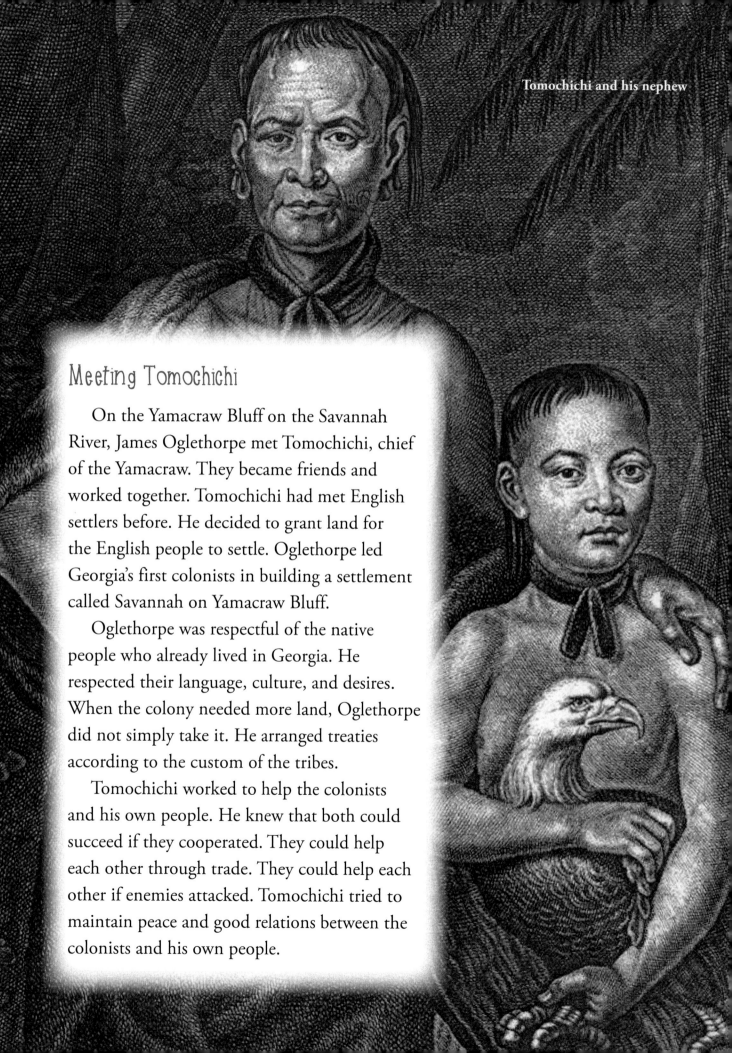

Tomochichi and his nephew

Meeting Tomochichi

On the Yamacraw Bluff on the Savannah River, James Oglethorpe met Tomochichi, chief of the Yamacraw. They became friends and worked together. Tomochichi had met English settlers before. He decided to grant land for the English people to settle. Oglethorpe led Georgia's first colonists in building a settlement called Savannah on Yamacraw Bluff.

Oglethorpe was respectful of the native people who already lived in Georgia. He respected their language, culture, and desires. When the colony needed more land, Oglethorpe did not simply take it. He arranged treaties according to the custom of the tribes.

Tomochichi worked to help the colonists and his own people. He knew that both could succeed if they cooperated. They could help each other through trade. They could help each other if enemies attacked. Tomochichi tried to maintain peace and good relations between the colonists and his own people.

Helping the New Colony

In July of 1733, Oglethorpe was surprised to see a ship arrive in Savannah. The ship brought forty-two Jewish people fleeing persecution in Europe. Oglethorpe welcomed them to the new colony. Doctor Samuel Nunes was part of the group. He was able to help save lives when colonists became sick with yellow fever. Many Christians who were persecuted in Europe also found a home in Georgia.

Oglethorpe stayed in Georgia for one year to help the colony. The government of England did not provide enough money for the colony at the beginning. Oglethorpe used his own money to help the colony get off to a good start.

James Oglethorpe introduces Yamacraw natives to the trustees.

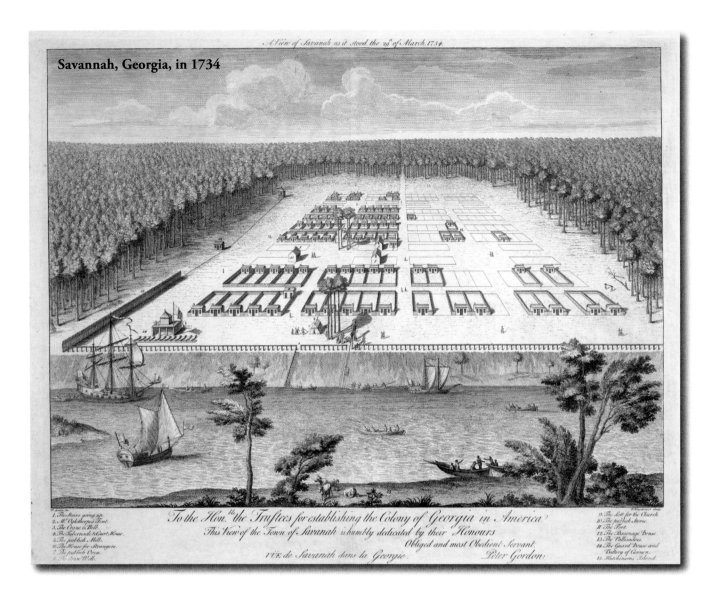

Savannah, Georgia, in 1734

A View of Savanah as it stood the 29.th of March. 1734

To the Hon.ble the Trustees for establishing the Colony of Georgia in America
This View of the Town of Savanah is humbly dedicated by their Honours
Obliged and most Obedient Servant
vüe de Savanah dans la Georgie.   Peter Gordon.

Not For Self, But For Others

When Oglethorpe returned to England, Tomochichi went with him.
Some of Tomochichi's family and representatives of the Lower Creek tribe
traveled with them. Tomochichi spoke with leaders in England on behalf
of his people. He asked that the English trade fairly. He also asked for help
bringing Christian education to his tribe. When Tomochichi returned to
Georgia, he spoke with other chieftains. He encouraged them to cooperate
with the English. Tomochichi met with English missionaries who visited
Georgia. He told them:

I shall be glad to see you at my town, and I would have you teach our Children, but we would not have them made Christians as the Spaniards make Christians, for they baptize without Instruction; but we would hear and be well instructed first; and then be baptized when we understand.

In 1736 English missionary Benjamin Ingham helped to establish a school near Savannah for Tomochichi's people. James Oglethorpe returned to Georgia several times to support the new colony. He and Tomochichi continued to work together for peace. Tomochichi died in 1739 when he was nearly one hundred years old.

The motto of the trustees of the Georgia colony was "not for self, but for others." James Oglethorpe and Tomochichi helped many people. They knew the strength of respect, service, and working together.

This I command you,
that you love one another.
John 15:17

Lesson Activities

- All Around the USA map: Find Savannah.

- Look at the map and chart of England's thirteen colonies on the next two pages.

- Rhythms and Rhymes: Enjoy "Hole in the Wall" on page 8.

- Student Workbook: Complete the Lesson 8 page.

- Literature for Units 1-4: *Benjamin West and His Cat Grimalkin*

Review Questions

- Why did James Oglethorpe want to start a new colony in America?

- What are some ways that James Oglethorpe helped the new colony of Georgia?

- Why do you think Tomochichi wanted Christian education for his people?

Hands-On History Ideas

- Pretend that you are the leader of a new colony. You will need to find a good place for the first settlement, help people build houses and find food, and cooperate with native people who already live in the area.

- Use building blocks to build a small settlement for a new colony.

Thirteen English Colonies

Lake Superior

Lake Huron

Lake Michigan

Lake Ontario

Lake Erie

New Hampshire

Massachusett

New York

Hudson River

Rhode Island

Connecticut

Pennsylvania

New Jersey

Delaware

Maryland

Ohio River

Appalachian Mountains

Virginia

North Carolina

South Carolina

Some colonies claimed land west of the Appalachian Mountains, but most colonists lived in the areas shown here.

Georgia

Atlantic Ocean

How Did We Get Thirteen English Colonies?

After James Oglethorpe founded Georgia in 1733, Great Britain had a total of thirteen colonies in America. This is the story of their beginnings.

Virginia – The first colony was Virginia. English settlers landed there in 1607. They called the first settlement in Virginia Jamestown.

Massachusetts – English Pilgrims founded Plymouth in Massachusetts in 1620. English Puritans founded the Massachusetts Bay colony (later Boston) ten years later.

New Hampshire – The first English settlers in New Hampshire came in 1623. They were merchants who set up a fishing business.

Maryland – Cecil Calvert brought two hundred settlers to Maryland in 1634. His title was Lord Baltimore.

Connecticut – The first settlers in Connecticut were from the Netherlands. John Eliot's friend Thomas Hooker from England brought one hundred settlers there in 1636.

Rhode Island – Minister Roger Williams came to Rhode Island in 1636. Soon other colonists who believed in freedom of religion settled there, too.

North Carolina – In 1663 King Charles II gave eight proprietors a large area of land which they named Carolina. One of the proprietors was Lord Cooper.

South Carolina – Lord Cooper founded Charles Town (later Charleston) in 1670. The proprietors sold Carolina to King George II in 1729. Carolina divided into two colonies.

Delaware – The first settlers in Delaware were from the Netherlands and Sweden. They called it New Sweden. The English took control in 1664.

New Jersey – New Jersey's first settlers were also from the Netherlands. The English also took control of New Jersey in 1664.

New York – New York's first settlers were from the Netherlands, too. They called the area New Netherland. After the English took control in 1664, they named it New York.

Pennsylvania – William Penn was a Quaker. He came to America in 1682 to found Pennsylvania.

Georgia – James Oglethorpe founded Georgia in 1733.

Governor's Palace of the Virginia colony in its capital of Williamsburg

Natives, Traders, & Beavers in New France

The colonies along the East Coast of North America were English. In 1666, the colonists were loyal subjects of England's King Charles II. He decreed that men who came to visit him must wear:

Breeches that were gathered at the knee,

A waistcoat (we call it a vest),

A cravat around his neck,

A periwig (a wig arranged in a fancy way),

A long coat,

A hat (when he was outside).

King Charles II

Fishermen and Natives

Not long after Columbus sailed to the New World, fishermen from Europe came to the coast of what later became Canada. They caught huge amounts of cod in those waters. The fishermen dried the fish to preserve them until they could sell them in Europe.

While the fishermen waited for the fish to dry onshore, they met native peoples who wanted to trade with them. The fishermen traded metal and fabric for furs and food.

Soon traders from France, the Netherlands, and England came to North America to trade with native people. They brought fishhooks, guns, knives, twine, kettles, beads, blankets, buttons, cloth, combs, mirrors, needles, scissors, spoons, and other items to trade.

The Abenaki tribe was one tribe that traded with Europeans.

Natives, Fur Traders, and Hatters

The best dressed men in England and other countries in Europe wore hats made from beaver fur. Millions of beavers lived in North America. People's desire for beaver hats made beavers an important item for trade in America for over 250 years.

Native people were trapping beavers long before Europeans arrived. They roasted beaver meat for food. They made coats, mittens, and moccasins from warm beaver skins. They even made dice out of beaver teeth.

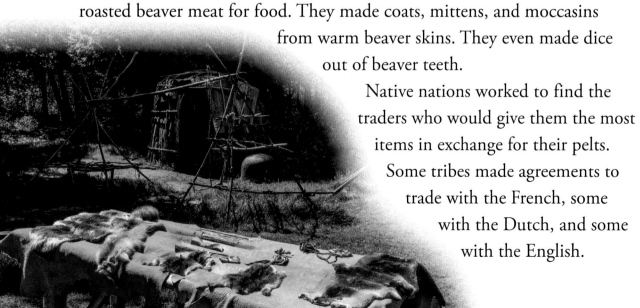

Native nations worked to find the traders who would give them the most items in exchange for their pelts. Some tribes made agreements to trade with the French, some with the Dutch, and some with the English.

Native people continued to do the trapping. They also prepared the beaver pelts to be shipped back to Europe. Natives prepared two types of beaver pelts: parchment beaver and coat beaver. To prepare parchment beaver, they simply dried beaver skins. To make coat beaver, they sewed pelts together to make a blanket. They wore the blanket around their shoulders for a year. This made the pelt oily and soft.

Verrazzano

Drying a beaver skin

European hatters removed the fur from the pelts and used it to make felt. The best felt had both parchment and coat beaver. Hatters used the felt to make hats.

New France in the New World

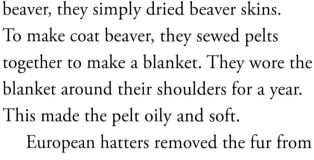

While English colonists founded the thirteen colonies, including the area called New England, French traders and settlers founded New France. New France grew to include a large area of North America. It included much of what is the United States of America today.

In 1524 King Francis I of France sent Giovanni da Verrazzano to North America. This was only 32 years after Columbus made his first voyage. Verrazzano and his crew crossed the Atlantic Ocean in the ship, *La Dauphine*. They sailed to Cape Fear in what is now North Carolina. Then they sailed north along the East Coast.

Making beaver hats

In 1534 Frenchman Jacques Cartier sailed into the St. Lawrence River. He began trading furs with local native tribes. In 1608 Samuel de Champlain founded Quebec City. This was one year after the English founded Jamestown, Virginia. Quebec City was the first permanent French settlement in North America.

At first, only a few people moved to New France to live as settlers and raise families. However, many fur traders came, as well as French Catholic missionaries who came to share the gospel with native people.

King Louis XIV Helps New France

Around 1634 twelve-year-old Pierre Boucher came to New France with his family. They settled along the St. Lawrence River. While Pierre was a teenager, he went to live in a settlement where Catholic priests taught the Huron tribe. Like Conrad Weiser in Pennsylvania, Pierre became an interpreter as an adult.

The kings and queens of England made many decisions about what happened in the English colonies. They sent soldiers to help them. However, King Louis XIV, who ruled as the French king from 1643 to 1715, was not very involved with the French settlers. The settlers wanted more help.

In 1662 the governor of New France sent Pierre Boucher to France to ask King Louis XIV to help them. The king agreed and sent soldiers to New France.

Most of the people living in New France were men. In 1663 the king sent unmarried women to New France. He gave them clothes and a hope chest. Inside each chest were a comb, scissors, needles, lace, gloves, a bonnet, and other items. Most of these women, who were called the King's Daughters, married settlers. Thousands of Canada's residents today are descendants of the King's Daughters.

Pierre Boucher departs from France.

King Louis XIV

Pierre Boucher

63

French Explore the Mississippi River

Louis Joliet was born in New France in 1645. He studied at Jesuit College in Quebec City. He became an organist, a teacher, and a fur trader.

Europeans were still looking for the water route to Asia that Columbus had hoped to find. In 1673 Joliet decided to explore the Mississippi River. He wanted to find out whether the river went to the Gulf of Mexico or to the Pacific Ocean. He also wanted to find natives who would trade furs.

Jacques Marquette was a Catholic priest who taught native people about Jesus. He decided to travel with Joliet so he could teach the natives who lived beside the Mississippi River.

Catholic nun teaches native women and children in Quebec.

New Spain

Pacific Ocean

N
W E
S

Lake Superior

Mississippi River

Missouri River

Lake Michigan

Lake Huron

Lake Erie

Lake Ontario

St. Lawrence River

Quebec City

Ohio River

New France

Land claimed by both France and Great Britain

Appalachian Mountains

British Territory

Atlantic Ocean

Mississippi River

Gulf of Mexico

Caribbean Sea

Great Britain, France, and Spain in America — 1650

Joliet, Marquette, and five boatmen called voyageurs traveled down the Mississippi River in two canoes. The native people treated the seven Frenchmen with kindness. Joliet, Marquette, and the boatmen reached what is now Arkansas. Native people assured them that the Mississippi flowed into the Gulf of Mexico.

Spain controlled the area where the Mississippi River emptied into the Gulf of Mexico. Joliet and Marquette turned around and went back north because they were afraid that Spanish soldiers might attack them.

In 1682 another Frenchman, Rene-Robert Cavalier de La Salle, and a small group of Frenchmen and native guides sailed down the Mississippi River. They reached the Gulf of Mexico. Even though the Spanish already claimed the area, La Salle claimed it for France.

French and Indian War

By 1754 French settlers and traders lived and traded alongside the St. Lawrence River, the Great Lakes, and the Mississippi River. By this time England was called Great Britain. Both Great Britain and France wanted to control more and more of North America. They began fighting a war in 1754. The British called it the French and Indian War.

On one side were France and native tribes who sided with the French. On the other side were Great Britain, American colonists, and tribes who sided with the British. The Iroquois Confederacy fought on the side of the British. Conrad Weiser joined the side of the British.

French and British troops fought in Europe, too. The war ended when the French and British signed the Treaty of Paris of 1763. Great Britain was victorious. France lost all of its territory in North America. Later that year, King George III issued the Proclamation of 1763. It set aside land west of the Appalachian Mountains for native people.

God gives us ways to make peace between people. The apostle Paul wrote:

Finally, brethren, rejoice, be made complete, be comforted, be like-minded, live in peace; and the God of love and peace will be with you.

2 Corinthians 13:11

Lesson Activities

- Timeline: Look at pages 4-7. You may also wish to review the previous pages you have learned about.

- Literature for Units 1-4: *Benjamin West and His Cat Grimalkin*

Review Questions

- Why did Europeans want to buy so many beaver pelts from the New World?

- Why did Louis Joliet want to explore the Mississippi River?

- Why do you think Europeans wanted to find a way to get to Asia by water?

Unit Review

- Student Workbook: Complete the Lesson 9 / Unit 3 Review page.

Hands-On History Ideas

- See the Unit 3 Project instructions on the next page.

Unit 3 Project
Charles II's Hat Shop

Supplies

- paper cups (approximately 2 inches across the bottom)
- ruler
- scissors
- black craft paint
- paintbrush
- black construction paper
- white glue or craft glue
- embellishments as desired (examples: felt, buttons, ribbons, lace, craft feathers, brads, sequins, stickers, etc.)

Directions

1. Mark cup 1 ¼ inches from the bottom. Cut to 1 ¼ inch height.
2. Paint cup black. (We found a package of black paper cups for $1.00 and only painted the bottom.) Let dry.
3. Trace and cut 3 ½ -inch circle from black construction paper. (We used a small bowl to trace.)
4. Place the cup base-down on construction paper. Trace around. Cut out inner circle.
5. Place glue along the inner circle.
6. Place cup cut-side down on glue. Let dry.
7. Glue embellishments to crown (cup) of hat as desired. Bend up brim of hat and glue securely. Use a clothespin to hold in place while glue dries.
8. Glue embellishments to outside of hat as desired. Let dry.
9. Creatively display hats in your hat shop!

How to make a felt feather:

1. Draw long leaf-shape on felt. Cut out.
2. Cut tiny snips toward center on both sides.
3. Gently pull on ends to spread feather out.

Unit 4

George Hewes
and the
Boston Tea Party

George Hewes walked through the snow down a familiar Boston street. Boston was his home. He was used to the brick buildings and the cobblestone streets. He was used to the crowds of people. He was used to the British soldiers milling about.

As he walked along on this snowy day, he spotted a little boy pushing a sled through the snow. The boy stopped to talk to John Malcom. Malcom was a British customs-house officer. Malcom did not want the boy to talk to him. He replied angrily, "Do you speak to me, you rascal?" He raised his cane to strike the boy's head. George Hewes spoke up just in time. "You are not about to strike that boy!" he exclaimed. "You may kill him!" Malcom turned to Hewes and called him a rascal just as he had the boy. "Do you presume, too, to speak to me?" Malcom demanded of Hewes in disgust.

Boston

Hewes replied, "I am no rascal, sir."
The officer then raised his cane and
struck Hewes on the head. The blow was
so hard it tore a hole in Hewes' hat and
knocked him to the ground.

A crowd soon gathered around Hewes.
Malcom was afraid of what the crowd
might do. He rushed away to hide in his
house. The angry citizens soon broke
into Malcom's house and brought him
back out into the street. They beat him
severely. They smeared him with tar. They
covered the tar with feathers. To "tar and
feather" was a way that people sometimes
punished and humiliated a person.

George Hewes

Colonists prepare to tar and feather John Malcom.

Anger in the Colonies

Trouble between British soldiers and American colonists was getting worse. Not long before the day Malcom attacked Hewes, British soldiers fired their guns into a group of angry Boston citizens. The soldiers killed five people. The tragedy was called the Boston Massacre.

Some colonists wanted to stay loyal to King George III of England. Others wanted to break free. Those who wanted to be free were called patriots. They thought the British government was treating them unfairly. Great Britain passed laws the colonists did not like. They made the colonists pay high taxes. They did not let representatives from the colonies help decide on the laws and the taxes. Many colonists resented this "taxation without representation."

King George III

Boston, 1770s

A Tax on Tea

The British government decided to tax shipments of tea to the colonies. This made many colonists angry. Tea was very popular, but many colonists stopped buying and drinking it. They wanted to show the British government they were not happy about the tax. Many colonial cities refused to accept shipments of tea so they would not have to pay the tax.

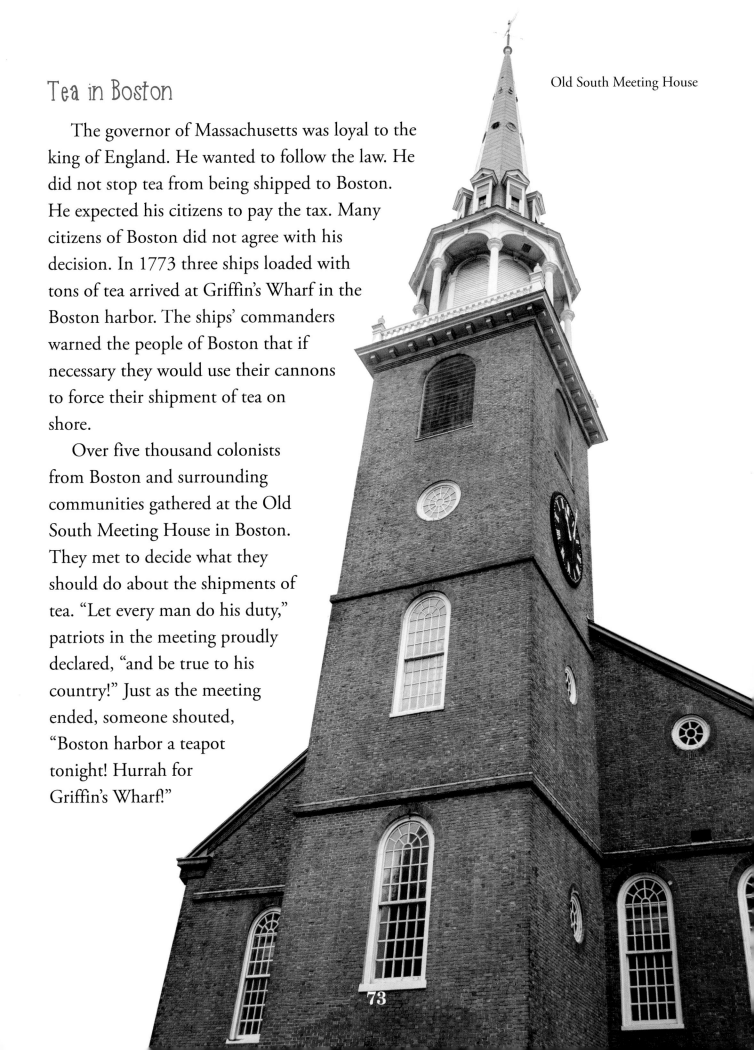

Tea in Boston

The governor of Massachusetts was loyal to the king of England. He wanted to follow the law. He did not stop tea from being shipped to Boston. He expected his citizens to pay the tax. Many citizens of Boston did not agree with his decision. In 1773 three ships loaded with tons of tea arrived at Griffin's Wharf in the Boston harbor. The ships' commanders warned the people of Boston that if necessary they would use their cannons to force their shipment of tea on shore.

Over five thousand colonists from Boston and surrounding communities gathered at the Old South Meeting House in Boston. They met to decide what they should do about the shipments of tea. "Let every man do his duty," patriots in the meeting proudly declared, "and be true to his country!" Just as the meeting ended, someone shouted, "Boston harbor a teapot tonight! Hurrah for Griffin's Wharf!"

That evening George Hewes and dozens of other patriots gathered their courage. They prepared to board the three ships. The men knew that if the British authorities found out who they were, they would arrest and punish them. That's why many disguised themselves as native people. After Hewes put on his disguise, he painted his face and hands with coal dust from a blacksmith shop. He picked up a hatchet and a club. He was ready for action.

Restored Tea Ship at the Boston Tea Party Ships and Museum in Boston

The Boston Tea Party

The men met at Griffin's Wharf and divided into three groups, one group for each ship. A crowd gathered to watch as the men boarded the ships. The men used their hatchets to break open the chests of tea. They threw the tea into the water.

One sixteen-year-old participant later recalled, "We were merry . . . at the idea of making so large a cup of tea for the fishes . . . . I never worked harder in my life."

As the men quietly headed home three hours later, 342 chests of tea bobbed up and down in Boston harbor. The people in the crowd went home. It was eerily quiet that night in Boston. The Boston Tea Party brought the American colonies and Great Britain one step closer to war.

Looking Back

When George Hewes was an older man, he recalled his memories about the Revolutionary War for a book called *A Retrospect of the Boston Tea-Party, with a Memoir of George R. T. Hewes, a Survivor of the Little Band of Patriots Who Drowned the Tea in Boston Harbour in 1773*. The book's author described Hewes as a man with "integrity of character." When a person has integrity he is honest and does what is right. The author wrote that without integrity of character, "independence and republican liberty are but empty names."

We are blessed to live in a country where we can enjoy freedom. More important than freedom, however, is integrity. Whether we live as citizens in a free country or as slaves in a land not our own, we must always strive to live a life of integrity and faith.

He who walks in integrity
walks securely,
but he who perverts his ways
will be found out.
Proverbs 10:9

Lesson Activities

- All Around the USA map: Find Boston.

- Rhythms and Rhymes: Enjoy "The Taxed Tea" on page 9.

- Student Workbook: Complete the Lesson 10 page.

- Literature for Units 1-4: *Benjamin West and His Cat Grimalkin*

Review Questions

- What happened at the Boston Massacre?

- What did patriots want the colonies to do?

- Do you think the Boston Tea Party was a good thing to participate in?

Hands-On History Ideas

- See the Unit 4 Project instructions on page 88.

Give Me Liberty
or
Give Me Death!

It was August of 1774. The weather was hot in the colony of Virginia. Patrick Henry leaned forward on his horse as he rode north. Edmund Pendleton, a respected lawyer, rode beside him. They rode through forests, fields, and streams until they came to Mount Vernon, home of George Washington. They spent the night there. The next morning they set off on their horses again. Washington rode with them. These three men were on their way to the Continental Congress in Philadelphia, Pennsylvania. Virginians had chosen them to represent Virginia as delegates, or representatives, at this important meeting.

Henry, Washington, and Pendleton
travel to Philadelphia.

Philadelphia

The First Continental Congress

Many colonists wanted to be free from the British. Twelve colonies sent representatives to meet together as the Continental Congress. They wanted to organize protests against the British government.

Patrick Henry was a young lawyer who had struggled through poverty for years. He searched for a job that would suit him and would provide for his family. He might have seemed an unlikely choice to represent Virginia at the Congress. The other men were accomplished and wealthy. Henry was not, but he had a skill that Virginians knew would be important in the Congress. They considered Henry the most eloquent man in Virginia. To be eloquent means to know how to choose the right words and to say them well.

Patrick Henry

The Continental Congress called its first meeting to order in Philadelphia on September 5, 1774. The delegates were on edge. They feared that if they said something, they might offend someone else. They sat in silence. The silence was so strong, someone said the men could hear their hearts beating.

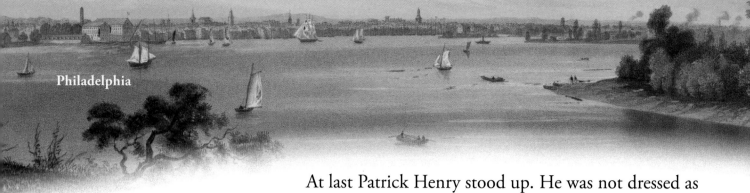
Philadelphia

From a poster
recruiting soldiers
for the Continental Army

At last Patrick Henry stood up. He was not dressed as well as the other men, but when he opened his mouth, he earned their respect. Henry calmly stated the reasons they were all gathered together. At the end of his speech, Henry declared, "The distinctions between Virginians, Pennsylvanians, New Yorkers, and New Englanders are no more. I am not a Virginian, but an American!"

The Continental Congress worked for peace with Britain, but they were not successful. Even the peace-loving delegates could sense that a war with England would probably happen soon. In October the members of the Continental Congress issued a declaration to inform the colonists they should "be in all respects prepared for every emergency." All across the colonies, patriots gathered ammunition, trained to become soldiers, and prepared to battle the British.

Patrick Henry in St. John's Church

After his service in the Continental Congress, Patrick Henry returned home. In March of 1775, Henry went to a meeting of men from all over Virginia. They met in St. John's Church in Richmond.

Patrick Henry wanted the men to make plans to form an army. He said they needed to prepare the soldiers for war.

Not all of the men at the meeting were ready for war. They knew that a war with Great Britain was probably going to happen, but they did not want to admit it. Some spoke up in protest. Patrick Henry was ready with an answer.

At this meeting, Patrick Henry spoke some of the most famous words in all of American history. He spoke about how the British had treated the colonists. He spoke passionately about the hardships the British government had caused. He told them he saw no way there could ever be a peaceful resolution to the problems with Great Britain.

As Henry spoke, the men listened. The following account is based on the memories of someone who heard Patrick Henry speak that day in St. John's Church:

Henry rose with an unearthly fire burning in his eye. He commenced somewhat calmly, but the smothered excitement began more and more to play upon his features and thrill in the tones of his voice. The tendons of his neck stood out white and rigid like whip-cords. His voice rose louder and louder, until the walls of the building, and all within them, seemed to shake and rock in its tremendous vibrations. Finally, his pale face and glaring eye became terrible to look upon. Men leaned forward in their seats, with their heads strained forward, their faces pale, and their eyes glaring like the speaker's.

St. John's Church

Patrick Henry in
St. John's Church

Patrick Henry ended his speech with these words:

The war is inevitable, and let it come! I repeat it, sir, let it come. . . . Gentlemen may cry, Peace, Peace—but there is no peace. The war is actually begun! The next gale that sweeps from the north will bring to our ears the clash of resounding arms! Our brethren are already in the field! Why stand we here idle? What is it that gentlemen wish? What would they have? Is life so dear, or peace so sweet, as to be purchased at the price of chains and slavery? Forbid it, Almighty God! I know not what course others may take; but as for me, give me liberty or give me death!

The men were convinced. They chose Patrick Henry to lead a committee to prepare for war. They gathered weapons and soldiers. They trained the soldiers to fight. The Revolutionary War soon began.

Patrick Henry's Legacy

Patrick Henry

Patrick Henry later served as governor of Virginia and as a member of the Virginia state legislature. He loved his state and his country. He served the public well.

Patrick Henry loved his family. He had six children with his first wife. After she died, Henry married again and had eleven more children. Henry enjoyed having his children and grandchildren around him. He loved to get on the floor and play with the little ones.

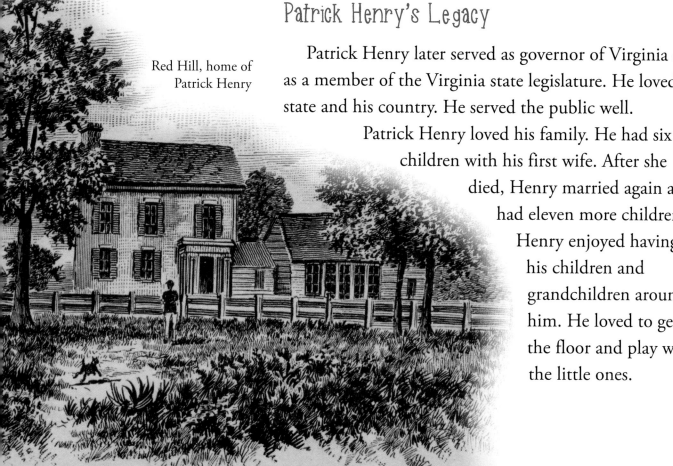

Red Hill, home of Patrick Henry

Sometimes Henry played his violin as the little ones danced around him. One of his grandsons said that Henry set a "good example of honesty, benevolence, hospitality, and every social virtue." On Sunday evenings he read aloud to his family from a book of sermons. After the reading everyone sang hymns together as Henry accompanied them on his violin.

Patrick Henry also loved his God and Savior. When Patrick Henry was an older man, he decided how to divide his money and land among his children and grandchildren after he died. He wrote these decisions in a document called a will. Henry ended his will with these words: "This is all the inheritance I can give to my dear family. The religion of Christ can give them one which will make them rich indeed."

Blessed be the God and Father
of our Lord Jesus Christ,
who according to His great mercy
has caused us to be born again
to a living hope through the
resurrection of Jesus Christ
from the dead, to obtain
an inheritance which is
imperishable and undefiled
and will not fade away,
reserved in heaven for you.
1 Peter 1:3-4

Lesson Activities

- All Around the USA map: Find Philadelphia and Richmond.

- Student Workbook: Complete the Lesson 11 page.

- Literature for Units 1-4: *Benjamin West and His Cat Grimalkin*

Review Questions

- Why were the delegates at the Continental Congress afraid to speak at first?

- What do you think Patrick Henry meant when he said, "Give me liberty or give me death"?

- What things did the colonies need to do to prepare for war with the British?

Hands-On History Ideas

- Pretend that you and one or two other people are riding horses on your way to an important meeting. What is the meeting going to be about? Where will you stay on the way? How long will it take you to get there?

- Use building blocks to build a church building.

Phillis Wheatley
and Her
Poetic Genius

The little girl clung nervously to the dirty cloth wrapped around her waist. She looked around her and wondered what might happen next. Already slave traders had snatched her from her home far away in Africa. They had marched her onto a ship with men, women, and other children. Already they had forced her to endure a miserable trip across the ocean. Already the traders had lined her up with her fellow passengers. Now, as they all stood side by side, white people were carefully looking them over. The little girl had no idea what would happen next.

Suddenly she noticed a lady's gentle eyes looking intently into her own. A man beside the gentle lady gave money to the slave trader. The little girl realized the lady had chosen her. The lady led her to a carriage nearby.

The little girl wondered why the lady had chosen her. There were other African girls at the market who were strong and healthy. She was sickly and thin. For some reason, this gentle and tender lady in the lovely dress had chosen her.

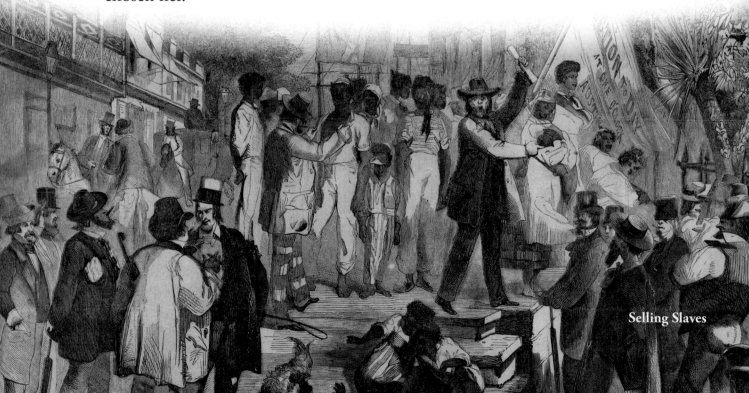

Selling Slaves

Boston

The carriage rumbled down the bustling streets of Boston. It finally stopped, and the kind lady led the girl into a house. She dressed the girl in new clothes. The kind lady did not know the girl's name nor her age. She did not know how to ask in a way the girl could understand. She decided to name her Phillis. Phillis was the name of the ship that had brought the girl to Boston. She saw that the girl had lost her front baby teeth, so she guessed she was about seven years old.

Phillis Wheatley at Home

Phillis soon learned how to cook and clean and do other chores around the Wheatley home. Mrs. Wheatley had chosen Phillis at the slave market because she looked humble and sweet. Not long after Phillis came, Mrs. Wheatley grew to be amazed at how quickly Phillis learned. Phillis was eager to learn. She wrote on the wall with a piece of chalk or a bit of charcoal, trying her best to copy the letters of the English alphabet. Mrs. Wheatley didn't mind. She was glad Phillis wanted to learn.

Cooking Pot

83

The Wheatleys loved Phillis. Mary, the Wheatleys' daughter, taught Phillis how to read and write. It was not common at this time for a white person to do this for an enslaved person. The Wheatleys did not give Phillis as many chores as their other slaves. They wanted her to have more time for her studies. Phillis became almost like a daughter to the Wheatley family.

It took Phillis only about a year and a half to become fluent in English. She loved to read the Bible. She studied Latin, astronomy, geography, literature, and history. She wrote poems. Mrs. Wheatley boasted about Phillis to her wealthy friends in Boston. They were amazed. They loved the beautiful poems Phillis wrote.

Phillis may have learned to read from lessons such as this.

Phillis Wheatley the Poet

In 1767, after Phillis had been with the Wheatleys for six years, a newspaper published one of her poems. Phillis was the first woman from Africa to have something published in America. Phillis became well-known for her beautiful poetry. Even though Phillis' poems were beautiful, no printer in America wanted to publish a book by an enslaved woman. Some people even doubted that Phillis had written the poems herself.

Boston, 1770s

In 1773 Phillis went on a journey to England. The English people gave her a warm welcome. A wealthy English lady, the Countess of Huntingdon, decided to pay for the printing of a book of Phillis' poems.

Before the printing was completed, Phillis learned that Mrs. Wheatley was dangerously ill. She hurried home to care for her beloved mistress. After she returned to Boston, the Wheatleys gave Phillis her freedom. Phillis continued to look after Mrs. Wheatley until she died the next year.

Phillis Wheatley

Phillis Wheatley the Genius

Times were hard in the colonies. Even though the colonists enjoyed the poems Phillis wrote, most people could not afford to buy her new book.

America soon fought the Revolutionary War with Great Britain. Phillis wrote a poem in honor of General George Washington, commander-in-chief of the colonial army. Her poem praised his heroic service. She sent the poem to General Washington, along with a letter in which she wrote:

Wishing your Excellency all possible success in the great cause you are so generously engaged in. I am, Your Excellency's most obedient humble servant,

Phillis Wheatley

Washington wrote Phillis a letter in reply. In his reply he wrote:

> *I thank you most sincerely for your polite notice of me, in the elegant Lines you enclosed; and however undeserving I may be of such [praise], the style and manner exhibit a striking proof of your great poetical Talents.*

Washington wrote in his letter that he wanted to publish the poem so that others could enjoy Phillis' "genius." He had not done so, however, because he was concerned that people would think he had published the poem to praise himself. Washington ended the letter by saying that if Phillis was ever near the army headquarters, he would be happy to have her pay him a visit. He signed the letter:

> I am, with great Respect, Your obedient humble servant,
>
> *G. Washington*

General George Washington

Statue of Phillis Wheatley in Boston

During a time when many did not treat women and slaves with the respect they deserved, Washington's letter shows how much he valued and appreciated Phillis Wheatley and her abilities.

The Bible teaches us about Joseph. Joseph's brothers sold him into slavery. It was a terrible thing for the brothers to do. God still brought much good out of the situation.

The slave trade that brought Phillis Wheatley to America was terrible. Even though Phillis came to America as a slave, she was grateful for where God had brought her. She realized that because she had been a slave, she had learned about Jesus. Phillis could have spoken the same words to the slave traders that Joseph spoke to his brothers:

As for you,
you meant evil against me,
but God meant it for good . . . .
Genesis 50:20

87

Lesson Activities

- All Around the USA map: Find Boston.

- Rhythms and Rhymes: Enjoy "Goliath of Gath" on page 10.

- Timeline: Look at pages 8 and 9.

- Literature for Units 1-4: *Benjamin West and His Cat Grimalkin*

Review Questions

- Why do you think most people did not teach slaves to read?

- Phillis Wheatley was the first woman from Africa to accomplish what in America?

- How did George Washington show respect to Phillis Wheatley?

Unit Review

- Student Workbook: Complete the Lesson 12 / Unit 4 Review page.

Hands-On History Ideas

- Pretend that you are teaching someone how to read. You might want to use chalk and a chalkboard or pencil and paper. You might use books to teach letters and words.

- Use building blocks to build a building similar to the Boston buildings you see on page 84.

Unit 4 Project
A Large Cup of Tea for the Fishes

Supplies

- 1 piece blue construction paper
- scissors
- black marker
- scraps of other paper
- 6 tea bags
- white glue
- brown paper
- tape
- glue stick

Directions

1. Cut waves across the top of the blue paper.
2. Draw waves on the rest of the blue paper.
3. Write "A large cup of tea for the fishes" across the top. (See page 74.)
4. Draw and cut out some small fish from paper scraps.
5. Glue tea bags on paper with white glue as shown.
6. Cut rectangles from brown paper (ours are 2 ½ x 4 inches.) Decorate to look like wooden crates. Write 3, 4, and 2 on the crates. (342 is the number of crates dumped at the Boston Tea Party.)
7. Tape sides of crates over tea bags as shown.
8. Glue fish around crates with glue stick.

Note: The tea in the real crates was loose and not in tea bags, but that might be a bit too messy for this project!

Unit 5

A Midnight Ride with Paul Revere

Across the countryside, people were on edge. They were waiting. Farmers tried to concentrate on their springtime work. They stopped every little while to strain their eyes into the distance. Neighbors made hurried visits, asking for news. Women looked anxiously from kitchen windows and over their clotheslines. Children peered from trees, hills, and upstairs windows. They wanted to be first to see a sign of the British. Everyone was tense, just waiting.

These farmers, craftsmen, and shopkeepers waited for the signal. They were ready to take up their weapons and fight. These English colonists in America were tired of being bossed by the British government far across the ocean. They were tired of unfair treatment. They were ready to defend their rights. America was the land they had made their own. They had become "Minutemen"—ready to fight at a minute's notice. But they had to wait for the signal.

Paul Revere

Late one April night, the signal came. Families lay asleep. Hoofbeats suddenly pounded into their yards. They heard shouts. Jumping from bed, they threw open their windows. House to house the message rang in the dark night: "The British are coming!" The moment for the revolution had arrived.

Paul Revere rode through the Massachusetts countryside on April 18, 1775. He warned his fellow American patriots that British soldiers were advancing in their direction. Other messengers sounded the alarm along different roads. The next day, America's Minutemen fought British soldiers at the towns of Lexington and Concord. They fired the first shots at Old North Bridge. It was the first battle of the American Revolution.

Who Was Paul Revere?

Paul Revere's father was born in France in 1702. He moved to Boston in 1716. He worked for a goldsmith to learn how to craft metal. Six years later, Paul Revere's father set up his own shop. He married Deborah Hitchbourn. Their son, Paul Revere, was born in December of 1734.

Paul Revere

Young Paul Revere learned how to craft metal objects in his father's shop. His father died when Paul was nineteen. Two years later, Paul Revere took over the family business.

Paul Revere was a skilled artist working with gold and silver. He was also a good businessman. He managed many employees and apprentices. His shop produced all kinds of metal objects: teapots, serving dishes, cups, tongs, spoons, buckles, buttons, rings, and beads. Revere also engraved designs on his metal objects.

Revere became a printer as well. He designed and printed labels and pictures for books, magazines, and newspapers. He even printed money for the Massachusetts government.

Paul Revere engraved this
January 1, 1770, newspaper.

Paul Revere engraved this picture, which
shows British ships in Boston harbor.

Silver Revere Pitcher

Paul Revere married Sarah Orne in 1757. They had eight children. Sarah died in 1773, soon after the birth of their eighth child. Later that year, Paul Revere married Rachel Walker. They also had eight children.

Son of Liberty

Paul Revere was a respected citizen of Boston. He raised his family and built his business. Meanwhile the American colonies had disagreements with their rulers in Great Britain. Revere became a trusted leader in Boston's secret group, "Sons of Liberty." The group met to plot against the British government. They organized public protests. Revere took part in their most famous protest, the Boston Tea Party. Paul Revere's midnight ride to warn the Minutemen was brave and dangerous.

Paul Revere knew that the British could punish or even execute him. He was working against the king of England. Revere took that risk because he believed in the cause of an independent America.

After the Revolution

After the war, Paul Revere continued to work in the silver and goldsmithing trade. Two of Paul Revere's sons and two grandsons joined the family business. The Revere family added bell-making to their business. They made hundreds of bells. Many Revere bells still ring in church towers. When he was sixty-five years old, Paul Revere started another business. He bought an old ironworking mill. He used it to produce sheets of copper. He had to continue learning the science of metals to perfect this process. The copper mill was successful. Shipbuilders used Revere copper to build ships for the new United States Navy. Paul Revere died in 1818 at the age of 83.

Paul Revere cast the bell in this church in Hancock, New Hampshire.

Revere statue in Boston

"Paul Revere's Ride"

Paul Revere was an important figure in Boston during his lifetime. As the fervor of the Revolution passed, so did his fame. In 1860 Henry Wadsworth Longfellow wrote a poem called "Paul Revere's Ride." A Boston newspaper published the poem. "Paul Revere's Ride" is one of the most popular American poems of all time. It made Paul Revere a famous figure in American history. It begins:

Listen, my children, and you shall hear
Of the midnight ride of Paul Revere,
On the eighteenth of April, in Seventy-five;
Hardly a man is now alive
Who remembers that famous day and year.

The patriots of 1774 fought for liberty. They wanted freedom to make their own decisions about their government. Keeping God's law and seeking His ways brings true liberty to a person's heart.

So I will keep Your law continually,
Forever and ever.
And I will walk at liberty,
For I seek Your precepts.
Psalm 119:44-45

Lesson Activities

- All Around the USA map: Find Boston, Lexington, and Concord.
- Rhythms and Rhymes: Enjoy "War Song" on pages 11-12.
- Student Workbook: Complete the Lesson 13 page.
- Literature for Units 5-9: *Toliver's Secret*

Review Questions

- What happened on the night of April 18, 1775?
- What did Paul Revere do in his business?
- Why do you think the citizens of Boston respected Paul Revere?

Hands-On History Ideas

- See the Unit 5 Project instructions on page 108.

Thirteen Colonies Declare Independence

Thousands of American soldiers gathered in New York City. The British army was approaching fast. But the orders for the evening of July 9, 1776, were not for battle. The orders were to march to the parade grounds. Officers would make an important announcement at 6 o'clock. General George Washington would be there. At the appointed time, officers read a printed document loudly and slowly:

When in the Course of human events, it becomes necessary for one people to dissolve the political bands which have connected them with another . . . .

We hold these truths to be self-evident, that all men are created equal, that they are endowed by their Creator with certain unalienable Rights, that among these are Life, Liberty and the pursuit of Happiness . . . .

That these United Colonies are, and of Right ought to be, Free and Independent States; that they are Absolved from all Allegiance to the British Crown . . . .

And for the support of this Declaration, with a firm reliance on the protection of divine Providence, we mutually pledge to each other our Lives, our Fortunes and our sacred Honor.

General Washington

96

Units of American troops had spread across the colonies. Congress sent them copies of the Declaration of Independence. Hearing the news, soldiers burst into cheers and celebrations. A new nation! Their own nation! No longer were they defending their rights as British colonists. They were fighting to be "free and independent states." The British army was the most powerful army on earth. Americans rose up to fight anyway. They burned with the spirit of freedom. This Declaration of Independence gave the American Army new zeal. In the words of their revered leader, George Washington:

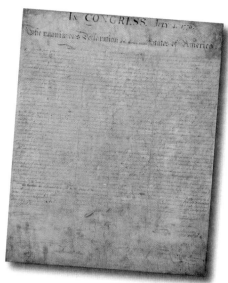
Declaration of Independence

> Perseverance and spirit have done wonders in all ages.

After Washington's troops in New York City heard the Declaration, they marched to Bowling Green Park. They were chasing down a victim: a statue of King George III of Great Britain. Jubilantly, defiantly, they pulled the statue down. King George was their king no more! The lead from his statue was too precious to waste. The Army melted it into bullets and cannonballs to shoot at the king's own army.

Washington's troops hear the Declaration of Independence.

Washington's troops pull down the statue of King George III.

97

PUBLISHED BY CURRIER & IVES   Entered according to act of Congress in the year 1876 by Currier & Ives in the Office of the Librarian of Congress at Washington   125 NASSAU ST. NEW YORK

WASHINGTON, APPOINTED COMMANDER IN CHIEF.

The Continental Congress, June 15th 1775, elected George Washington, Commander in Chief, of all the forces raised, or to be raised, for the defence of the Colonies. He being then 43 years of age, and a member of that body, when President Hancock announced to Washington his appointment, he modestly and with great dignity signified his acceptance of the important trust.

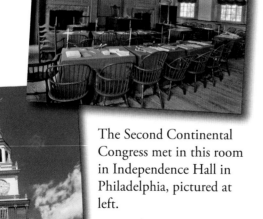

The Second Continental Congress met in this room in Independence Hall in Philadelphia, pictured at left.

The Second Continental Congress

Representatives from all thirteen colonies met in Philadelphia in May of 1775 for the Second Continental Congress. Difficulties between Americans and the British were growing worse. Americans chose to fight for better treatment from Great Britain. The Second Continental Congress chose George Washington to command the Continental Army.

The Declaration of Independence

British and American soldiers clashed in Lexington and Concord, Massachusetts, on April 19, 1775. Peace with Britain looked more and more hopeless. The next year the Continental Congress decided it was time to start a new country. This country would be the United States of America. Congress decided to announce to Great Britain and the world that the colonies were now an independent country. Congress chose a committee of five men to write a Declaration of Independence. Thomas Jefferson was the main author.

Jefferson represented the colony of Virginia at the Continental Congress. He was thirty-three years old, one of the youngest delegates. Jefferson already had a reputation as a gifted writer. While staying in Philadelphia, Jefferson rented two rooms in the home of bricklayer Jacob Graff. Jefferson brought in a custom-made portable writing desk and swivel chair. There he composed some of history's most important words.

British and American troops fired the first shots of the American Revolution at the Old North Bridge over the Concord River.

Committee Members: Benjamin Franklin, John Adams, and Thomas Jefferson

The Continental Congress adopted the Declaration of Independence on July 4, 1776. This is why we celebrate July 4 as America's birthday. Congress asked local printers to make copies. They sent copies all over the colonies.

Fifty-six men of the Continental Congress signed their names on the Declaration of Independence. They were taking a bold and dangerous step. To the British, they were traitors to their king. If the British won the war, they could be executed for their act of treason. Those brave delegates put their lives, fortunes, and honor at risk. They took that risk for a free and independent America.

Signing the Declaration of Independence

The American Revolution

British and American armies fought battles up and down the colonies. Americans struggled through six years of war. The American Army was continually low on money, supplies, and training. But they had George Washington. He was a leader they believed in. They also had "perseverance and spirit." They did not give up.

British General Cornwallis surrenders to American General George Washington at Yorktown.

In 1778 France joined the American side. In October 1781, the American and French armies trapped the British at Yorktown, Virginia. British General Cornwallis knew his army could not defeat the combined armies. He sent out an officer bearing the white flag of surrender.

Britain was shocked. This raggle-taggle band of colonists had put up quite a fight. How dare they call themselves an independent country? Was it possible the Americans had won? Britain could have sent more troops and continued the war. They were fighting in other wars across the globe. They decided to give up the fight. Great Britain recognized America as a separate nation. Perseverance and spirit claimed victory once again.

The Declaration of Independence states that all men are created equal.

God created man in His own image, in the image of God He created him; male and female He created them.
Genesis 1:27

Lesson Activities

- All Around the USA map: Find New York City, Philadelphia, and Yorktown.

- Rhythms and Rhymes: Enjoy "Yankee Doodle" on page 13.

- Student Workbook: Complete the Lesson 14 page.

- Literature for Units 5-9: *Toliver's Secret*

Review Questions

- The Declaration of Independence declared the colonies independent of what country?

- Why do you think that the Continental Congress wanted all American soldiers to hear the Declaration of Independence?

- Why was it bold and dangerous for men to sign the Declaration of Independence?

Hands-On History Ideas

- Pretend that you have to deliver an important message to units of soldiers scattered across the countryside. Hope you can find a fast horse! Hope you can sneak past the British soldiers!

- Use building blocks to build a desk and chair for Thomas Jefferson.

James Madison
and the
Constitution

Two trunks full of books. What a treasure trove! So much to learn! James Madison loved to read, study, and learn. What fun to unpack the trunks. He held each volume. He marveled at the discoveries that lay before him. These trunks had traveled from France to Madison's home in the Virginia countryside.

James Madison's friend Thomas Jefferson was in France, serving as the U.S. ambassador. Jefferson told Madison that he would be glad to purchase books for him. Jefferson looked for books that were "old and curious, or new and useful." In the late 1700s, it was hard to get a particular book you wanted to read. Many books were available only in Europe.

Madison accepted Jefferson's offer. He requested books about "the ancient or modern federal republics, on the law of Nations, and the history natural and political of the New World."

James Madison had a special reason for collecting books. He had an important project underway. He was trying to learn the best way to govern a nation.

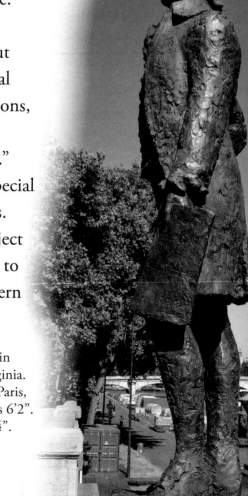

Madison statue in Harrisonburg, Virginia. Jefferson statue in Paris, France. Jefferson was 6'2". Madison was 5'4".

A Weak Government

The United States of America declared independence from Great Britain in 1776. During the Revolutionary War, the Continental Congress made decisions for the new nation. Each state sent delegates to the Congress. In 1777 the Continental Congress wrote the Articles of Confederation. This was a basic plan for a government of the United States.

The Articles of Confederation left most decisions to each state. The new country had many problems. Americans disagreed over many issues. America had been founded with great hope and courage. Now Americans were afraid their new nation would crumble.

The Education of James Madison

James Madison was born on March 16, 1751. For his whole life, the same corner of Virginia countryside was his home. When Madison was about ten years old, his parents built Montpelier, a grand brick home. Montpelier was the center of a huge plantation. The plantation had many slaves. Slaves bore the work of building, farming, and taking care of the household. The Madison family passed down these human beings as property from father to son.

James Madison

On the grounds of Montpelier

Montpelier

College of New Jersey

James Madison was always eager to learn. His family was able to provide him with a good education. His mother was most likely his first teacher. At age eleven young James went to the school of Donald Robertson. Robertson had come to Virginia from Scotland. Many of his students grew up to be leaders in America's early days. Robertson introduced young James to a host of fascinating subjects. Robertson guided him in studying from history's greatest thinkers and writers.

As an elderly man, Madison said of his teacher, "All that I have been in life I owe largely to that man." After attending Robertson's school, Madison went to the College of New Jersey, now Princeton University. He excelled in his studies there.

James Madison soon began to work in government. He first served in his home county. Then he served in the government of the Virginia colony. Virginians chose him to attend the Continental Congress. Madison's fellow leaders respected his knowledge and clear thinking. He was able to help people with different points of view work together.

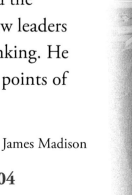

James Madison

Making Plans for a New Government

James Madison's cousin Francis Taylor visited Montpelier in March of 1787. Francis complained in his diary that his cousin spent whole days in his room. Madison was buried in urgent business. He was worried. He had watched anxiously as the states failed to work together. He was afraid the "American experiment" would turn out to be a disaster. He was studying ideas about government. What works? What doesn't work? What could he do to make things better?

This medallion shows James Madison at his desk.

The idea of a government that served its people was a new idea. Kings and queens had ruled most people in the history of the world. Most people had never considered the idea of people choosing their own leaders. Madison was determined to save the country Americans had fought for. He made good use of his blessings. He had an excellent education. He had experience. He had wise friends. He had a good library, expanded thanks to Thomas Jefferson. Madison studied history and government. Madison wrote down his ideas about how to help the United States.

The Constitutional Convention

Meanwhile, Madison worked to arrange a meeting. He thought representatives from all the states should meet. All states except Rhode Island sent representatives to a convention in Philadelphia. The representatives met to work out a better government for the new country. Meetings began on May 25, 1787. Madison was ready with a new idea for government. Madison's plan was for three branches of government. The three branches were executive (president), judicial (judges and courts), and legislative (lawmakers).

The Constitutional Convention met at Independence Hall.

George Washington sat in this chair at the Constitutional Convention.

James Madison

The Constitutional Convention worked through a long, hot Philadelphia summer. They considered, argued, debated, and resolved. Finally they wrote a Constitution for the United States. Representatives signed their names on the Constitution on September 17, 1787. The Convention had made many changes to Madison's original proposal. Still, his ideas formed the foundation of the Constitution. The Constitution still governs the United States of America.

The first paragraph of the Constitution explains why America's leaders crafted it. It affirms the belief that government works best when people choose their own government.

We the People of the United States, in Order to form a more perfect Union, establish Justice, insure domestic Tranquility, provide for the common defence, promote the general Welfare, and secure the Blessings of Liberty to ourselves and our Posterity, do ordain and establish this Constitution for the United States of America.

James Madison worked to "secure the blessings of liberty" for his country. Meanwhile dozens of slaves worked at his family's plantation. Slave owners treated other human beings as property. They separated families. They forced slaves to work hard without pay. Sometimes they punished slaves cruelly.

Many of the early leaders of the United States owned slaves. Leaders argued over slavery at the Constitutional Convention. James Madison was not comfortable with slavery. He wanted slavery to end. He spoke against it. Sadly, he did not carry his convictions into action. He did not free his own slaves.

The Constitution Becomes Law

The Constitution stated that nine states must agree to it before it would become law in the United States. New Hampshire became the ninth state to accept the Constitution on June 21, 1788. On July 2, the Continental Congress announced that the Constitution was now the law. The nation prepared for peaceful elections as directed in the Constitution.

James Madison had accomplished what he set out to do. He had sat at his desk at Montpelier. He had surrounded himself with books. He had studied the ideas of the great thinkers of history. He had formed a vision for a new kind of government. James Madison's vision had become real.

God wants people to honor those who work in government. The apostle Paul told Titus to remind Christians about that.

Remind them to be subject
to rulers, to authorities,
to be obedient, to be ready
for every good deed.
Titus 3:1

Lesson Activities

- All Around the USA map: Find Montpelier and Philadelphia.
- Timeline: Look at pages 8-11.
- Literature for Units 5-9: *Toliver's Secret*

Review Questions

- What group made decisions for the new United States during the American Revolution and the early years as a nation?
- Why was James Madison worried about his country in 1787?
- What helped to prepare James Madison to be a leader in working out a new Constitution?

Unit Review

- Student Workbook: Complete the Lesson 15 / Unit 5 Review page.

Hands-On History Ideas

- Pretend you are a teacher. What would be important to teach future leaders of your country?
- Use building blocks to build a trunk to carry books across the Atlantic Ocean.

Unit 5 Project
Revere and Son Shop Window

Supplies

- 3 pieces white cardstock
- tape
- 1 piece of aluminum foil
  (a little larger than a piece of cardstock)
- pencil
- glue stick
- ruler
- marker
- white glue
- 22 popsicle sticks

Directions

1. Tape two pieces of cardstock together with longer sides meeting to make one large piece. Flip over to put taped side on the back.

2. On the third piece of white cardstock, draw objects that can be made of silver, such as teapots, coffee pots, goblets, mugs, spoons, vases, bowls, and serving platters. See second picture.

3. Glue cardstock with drawings to aluminum foil with glue stick.

4. When glue is dry, cut out objects. Handles can be cut separately as shown for easier cutting. See third picture.

5. You can "engrave" your silver objects by pressing down designs with a pencil if you wish.

6. Using a ruler, draw lines as a "shelf" for the objects, as shown in the fifth photo.

7. Glue silver objects onto the "shelf" with glue stick.

8. Write "Revere and Son" across the top with a marker.

9. Use white glue to glue popsicle sticks in a window pattern.

Unit 6

The White House and
Washington, D.C. in 1803

George Washington at Mount Vernon

Sunrise light spilled onto the gently flowing waters of the Potomac River. The quiet stillness of night gradually faded. Though the morning had just arrived, men and women were already walking to their day's work. The rustle of hooves tramped across the fields. An overseer rode by on his horse. Mount Vernon was awake.

George Washington was master of this little world. He sat at the breakfast table. His plate of hoecakes was swimming in butter and honey. Family and guests filled other chairs around the elegant table. Washington was quiet and focused, but cheerful. Breakfast was a pause in the busy work of his day. Every corner of this house mattered to him. His mind ranged over every acre of his farm. This was the home he had made for his family. This was the estate he carefully managed. This was the place his heart was at home.

Washington gave years of service to his country. His service had always meant leaving this place. He had gone where his country needed him. He was an old man now. Finally, he could look at the years ahead and see himself at home. Breakfast was over. He went outside to mount his horse. He would check on fields, workmen, and projects underway. Washington was always busy making improvements. He gave instructions, checked on progress, and corrected workers. He even got his hands dirty helping.

Mount Vernon

George and Martha Washington with two of their grandchildren and an enslaved person.

A Self-Sufficient Estate

Washington owned 8,000 acres of land. Large and small buildings looked like a village surrounding the large mansion. Slave workers and free workers lived with their families in homes scattered throughout the estate. The many outbuildings included barns, stables, and a coach house. There was a spinning house for making yarn and cloth. There was a gristmill for grinding grain into flour. There was a smokehouse for preparing meat. There was a blacksmith shop, a salt house, and a greenhouse.

Mount Vernon Plantation

Washington's goal was a self-sufficient plantation. Mount Vernon's work force produced almost everything the Washington family and their workers needed. They also produced extra goods to sell for cash. Cobblers made shoes and seamstresses made clothing right on the estate. Gardeners grew abundant fresh vegetables. Orchards produced apples, pears, cherries, peaches, and apricots. Fields yielded crops of corn, tobacco, and wheat.

The noise and smell of animals were everywhere: horses, mules, cows, sheep, hogs, dogs, cats, chickens, turkeys, and geese. Down by the river, warehouses stood ready for fishing season. Each spring workers caught and preserved over a million fish. Washington had many managers and overseers. Even so, he stayed personally in touch with operations at his estate.

Slavery at Mount Vernon

Over three hundred enslaved persons lived on George Washington's estate. Slaves worked in every aspect of farm and household operations. Generations of slave families served the extended Washington family. Some slaves lived in large dormitories. Others lived in small cabins. A slave cabin usually had a tiny garden and a few chickens outside the door.

Washington inherited ten slaves when he was eleven years old. He bought more slaves as a young adult. His wife Martha brought many more slaves onto the estate. They were part of her property from her first marriage.

In George Washington's world, slavery was normal. His attitude changed as he grew older. He eventually decided to stop buying and selling human beings. He hoped that the institution of slavery would someday end in America. He gave instructions in his will for his slaves to be freed at the time of his wife's death. Still, the Washington family depended on the labor of enslaved people for their comfortable lifestyle.

This man is probably Hercules, the enslaved person who worked as the Washingtons' cook.

Washington's Childhood and Marriage

George Washington was born in 1732 at Pope's Creek, Virginia, on the Potomac River. Washington's father died when George was eleven. His father left young George a 280-acre farm.

Washington started working as a surveyor when he was a teenager. Surveyors study the geography of a given area. They determine accurate locations and produce maps. At age 21, Washington joined the British army stationed in America. He loved the adventurous life of a soldier. He served with courage and excellence.

George Washington married Martha Custis in 1759. She was a young widow. She had a young son and daughter. Washington loved and raised them as if they were his own children. Soon after his marriage, George Washington inherited his family's estate at Mount Vernon.

Wedding of George Washington and Martha Custis

General and President

Washington served for fifteen years in the colonial government of Virginia. The Continental Congress chose George Washington to command the American Army in June of 1775. Washington told Martha that he expected to be safely back at Mount Vernon that fall. It was eight years before he could return home. Washington was the leader the country needed. He encouraged the struggling Army and new nation to keep going. After the American Revolution, Washington resigned from command of the Army. He returned home to Mount Vernon.

In 1787 Washington reluctantly left home again to help his struggling new nation. The Constitutional Convention was meeting in Philadelphia. The Convention asked him to serve as president of the Convention. People had more trust in the Convention because Washington was there. Washington hoped the Convention would complete his service to his countrymen.

The United States asked Washington to do one more thing. With the new Constitution in action, America chose George Washington to be the first President of the United States. He served for eight years. He set the example of what it means to be president. Washington earned the title, "Father of His Country," because he led and served.

George Washington becomes the first president.

Home to Mount Vernon

In 1797 George and Martha Washington returned home to Mount Vernon to stay. Washington stayed active managing his estate. December 12, 1799, was a cold and rainy day. After spending much of the day riding around his estate on his horse, Washington became sick.

Mount Vernon weathervane

114

Washington's illness quickly grew serious. Two days later, Washington died in his own bedroom at Mount Vernon. Many of his loved ones were with him.

A Dove of Peace

A gold dove with an olive branch in its mouth flies above the highest point of Mount Vernon's roof. George Washington designed this weathervane himself. He ordered it from a master craftsman in Philadelphia. The dove symbolized Washington's hopes for peace for his country.

Mount Vernon was George Washington's place of peace. It was the place to which he always yearned to return. Yet, for long years as soldier and statesman, he sacrificed his own peace. Washington left Mount Vernon for the good of his country. He guided America to a place of peace.

George Washington was a man of prayer. Paul taught Christians in Colossae:

Devote yourselves to prayer,
keeping alert in it
with an attitude of thanksgiving.
Colossians 4:2

Lesson Activities

- All Around the USA map: Find the Potomac River, Mount Vernon, and Philadelphia.

- Rhythms and Rhymes: Enjoy "Minuet" on page 14.

- Student Workbook: Complete the Lesson 16 page.

- Literature for Units 5-9: *Toliver's Secret*

Review Questions

- Why is George Washington known as the "Father of His Country"?

- Why did George Washington spend so much time away from Mount Vernon?

- What does the peace dove weathervane on the top of Mount Vernon symbolize?

Hands-On History Ideas

- See the Unit 6 Project instructions on Page 128.

A Home for the President

Busy workmen heard a coach arriving. Tools in hand, they went to the windows to look. The president is here! The house did not look very presidential. It smelled like wet plaster and paint. Most of the rooms were unfinished. The mess of construction spilled outside. The yard was full of trash piles. Large holes pocketed the ground where workers had dug clay to make bricks. But President John Adams had arrived. Ready or not, from this day forward, this would be the home of every President of the United States.

John Adams had left a comfortable house in Philadelphia and all the luxuries of a big city. He had just moved to Washington, America's new capital city. The so-called city contained muddy roads, a few houses, and half-built government buildings. See the illustration on page 109.

After dinner, John Adams carried a candle up a back staircase. He went to the lonely living quarters. That night he became the first president to sleep in the White House. The next day he wrote a letter to his wife Abigail:

Washington, D.C., and the United States Capitol Building, 1800

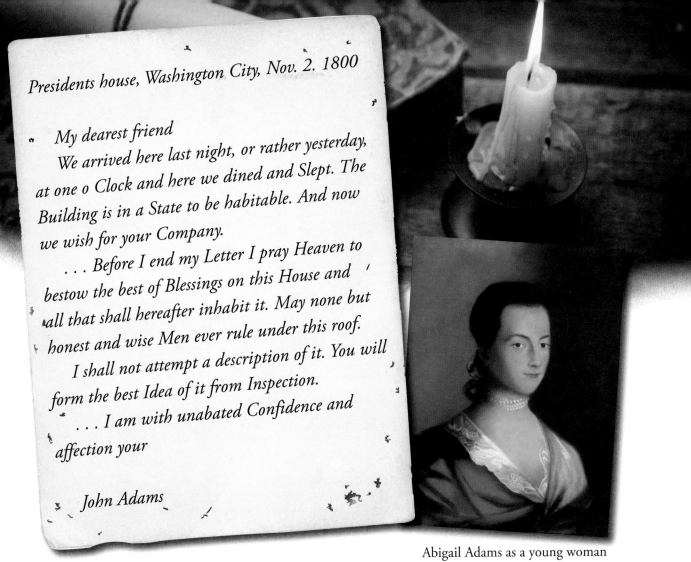

Presidents house, Washington City, Nov. 2. 1800

My dearest friend
   We arrived here last night, or rather yesterday, at one o Clock and here we dined and Slept. The Building is in a State to be habitable. And now we wish for your Company.
   . . . Before I end my Letter I pray Heaven to bestow the best of Blessings on this House and all that shall hereafter inhabit it. May none but honest and wise Men ever rule under this roof.
   I shall not attempt a description of it. You will form the best Idea of it from Inspection.
   . . . I am with unabated Confidence and affection your

John Adams

Abigail Adams as a young woman

Choosing a Capital City

The new United States had agreed on the Constitution. They had created a bold and imaginative new form of government. They had also created a lot of work to be done! Each new department needed an office. They had to hold elections to fill dozens of government posts. What about the courts? What about the military? What about the post office? One first step was to establish a capital city.

America's leaders had argued for years about where the capital city should be. Should it be in the North or the South? Should they choose an established city or start from scratch? Everyone had an opinion.

George Washington spent his terms as president first in New York City and then in Philadelphia. In 1790 Congress reached a decision. They gave Washington the job of choosing a ten-mile-square site where the government would build a new capital. The capital would move to the new site in ten years. Until then the government would continue to function in Philadelphia.

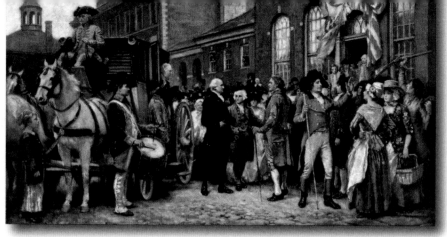

Washington took the oath of office for his first term as president at Federal Hall in New York City.
He took the oath of office for his second term as president at Congress Hall in Philadelphia.

Planning the Capital City

Washington chose a site along the Potomac River. He appointed his friend, surveyor Andrew Ellicott, to map out the area for the capital district. Ellicott worked with his brother Joseph and their friend Benjamin Banneker, pictured at right. The surveying team laid stones every mile to mark the site. Benjamin Banneker was the son and grandson of freed slaves. Banneker learned to read and write from his mother and his grandmother, who had come to America as an indentured servant. Banneker learned surveying, mathematics, and astronomy from borrowed books.

L'Enfant shows President Washington his plans for the capital city.

George Washington announced the location of the new capital on January 24, 1791. Washington called the little piece of wilderness "Federal City." Congress appointed a committee to establish the new capital. They named the new capital city "Washington."

George Washington chose another friend to design the city of Washington. Pierre Charles L'Enfant was born in France. He came to the United States to help fight in the Revolutionary War. After the war, he worked as an architect. Architects draw plans for buildings. L'Enfant made plans for a beautiful capital city for the new nation.

A Design for the President's House

Thomas Jefferson proposed a contest for a design for the president's house. The prize was $500. Architect James Hoban submitted the winning design. Hoban was born in a humble cottage in Ireland in 1758. He emigrated to the United States after the American Revolution.

Workers laid the cornerstone for the president's house on October 13, 1792. The eight-year construction project began. Builders lived in small huts and cottages grouped around the construction site. They formed Washington's largest neighborhood. Workshops, storehouses, a cookhouse, and stacks of building supplies added to the clutter. The largest building in the makeshift village was "carpenter's hall." It served as a church on Sundays.

James Hoban moved to Washington. He supervised the construction and managed workers, both slave and free. Hoban married Susanna Sewall on January 12, 1799. James Hoban settled permanently in Washington. He served the city in many ways. He and Susanna had ten children.

L'Enfant's design

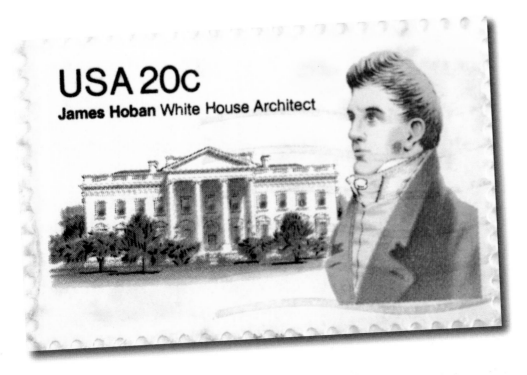

Architect's drawing of the White House

President John Adams

John and Abigail Adams in the White House

John Adams was the second President of the United States. He began his term in Philadelphia in 1797. He announced that he would move from Philadelphia to Washington in November of 1800. The ten-year deadline had arrived. It was time for the government to move to the new capital.

Abigail Adams joined her husband two weeks after he arrived. Fortunately, the Adams had simple tastes. They were used to making do. They had served their country at home and overseas. They had moved and set up housekeeping many times. Abigail wrote a letter to her daughter soon after her arrival. She complained about the mess of the city and the president's house. Yet she was determined to make the best of it.

> You must keep all this to yourself, and, when asked how I like it, say that I write you the situation is beautiful, which is true. The house is made habitable, but there is not a single apartment finished . . . . We have not the least fence, yard, or other convenience, without, and the great unfinished audience-room I make a drying-room of, to hang up the clothes in.

Abigail Adams

The principal stairs are not up, and will not be this winter. Six chambers are made comfortable; two are occupied by the President and Mr. Shaw [the president's secretary]; two lower rooms, one for a common parlour, and one for a levee-room. Up stairs there is the oval room, which is designed for the drawingroom, and has the crimson furniture in it. It is a very handsome room now; but, when completed, it will be beautiful. . . . It is a beautiful spot, capable of every improvement, and, the more I view it, the more I am delighted with it.

With this beginning, the new government and the new city had a new house that today still serves as the home of the president: the White House.

As you read in the letter President Adams wrote to his wife Abigail after his first night in the White House, he prayed for God's blessings on the president's house and all who would live there in the future.

Unless the Lord builds the house,
They labor in vain who build it;
Unless the Lord guards the city,
The watchman keeps awake
in vain.
Psalm 127:1

Lesson Activities

- All Around the USA map: Find Philadelphia, Washington, D.C., New York City, and the Potomac River.

- Rhythms and Rhymes: Enjoy "Oh, Dear! What Can the Matter Be?" on page 15.

- Student Workbook: Complete the Lesson 17 page.

- Literature for Units 5-9: *Toliver's Secret*

Review Questions

- What did John Adams pray for in his letter to his wife Abigail?

- What two cities hosted the United States government before the capital moved to Washington?

- List five tasks that were involved in establishing the city of Washington.

Hands-On History Ideas

- Pretend that you are overseeing the construction of an important government building. You will have to plan what to do when, hire and manage workers, and get supplies.

- Use building blocks to build the White House. It is pictured in the stamp on page 119.

Blazing Trails
with
Daniel Boone

Daniel Boone was bold, courageous, and independent. He tramped through endless forests with his rifle and wilderness know-how. He stood high on the cliffs of the Appalachian Mountains. He saw America stretching far beyond. Many Americans like Daniel Boone daydreamed about the West. They wanted adventure. They wanted land. They wanted new opportunities. Daniel Boone blazed their trail, opening the way to the West.

English colonists had settled along the East Coast of America. The Appalachian Mountains stood like a fence to the west. God spread this beautiful forest-covered barrier from Canada to Alabama. The expanse on the other side was mysterious and fascinating. The colonies from New Hampshire to Georgia gradually filled with towns, farms, and people. The West had wide open spaces. Americans grew all the more eager to go there.

Young Daniel Boone

Daniel Boone was born on November 2, 1734, in Exeter Township, Pennsylvania. He was the sixth of eleven children. Daniel led his family's cows to graze in the woods each day. He loved to be outdoors.

Daniel did not have much formal schooling. His brother's wife taught him to read and write. He became an expert on animals and birds. He hunted with a club. At age thirteen he got his own rifle. He helped put meat on his family's table.

Appalachian Mountains

In 1750 Daniel Boone was 15. His family left Pennsylvania for North Carolina. North Carolina had more open space for settlement. However, native people had lived and hunted there for many generations. They were not willing to let British settlers take over without a fight. In North Carolina, Daniel Boone joined the county militia. He had his first experience fighting against native people.

Daniel Boone's Birthplace

The French and Indian War

Boone joined the British army in America in 1755. He fought on the British side in the French and Indian War. Boone hauled supplies with a wagon and horses. His militia marched to attack the French Fort Duquesne in Pennsylvania. George Washington's militia joined Boone's militia in the same march. Washington had been born in 1732, two years before Daniel Boone.

Fort Duquesne

The French attacked south of the fort. They utterly defeated the British. In the crush of battle, Daniel grabbed a horse from his wagon team. He raced away and escaped with his life.

Daniel and Rebecca

Daniel Boone returned home to North Carolina. He married a girl from a neighboring family. Rebecca Boone was soon managing a busy frontier household. Daniel and Rebecca had four daughters and six sons. Rebecca Boone often ran the household alone. Daniel Boone made his living hunting and trapping animals for their fur. His trips into the wilderness lasted for days or even months.

"Daniel Boone Escorting Settlers through the Cumberland Gap" by George Bingham

Explorer, Businessman, and Pioneer

Boone explored the region west of the Appalachian Mountains. He worked with businessmen who hoped to make money by selling land to new settlers. Settlers needed a way to reach new farms on the other side of the mountains. It was hard to take wagons and livestock over the mountains. Boone led a team of thirty woodcutters. They cut a trail through the wilderness. Settlers called the trail the Wilderness Road. It passed through the Cumberland Gap.

Daniel Boone helped to establish a settlement at the end of the Wilderness Road. He named it Boonesborough. He moved his family there. The first residents of Boonesborough were in constant danger. Native people who lived in the area might attack any time. In faraway Philadelphia, the United States declared independence from Great Britain. The British army encouraged native tribes to fight the American settlers even harder.

FORT BOONESBOROUGH

Fort Boonesborough

124

In 1779 Daniel Boone led thirty men from Boonesborough to Blue Licks. Blue Licks was a natural salt deposit. They went there to harvest salt. Shawnee natives attacked. The Shawnee took Boone and most of his men prisoner. The Shawnee took them to faraway villages. Daniel Boone lived as a prisoner of the Shawnee from February until June.

As a prisoner, Daniel Boone paid close attention. He learned that the Shawnee were planning an attack on Boonesborough. Daniel Boone secretly crept away from the village. He traveled an amazing 160

Boone escapes from the Shawnee.

miles in four days. He reached Boonesborough and warned the settlers to prepare for attack.

Boone learned that his family had gone. Rebecca Boone thought the Shawnee had killed her husband. She had moved her children back to North Carolina. When the Shawnee attacked Boonesborough, the settlers were prepared. The settlers won even after the Shawnee held them under a ten-day siege. Daniel Boone then joined his family in North Carolina. Boone was never settled for long. Sometimes he tramped alone in the wilderness. Sometimes he packed up his family for another move. They moved between Kentucky, North Carolina, and Virginia.

Boone leads settlers to Kentucky.

Boone the American Hero

Boone became a hero to his fellow Americans. They admired his bravery, skill, and spunk. People loved books about Daniel Boone. Authors created stories about Boone's wild adventures. Many of these were "tall tales." Authors imagined some stories. They changed other stories to make them sound more exciting. Daniel Boone was embarrassed by these false "biographies." His real life was adventurous enough to make a good tale!

Daniel Boone
portrait by Charles Harding

In 1799 Boone was sixty-four years old. He pushed even farther west. Daniel and Rebecca Boone moved with several of their grown children and their families. They settled in Upper Louisiana, which was then under Spanish control. This region is now in the state of Missouri. The Spanish gave Boone 850 acres of land. They appointed him a judge. He settled disputes among settlers. He held court under a tree on his son's land. This time Daniel Boone had gone west to stay.

In 1812 the United States and Great Britain began fighting the War of 1812. Daniel Boone volunteered to fight. He was seventy-eight years old. The Army declined his offer. Rebecca Boone died in 1813. She and Daniel had been married for fifty-six adventurous years. In 1817, Daniel Boone went on his last long hunt in the wilderness. He took one of his grandsons along.

PIONEER LIFE IN MISSOURI IN 1820.

In 1820 Charles Harding was working in St. Louis, Missouri. He was a portrait artist. He traveled around painting portraits of famous people. He heard that Daniel Boone lived close by. Harding set out to track him down. He found Daniel Boone living in an old house miles away from the main road. Boone was eighty-five years old. Charles Harding asked if he would pose for a portrait. This portrait, shown at left, was the only portrait made of Daniel Boone in his lifetime.

While Boone sat for the portrait, Charles Harding asked if he had ever been lost. Boone answered, "No, I can't say as ever I was lost, but I was bewildered once for three days." Daniel Boone died just a few months later, on September 26, 1820.

A few years before he died, Daniel Boone wrote about his faith in a letter to his sister. He told her that he loved God and believed in Jesus Christ. Jesus said:

I am the resurrection and the life;
he who believes in Me will live
even if he dies.
John 11:25

Lesson Activities

- All Around the USA map: Find Exeter Township, the Appalachian Mountains, Wilderness Road, Boonesborough, and St. Louis.

- Timeline: Look at pages 10-13. You may also wish to review the previous pages you have learned about.

- Literature for Units 5-9: *Toliver's Secret*

Review Questions

- In what war did Daniel Boone serve alongside George Washington?

- How did Daniel Boone help settlers move across the Appalachian Mountains?

- Why do you think Daniel Boone became an American hero?

Unit Review

- Student Workbook: Complete the Lesson 18 / Unit 6 Review page.

Hands-On History Ideas

- Pretend that you are Daniel Boone or a member of his family, exploring, hunting, trapping, and preparing the way for new settlers.

- Use building blocks to build a wilderness fort with a few houses and a wall surrounding them.

Unit 6 Project
George Washington's Breakfast

George Washington loved hoecakes "swimming in butter and honey" for breakfast. Hoecakes are pancakes made with cornmeal. Try these cornmeal pancakes. And go ahead and let them swim in butter and honey (or maple syrup), too!

This recipe requires adult supervision and involvement. Makes about 40 small (3 ½ inch) pancakes.

Ingredients

- 1 ¾ cups cornmeal
- 1 ½ cups flour
- ¼ cup sugar
- 2 tablespoons baking powder
- ½ teaspoon salt

- 2 ¼ cups milk
- 1 tablespoon vinegar
- 2 eggs, well beaten
- ¼ cup oil

- oil for skillet
- butter and honey or maple syrup for serving

Directions

1. Mix dry ingredients in bowl.
2. Mix wet ingredients in another bowl.
3. Add the dry ingredients to the wet ingredients. Stir gently. Gently press out any large lumps until just blended.
4. Heat a frying pan on the stove to medium heat. Lightly coat the bottom with oil.
5. Test the skillet's heat with a small drop of batter. Batter should begin to cook immediately, but not burn.
6. Using a large serving spoon, pour batter in three small circles. Cook on the first side until the surface has bubbles all over it.
7. Gently slide a spatula under each pancake and flip to cook the other side. Remove from skillet when golden brown.
8. Add a small coating of oil to skillet before cooking each batch. Continue until you use all the batter.
9. Keep pancakes warm in a low-heat oven until ready to serve.
10. Serve hot with plenty of butter and honey or maple syrup.

29 USA

Unit 7

129

SACAGAWEA

Circuit Riders
and
Camp Meetings

A pioneer girl in a calico dress leaned against the big oak tree in the front yard. She looked at the wagon track leading from the dark woods. She waited for the preacher to ride into the yard on his tall brown horse. The preacher coming was the biggest thing that happened in her family. He visited many families scattered in the hills. She liked to think this was his favorite stop. He always said Mother's dinner was the best ever set on a Kentucky table.

A horse appeared from among the trees. Preacher's coming! She jumped and waved. She was the first one to spot him! His loud, joyful greeting brought the family running. They all chattered, exchanging news and asking questions. He helped with the chores until Mother called them to supper.

Saturday evening by the fire, Preacher told stories. He shared news of their relatives and friends. Mother passed around company tea, company sugar, and fresh berry pie on the company dishes.

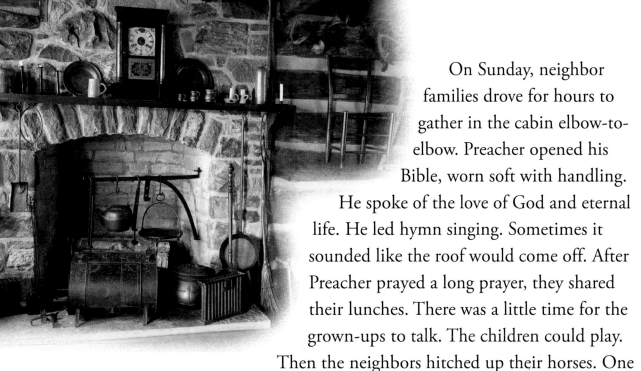

On Sunday, neighbor families drove for hours to gather in the cabin elbow-to-elbow. Preacher opened his Bible, worn soft with handling. He spoke of the love of God and eternal life. He led hymn singing. Sometimes it sounded like the roof would come off. After Preacher prayed a long prayer, they shared their lunches. There was a little time for the grown-ups to talk. The children could play. Then the neighbors hitched up their horses. One by one, their wagons disappeared up the forest path. It would be weeks before they would gather again.

Preacher shared their breakfast the next morning. Then he saddled his horse. He gave them each an encouraging word. He looked back and waved before he rode out of sight. The family would think about and talk over all he'd said until he came riding up again.

Faith on the Frontier

American families who settled the lonely wilderness spread far apart. For weeks at a time, all a pioneer family had was each other. They stayed busy on tiny farms tucked in the mountains. It was hard to travel, even to visit a neighbor. Most lived far from Christian teaching and fellowship.

In the early days of the colonies, church and religion were at the center of life. That changed as America changed. People taught new ideas about man's right to be independent. Some people decided they wanted to be independent from God and His laws.

Americans became greedy for land and wealth. Greed was at the heart of the cruel way people treated enslaved persons and native people. Some Americans moved to the West to live a wild life away from the law.

Frontier Missionaries

Church leaders in the East sent missionary preachers over the Appalachian Mountains. These "circuit riders" rode from house to house. They held church services in cabins. Slowly, as towns and communities grew, Christian congregations grew also. Some built log meeting houses with a simple wooden pulpit and benches.

Preachers rotated services at multiple churches. Congregations might have a preacher only once in several weeks. Most circuit riders and churches on the frontier were Presbyterian, Methodist, or Baptist.

Christians built the Mulkey Meetinghouse, pictured above, in Kentucky in 1804. The grave of Daniel Boone's sister is in its cemetery.

132

The Birth of Camp Meetings

The Presbyterian church had a tradition of yearly communion services. These lasted from Friday to Monday. Congregations took turns hosting the service. Members of other churches visited for the weekend. They stayed in the homes of local church members.

Around 1800, communion services began to attract larger crowds. Church members ran out of room to host visitors. People camped near the church in tents and wagons. Communion services grew into "camp meetings."

At camp meetings, people gathered to hear sermons, sing hymns, and celebrate communion. Local ministers invited other frontier preachers to come preach. People were used to quiet, solemn communion services. Camp meetings were different. Preachers gave energetic sermons. New believers were loud and lively.

Many heard the truth of Christ and found new life. People went home from camp meetings excited. They spread the word. More churches hosted camp meetings. More and more people came to participate.

Cane Ridge

In 1790 a small group of Presbyterian settlers left North Carolina. On the advice of Daniel Boone, they settled in northern Kentucky. In 1791 they built Cane Ridge Meeting House. Barton W. Stone served as minister of the churches at Cane Ridge and Concord, Kentucky. In 1801 Stone went to a camp meeting. He got excited about the Lord's work. He decided to host a camp meeting at Cane Ridge.

Rain fell in buckets on Friday, August 6. People still flocked to Cane Ridge Meeting House. Preaching, prayers, and singing continued for several days, almost without stopping. Preachers spoke from simple pulpits scattered in the woods. Several preached at the same time. People gathered around to hear and watch.

At night, the camp was bright with bonfires, lamps, and candles. People carried torches as they walked. The preachers kept right on preaching. People miles away heard the shouts of thousands of people worshiping.

Cane Ridge meeting house

Barton W. Stone

Between 20,000 and 30,000 people gathered around Cane Ridge Meeting House. They were young and old, black and white, rich and poor. Preachers urged them to repent of their sins and put their faith in God. Many became followers of Christ. God was sending rain on the dry spiritual desert of the frontier.

Peter Cartwright's Story

Peter Cartwright

Peter Cartwright was raised on a Kentucky pioneer farm. When Peter was nine, a circuit rider visited his family. He asked to hold church in their home. Peter's parents sent Peter out to invite the neighbors. Neighbors filled the cabin to overflowing.

Peter was sixteen in 1801. Revival was sweeping Kentucky. Peter went to a camp meeting. He repented of his sins and became a follower of Christ.

As an elderly man, Peter remembered,

My mother raised the shout, my Christian friends crowded around me and joined me in praising God.

In 1804 Peter Cartwright became a circuit rider. He brought the good news of the gospel to frontier families like his own. He preached in Kentucky, Indiana, Tennessee, and Ohio. He wrote his autobiography at the age of seventy-one. He remembered the revival that fanned out after Cane Ridge,

From this camp-meeting . . . the news spread through all the churches, and through all the land, and it excited great wonder and surprise; but it kindled a religious flame that spread all over Kentucky and through many other states.

And He said to them,
"Go into all the world and preach the gospel to all creation."
Mark 16:15

Lesson Activities

- All Around the USA map: Find the Appalachian Mountains and Cane Ridge.

- Rhythms and Rhymes: Enjoy "Hymn III" on page 16.

- Student Workbook: Complete the Lesson 19 page.

- Literature for Units 5-9: *Toliver's Secret*

Review Questions

- Why did many frontier preachers ride a circuit to hold church services, teach, and encourage, instead of ministering in one place?

- What was the purpose of camp meetings?

- If you lived in Kentucky in 1801, would you want to attend a camp meeting? Why?

Hands-On History Ideas

- Pretend you are attending a camp meeting. You will need to set up your camp and cook your own food. You can choose which preacher you'll listen to of the many preaching at the same time. You can even start preaching or leading songs yourself!

- Use building blocks to build a frontier meeting house.

Exploring the West with Lewis and Clark

America's youngest explorer set out on the Missouri River at just two months old. He was born in what is now North Dakota. Before his first birthday, Jean Baptiste Charbonneau had traveled all the way to the Pacific Ocean. He explored the American West strapped to his mother's back. He was a member of the Lewis and Clark Expedition.

Plans for Exploration

Is there a route to the Pacific Ocean by river? What native nations live in the far West? What animals and plants are there? President Thomas Jefferson thought Americans ought to know.

Jefferson asked Congress to pay for an expedition to explore from the Mississippi River to the Pacific Ocean. Jefferson asked his friend and secretary Meriwether Lewis to lead the expedition. Lewis jumped right in. He went to Philadelphia to study with the top scientists of the day. He studied medicine, the human body, plants, fossils, mapmaking, mathematics, and surveying.

Lewis had a lot of shopping to do. He gathered mathematical tools, reference books, paper, pens, ink, weapons, clothing, camping gear, hunting gear, cooking gear, and medicine.

Lewis bought hundreds of gifts for native people he expected to meet, such as mirrors, beads, ribbons, needles, thread, scissors, belts, knives, and jewelry. President Jefferson provided peace medals.

Front and Back of Jefferson Peace Medal

Lewis asked William Clark to join him in leading the expedition. Lewis and Clark had served in the Army together. They chose men who had useful skills for the journey. They called the group "Corps of Volunteers for North West Discovery."

The Louisiana Purchase

By this time, France controlled the Louisiana Territory, including the Mississippi River and the city of New Orleans. As more Americans moved west, the Mississippi River grew more important. People used the river for travel and for sending and receiving goods. New Orleans had a busy port with loaded ships coming and going.

Jefferson sent representatives to France hoping to buy New Orleans and what is now Florida. The French offered to sell the entire Louisiana Territory, including New Orleans, the Mississippi River, and 827,000 square miles of land. The price that the U.S. paid was fifteen million dollars, or four cents per acre. The United States doubled in size all at once! Lewis and Clark had all the more reason to go exploring. They would be learning about the newest section of the United States.

Meriwether Lewis

William Clark

Signing the
Louisiana Purchase Treaty

Lewis and Clark carried this map with them.

Patrick Gass explored with Lewis and Clark. He drew this picture of them holding a council with native people.

Statue of Sacagawea and Jean Baptiste Charbonneau in the United States Capitol

Beyond the Mississippi River

On May 14, 1804, the Lewis and Clark Expedition set off for adventure! From near St. Louis, Missouri, they traveled north on the Missouri River. At the end of October, they reached a large Hidatsa and Mandan community. They built Fort Mandan across the Missouri River from the community. The fort was home for the winter.

Toussaint Charbonneau lived with the Hidatsa and Mandan. He was a French Canadian fur trader. His wife Sacagawea was from the Shoshone tribe of the Rocky Mountains. When she was twelve years old, Hidatsa natives captured her and brought her to North Dakota.

Lewis and Clark asked Charbonneau and Sacagawea to join the expedition. They wanted their help communicating with native tribes. Sacagawea gave birth to her first child, Jean Baptiste Charbonneau, on February 11, 1805, in Fort Mandan.

On April 7, 1805, the expedition left Fort Mandan. As they traveled, they made detailed notes about plants, animals, and geography. They made maps of the rivers and streams. They met with native tribes. They hunted and cooked their food on campfires. They treated their own illnesses and injuries. They pushed farther and farther west.

Sacagawea

Sacagawea was a helpful member of the expedition in many ways. As Clark wrote in his journal, "A woman with a party of men is a token of peace." Her presence was a sign that the expedition was friendly. Native tribes knew a war party would never bring along a woman with a baby.

Sacagawea knew about useful plants for food and medicine. She showed the men how to make leather clothing and moccasins. In May of 1805 the expedition was traveling along the Missouri River. Sacagawea was riding in one of the larger boats. Strong wind suddenly struck the boat's sail. The boat thrashed to the side. Supplies dumped into the water. Sacagawea reached out and saved priceless tools, books, papers, and medicine.

In August of 1805, Sacagawea saw they were nearing her Shoshone homeland. Lewis and Clark were counting on buying horses from the Shoshone. They needed horses to travel through the Rocky Mountains. The expedition soon found a band of Shoshone. They arranged a meeting with Chief Cameahwait. Sacagawea arrived at the meeting to help translate. She suddenly jumped and ran to embrace the chief. Cameahwait was her brother! She had not seen him since her capture five years before.

Over the Rocky Mountains

Riding Shoshone horses, the expedition pressed on. They struggled bravely through the cold, rugged Rocky Mountains. They ran dangerously low on food and water. At last they reached flat land on the other side.

On the Weippe Prairie, the expedition met the Nez Perce tribe. They asked the Nez Perce for help building canoes. With six new canoes, the expedition traveled on the Clearwater and Columbia Rivers.

Members of the Nez Perce tribe, along with Nez Perce canoe, cradleboard, and tipis

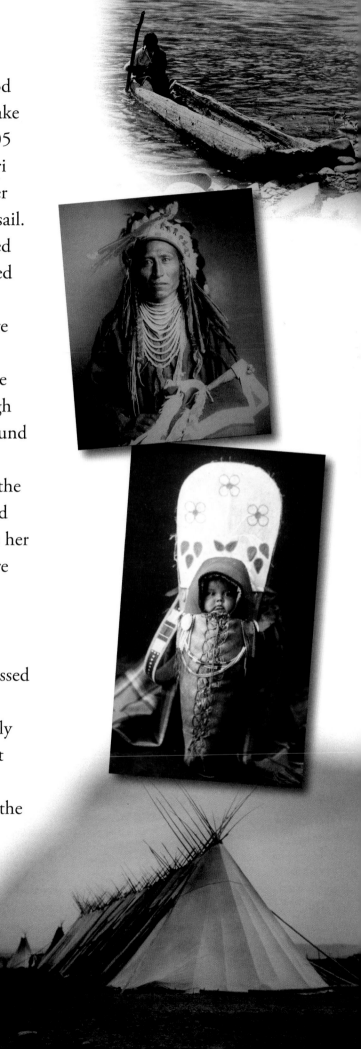

"Lewis and Clark on the Columbia River"
by Frederic Remington

Reconstructed Fort Clatsop

Finally, in November 1805, they reached the endless gray-blue expanse of the Pacific Ocean. They built Fort Clatsop in what is now Oregon. There they spent the long, cold, rainy winter.

Homeward Bound Journey

On March 23, 1806, William Clark wrote in his journal:

> . . . we loaded our canoes and at 1 p.m. left Fort Clatsop on our homeward bound journey. . . .

William Clark and baby Jean Baptiste became great friends. Clark nicknamed him Pompy. On the journey east, the expedition came to a huge rock tower beside the Yellowstone River. Clark named it "Pompy's Tower." There, the expedition left the only mark that is still visible today. Clark carved, "Wm. Clark July 25, 1806."

140

On August 14, 1806, the expedition returned to the Hidatsa and Mandan community. They said goodbye to Charbonneau, Sacagawea, and Jean Baptiste. Surely no one has had more adventure in his first nineteen months of life! The expedition arrived in St. Louis on September 23, 1806. Townspeople cheered from the bank of the Mississippi River. The explorers learned that their countrymen had given them up for dead. They had been away exploring for two years. Yet they had returned safe and sound! They brought a wealth of knowledge, stories, artifacts, maps, and new connections. Meriwether Lewis sat down to write Thomas Jefferson:

> Sir, It is with pleasure that I announce to you the safe arrival of myself and party at 12 o'clock today at this place with our papers and baggage. In obedience to your orders we have penetrated the Continent of North America to the Pacific Ocean . . .

Genesis 1 describes when God made land and the seas on the third day.

> . . . God said, "Let the waters below the heavens be gathered into one place, and let the dry land appear"; and it was so.
> Genesis 1:9

141

Lesson Activities

- Student Workbook: Complete the Lesson 20 page.
- Literature for Units 5-9: *Toliver's Secret*
- Look at the map of the Lewis and Clark Expedition on pages 142-143.

Review Questions

- What was one reason Thomas Jefferson wanted an expedition to explore the West?
- What country did the United States buy the Louisiana Territory from?
- Why were people in St. Louis and other places in the United States surprised to see the expedition return?

Hands-On History Ideas

- See the Unit 7 Project instructions on Page 150.

Fort Clatsop

Columbia River

Clearwater River

Oregon
Country

Nez
Perce

Snake River

Shoshone

Missouri River

Fort Manda[...]

Yellowstone River

Pompy's Tower

Rocky Mountains

Missouri River

Louisiana
Territory

1804-1805 Journey to Pacific Ocean — — —

Lewis and Clark followed the same route back
with a few exceptions. On part of the return
journey they were together ——— and on part
they split up with Lewis – – – going one way
and Clark ⋯⋯ going a different way.

Spanish Territory

Pacific
Ocean

Lewis and Clark Expedition

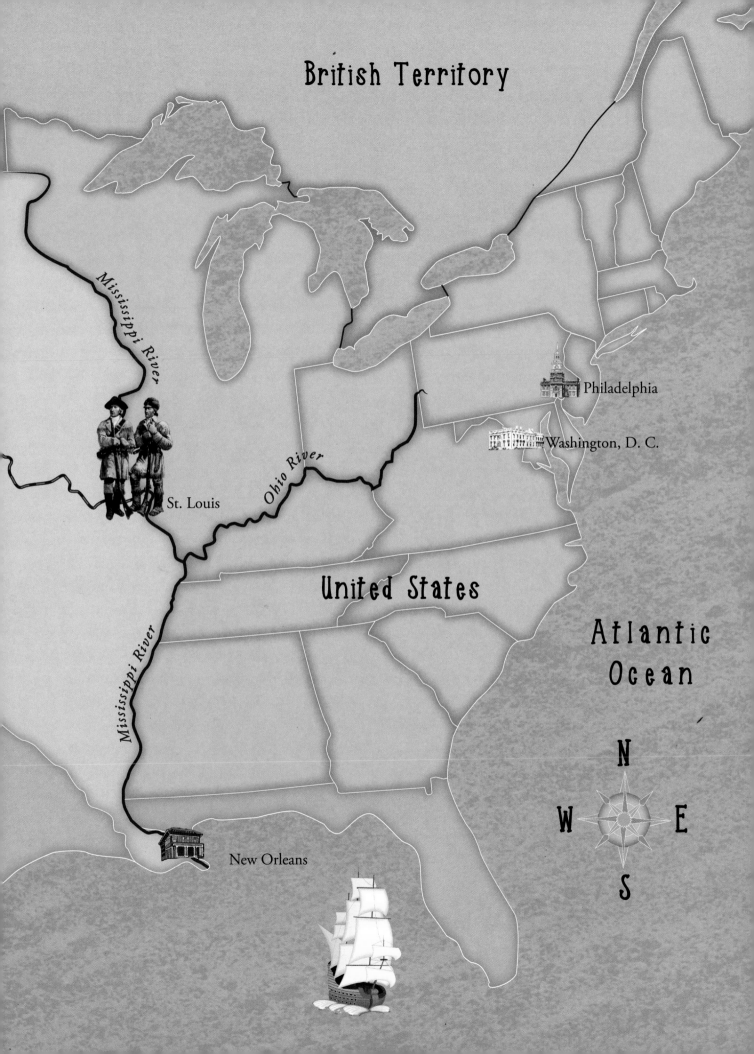

British Territory

Mississippi River

Ohio River

St. Louis

United States

Philadelphia

Washington, D. C.

Atlantic
Ocean

Mississippi River

New Orleans

N

W   E

S

Robert Fulton
and His
New Ideas

Robert often went fishing with his friend Christopher and Christopher's father. The fishing part was fun. It was fun to be outside. It was fun to be out of school. But the boys got tired. Christopher's father made them work hard! They pushed poles against the bottom of the creek to make the boat move. Christopher and Robert strained and sweated. The boat sloshed heavily forward, little by little. Robert started thinking. What would work better?

Robert built a model boat with paddle wheels. The paddle wheels turned in the water and moved the boat forward. Robert built full-size paddle wheels for the fishing boat. They worked! He turned a crank and the paddles moved the boat through the water. Robert and Christopher were done with those dreaded poles!

Robert Fulton and his friend Christopher

Robert Fulton's Birthplace in Lancaster, Pennsylvania

Quicksilver Bob

Robert Fulton was born in 1765. He grew up in Lancaster, Pennsylvania. His father died when Robert was three. He didn't leave much money. Robert's mother bravely raised Robert, his three sisters, and brother alone.

Robert learned first at home with his mother. When he attended a school at age eight, Robert struggled. He didn't pay attention. His head was full of new ideas! He wanted to use his hands. He wanted to make things. His friends called him "Quicksilver Bob" because he bought mercury, called quicksilver, from the local pharmacist. He used it for secret experiments.

Robert's boyhood overlapped with the Revolutionary War. Robert loved to hang around a local gun shop. The gunsmiths stayed busy filling orders for the American Army. They welcomed young Quicksilver Bob. They even listened to his suggestions. Robert drew new designs for guns. The gunsmiths tried his ideas. His designs worked!

Quicksilver Bob saw problems to be solved as possibilities. With his hands, he could make his ideas come to life! Robert tried out a friend's set of paints. He discovered a new talent. He was good at painting! He decided to be an artist.

145

Benjamin West's painting of his family includes his wife, two children, father, and uncle. West is standing with his palette.

Becoming a Painter

Robert Fulton moved to Philadelphia when he was seventeen. He set up shop as a portrait painter. He painted Benjamin Franklin's portrait. They became good friends. Robert Fulton supported himself by painting. He built up savings, too. When he turned twenty-one in 1786, he bought a farm for his mother and sisters. He made sure they were settled and comfortable. Then he was off to London!

In London, Fulton lived with Benjamin West and his family. West was an American artist. He had moved to England years before. He was one of the world's best painters. Robert Fulton studied painting with West.

Becoming An Inventor

Robert Fulton traveled around England. He made many friends. One new friend owned rich coal mines. The coal was valuable but hard to transport to buyers. Workers put the coal into bags. Horses carried the bags away from the mines. This method was too slow. This was just the kind of problem to capture Robert Fulton's attention!

Fulton's new friend was digging canals on his property. Canals are man-made rivers. With canals the coal could travel by boat. Fulton jumped right in to help. Their canals were successful!

Soon Robert Fulton was busy with more ideas. He designed many machines, like a canal-digger, a rope twister, and a machine to move boats over land. Robert Fulton had a new job. He had become an inventor!

Fulton statue in the Library of Congress

Robert Fulton had struggled in school, but that didn't stop him from learning. He drew excellent diagrams of his inventions. He could explain his ideas in writing. He wrote a little book about canals. He explained how canals could help with transportation and trade. Fulton sent copies of his book to the United States. He wanted to help his own country. He sent one to the governor of Pennsylvania. He sent another to George Washington, who was serving as America's first president.

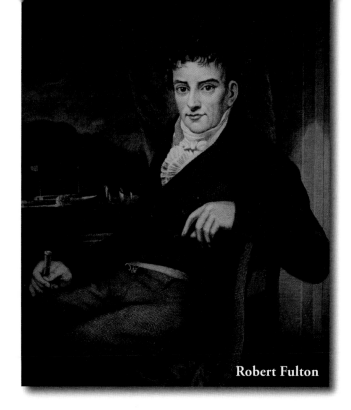

Robert Fulton

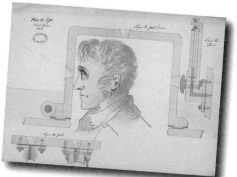

Fulton's illustrations

Learning in France

Robert Fulton moved to France. He kept right on learning and inventing. He learned to speak French, German, and Italian. He studied math, physics, and chemistry. He became friends with Robert Livingston. Livingston was in France to represent the United States. Livingston helped arrange the Louisiana Purchase with the French government.

Fulton and Livingston set up a business partnership. Inventors had been working on steam engines for many years. Steam engines produce power from the heat created by boiling water. Steam engines could power many things, including steamships. Fulton and Livingston wanted to turn steamships into a way to make money.

Robert Fulton spent years on his experiments with steamships. Things did not always go smoothly. Sometimes his experiments fell apart. He never stopped trying. Finally, he created a design that worked. He returned to the United States. He was eager to see what he could do with steamships in his own country.

147

A Steamship in America

Robert Fulton supervised the building of a steamship in New York City. People laughed. It looked so different from other ships. "That thing will never go anywhere!" they said. People called the ship, "Fulton's Folly." Even his friends thought he would fail. Fulton said, "Like every enthusiast, I have no doubt of success." He worked for months while people mocked him.

At last his steamship, the *Clermont*, was ready. On the morning of August 17, 1807, people crowded the wharf in New York City. They even climbed to the rooftops to watch. Some were still laughing. *Clermont's* engine sent out a burst of sparks. She was off for Albany!

The first voyage of the *Clermont* was a stunning success! The passengers were delighted. Robert Fulton was victorious and jubilant! "Fulton's Folly" traveled 150 miles on the Hudson River to Albany and back. The steamship made the trip in one-third the time it took a sailing ship! Fulton had shown the world a new, fast, modern way to travel.

Robert Fulton's "Clermont." First Vessel ever Propelled by Steam. 1807.

Fulton married shortly after his *Clermont* victory. He and his wife Harriet had one son and three daughters. Fulton was busy with new ideas and innovations when he died suddenly in 1815.

It Will Come

Around 1810, Fulton was traveling to Washington, D.C., on a stagecoach. The coach had to stop at a tavern to change horses. The travelers had a long wait. A lady asked, "Oh, Mr. Fulton, you have invented a way to travel quickly over the water. Why can you not invent a way to carry us quickly over the land?"

Fulton bowed to her and said, "Madam, it will come." Robert Fulton didn't live to see that day. What would he have invented to travel over land? He always had a new idea.

In all labor there is profit,
But mere talk
leads only to poverty.
Proverbs 14:23

Lesson Activities

- All Around the USA map: Find Lancaster, Philadelphia, New York City, Albany, and the Hudson River.

- Rhythms and Rhymes: Enjoy "The Glendy Burk" on page 17.

- Timeline: Look at pages 14-15.

- Literature for Units 5-9: *Toliver's Secret*

Review Questions

- How did Robert Fulton's training in art help him when he later became an inventor?

- What did Robert Fulton do when people laughed at his steamship?

- Why do people want faster and easier ways to travel?

Unit Review

- Student Workbook: Complete the Lesson 21 / Unit 7 Review page.

Hands-On History Ideas

- Pretend that you are the pilot of a steamship. Your passengers will be amazed at how quickly it travels!

- Use building blocks to build your own idea for a new invention.

Lewis and Clark Observation Journal

Supplies

- notebook or journal
- writing and drawing utensils

Lewis and Clark observed and recorded what they saw in the West. They filled hundreds of journal pages with their research. They drew pictures and took notes on everything from animals and plants to the homes and tools of native peoples. Imagine that Lewis or Clark came to the place where you live. Imagine that almost everything he sees is new to him. Make a journal with drawings and notes of everyday things from your life, both inside and outside your house. Draw and write notes on at least ten objects.

Unit 8

Lesson 22 - Tecumseh and William Henry Harrison
Lesson 23 - The Pickersgill Family and the War of 1812
Lesson 24 - America's First School for the Deaf

Tecumseh
and
William Henry Harrison

In a grove of walnut trees in Indiana, old ways and new ways faced each other. Tecumseh was there to speak for the Shawnee and other native tribes. William Henry Harrison represented the United States government. Tecumseh was asking the United States to return land taken from native people. Harrison's job was to protect and enlarge United States territory. Native tribes wanted land to be open for their way of living. Americans wanted to buy farms and build cities. Tecumseh and Harrison each brought his own goals and outlook to the meeting in the walnut grove. They talked. They argued. They got angry. They left without changing each other's minds.

Tecumseh

Tecumseh was a member of the Shawnee tribe. The Shawnee lived mainly in what is now Ohio. Tecumseh was born in 1768. By that time, the Shawnee were already fighting to keep their homeland. When Tecumseh was six years old, settlers killed his father. Tecumseh promised he would grow up to be a warrior like his father.

Chief Blackfish adopted young Tecumseh. Blackfish raised Tecumseh alongside several white "brothers." Blackfish had captured these boys from American families. Five times during Tecumseh's childhood, his family had to flee to escape invading armies. When Tecumseh was about fourteen, he joined Chief Blackfish in fighting the Americans. They fought with the British army during the Revolutionary War. They believed the British would allow them to keep their lands. After the United States won the Revolutionary War, native tribes rapidly lost more land.

Tecumseh soon became a war chief. A war chief's job was to lead his tribe in battle. Tecumseh fought in battles large and small. He fought settlers, traders, and the United States Army.

Tecumseh

Shawnee warrior

153

In 1808 Tecumseh settled at Tippecanoe in Indiana Territory. He embarked on a quest. He wanted to convince all native tribes to band together. He wanted them to defend their homeland and their way of life. Tribes had fought against each other for hundreds of years. If they worked together, could they be strong enough? Could they stop American settlers from taking their lands?

Tecumseh traveled thousands of miles to meet with native tribes. He went north all the way to New York. He went south all the way to Florida. He convinced many tribes to join the cause. He became a leader and spokesman for native people across the country. Many of Tecumseh's followers gathered at Tippecanoe. This was the headquarters of the alliance.

Tecumseh

William Henry Harrison

William Henry Harrison came from a wealthy Virginia plantation family. He was the youngest of seven children. He was born in 1773 to Benjamin and Elizabeth Harrison. Benjamin Harrison was a longtime governor of Virginia. He was a member of the Continental Congress. He signed the Declaration of Independence. The Harrisons were close friends with George Washington and his family.

Plantation of the Harrison family in Virginia

William Henry Harrison joined the United States Army in 1791. He was eighteen years old. He was soon fighting battles against native tribes. He served in the Army until 1798.

Harrison became the first governor of Indiana Territory. He moved to the new capital of Vincennes in 1801. He brought his wife Anna and their three children. They built a mansion named Grouseland. It was the first brick house in Indiana Territory. William Henry and Anna Harrison eventually had ten children. Five were born at Grouseland.

William Henry Harrison

Harrison worked to get more land for American settlers. The U.S. government bought land from native tribes. Land sales brought disagreement. In traditional native cultures, individuals did not own land. A few tribal chiefs might sign a treaty and receive payment. Others in the tribe claimed those chiefs did not have the authority to sell. Government officials often forced native peoples to sell their land through tricks, lies, and threats. Native leaders signed many treaties in the Council Chamber at Grouseland. Harrison added millions of acres to the United States.

Tecumseh and Harrison

In August of 1810, Tecumseh and a band of followers came to Grouseland. It was the first meeting between William Henry Harrison and Tecumseh. They did not meet in the Council Chamber. They met outdoors in a grove of walnut trees near the house. Tecumseh argued passionately. He championed the rights of native people to their land and way of life. He told Harrison that he spoke for all native people.

Grouseland

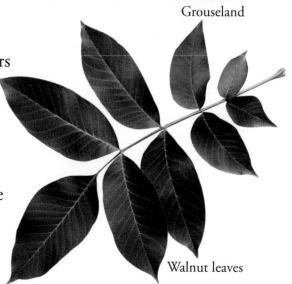

Walnut leaves

To Tecumseh, land belonged to all, like air and water. He did not believe land could be sold. Tecumseh warned Harrison that war was coming if he continued to acquire land. Harrison told him that all treaties he had arranged were legal. Tecumseh called Harrison a liar. Tempers flared! Many in the assembly grabbed their weapons. The men challenged each other, but they did not fight.

Harrison and Tecumseh had opposite perspectives. Their meeting only caused each of them to push harder for their goals. Tecumseh continued to recruit native people for his alliance. Harrison wrote to the United States government asking for more soldiers. Tecumseh's leadership impressed him. Tecumseh's followers at Tippecanoe had grown into a large community. White settlers in the area were frightened. They demanded that the United States government protect them.

The Battle of Tippecanoe

In July of 1811, Tecumseh left Tippecanoe. He traveled south to recruit more people to join his alliance. On his way, he visited Harrison. Tecumseh asked Harrison not to acquire any more land until he returned. Thus Harrison knew that Tecumseh would be away for a while. Harrison assembled an army. His 950 men were a mix of soldiers and local volunteers. Harrison led his army north from Vincennes to Tippecanoe. They set up camp near the town.

Harrison's camp lay sleeping at 4:00 a.m. on November 7, 1811. Native warriors made a surprise attack! They fought in the dark for two hours. Native warriors fell back to reorganize. Then Harrison's army attacked.

Battle of Tippecanoe

The surprised native warriors scattered. American troops chased them on horseback. Harrison's army burned the town. His army left victorious. Many native people had shared Tecumseh's dream. They went home to their villages defeated. The alliance of native people was never as strong again.

Two Different Worlds

Tecumseh and William Henry Harrison represented two different worlds. Those worlds had different goals and beliefs. Both sides could not have what they wanted. Tecumseh came from an old order that was fading. Harrison came from a new order that was quickly gaining power. Tecumseh died in 1813 in another battle with the U.S. Army. Twenty-eight years later, Harrison became President of the United States.

The Bible teaches us the right way to work out our differences.

Let all bitterness and wrath
and anger and clamor and slander
be put away from you,
along with all malice.
Be kind to one another,
tender-hearted,
forgiving each other,
just as God in Christ
also has forgiven you.
Ephesians 4:31-32

Lesson Activities

- All Around the USA map: Find Tippecanoe and Vincennes.
- Student Workbook: Complete the Lesson 22 page.
- Literature for Units 5-8: *Toliver's Secret*

Review Questions

- What did Tecumseh encourage the various native tribes to do?
- Why did American settlers want more land?
- What do you think is the best way to settle disagreements?

Hands-On History Ideas

- Pretend that you are with Tecumseh and William Henry Harrison when they first meet and argue in the walnut grove. What will you do to help them cooperate? What will you tell each of them that will be helpful?
- Use building blocks to build a house similar to Grouseland, shown on page 155.

The Pickersgill Family
and the
War of 1812

Caroline Pickersgill's mother Mary was famous for making flags. One summer day in 1813, military officers visited her shop in Baltimore, Maryland. Lieutenant Colonel George Armistead was in charge of the American soldiers at nearby Fort McHenry. Armistead sent the officers to the flag shop with a special order. He wanted an American flag that was thirty feet tall and forty-two feet wide! He wanted it "so large that the British will have no difficulty seeing it from a distance." Make a flag larger than her house? Of course! Mary Pickersgill was up to the challenge. Her daughter Caroline was ready to help. Two teenage nieces and a teenage indentured servant also assisted in the enormous project.

The ladies sewed for six weeks. Their hands ached. Their backs and necks grew sore. They used yards and yards of red, white, and blue woolen cloth. Each red and white stripe was two feet wide. Each white cotton star they stitched in place was two feet across.

Pickersgill house today

America was in the middle of a war with Great Britain. As they sewed, all the women wondered when the British would attack Baltimore. It was sure to be soon. The Pickersgill family's house was not large enough to piece the flag together. The ladies spread out their project on the floor of a large building nearby. They often worked until midnight. Finally they finished their task. The flag was the largest in the world.

Mary Pickersgill presented the fifty-pound flag to the soldiers at Fort McHenry. It took nine of the soldiers to raise it up above the fort, where it waved proudly. They paid Mary Pickersgill $405.90 for the flag.

Fort McHenry

The War of 1812

America had been at war with Great Britain for a year. The war began in 1812 and came to be called the War of 1812. For some time the British navy had been stopping American ships at sea. They captured American sailors. The British had also supplied native tribes with weapons to fight against American settlers.

Much of the fighting during the War of 1812 took place at sea. The Pickersgills and the rest of America received news about one battle after another.

War of 1812 reenactors
at Fort McHenry

Burning Washington, D.C.

In August of 1814, British troops set Washington, D.C. on fire. They burned the U.S. Capitol and the White House. Countless books, manuscripts, and paintings turned into ashes. Residents of Baltimore, where the Pickersgills lived, could see the orange glow of the burning capital city. They were on edge. The British army was close, and getting closer. They approached by land and by sea. The American soldiers at Fort McHenry prepared for battle. Mary Pickersgill's enormous flag waved boldly above them.

"Our Flag Was Still There"

Around sunrise on September 13, 1814, the British began their attack on Fort McHenry. The British ships were anchored in Chesapeake Bay about two miles from the fort. All day and throughout the night, the British fired at the fort from their ships. The American soldiers bravely endured the almost constant explosions.

An American Army general ordered the soldiers at Fort McHenry to surrender to the British. The general didn't think the Americans could possibly win. Lieutenant Colonel Armistead was not ready to give up. He knew he could get in trouble if he went against the general's orders, but he was determined to stand strong.

Not long before the British attack began, a lawyer named Francis Scott Key traveled to Baltimore. He visited one of the British ships near Fort McHenry. Key talked to the British about releasing an American doctor they had captured.

Francis Scott Key

The British agreed to release the doctor, but they would not let the men return to land until the attack on Fort McHenry was over.

From a ship in the Chesapeake Bay, Francis Scott Key watched the attack on the fort. Key told a friend about his experience. The friend wrote this account:

[They] remained on deck during the night, watching every shell from the moment it was fired until it fell, listening with breathless interest to hear if an explosion followed. But it suddenly ceased before day, and as they had no communication with any of the enemy's ships they did not know whether the fort had surrendered or the attack been abandoned. They paced the deck for the remainder of the night in painful suspense, watching with intense anxiety for the return of day, and looking every few minutes at their watches to see how long they must wait for it; and as soon as it dawned, and before it was light enough to see objects at a distance, their glasses were turned to the fort, uncertain whether they should see there the stars and stripes or the flag of the enemy. At length the light came, and they saw that "our flag was still there." . . . At length Mr. Key was informed that the attack on Baltimore had failed and the British army was [leaving] . . . .

Bombardment of Fort McHenry

This is how Mary Pickersgill's Star-Spangled Banner looks today. Look at the silhouette of a girl who is forty-eight inches tall at right. She is about the height of two stripes on the flag.

After the War of 1812, the flag continued to fly over Fort McHenry. Before long, it became the personal property of Lieutenant Colonel George Armistead. The Armistead family passed the flag down as a treasured heirloom until one family member donated it to the Smithsonian Institution in 1912.

The original flag was much wider than the flag that remains today. Parts of the flag are gone due to weather and age. Other portions were snipped off and given away as souvenirs. The flag is now kept safe on display in the Smithsonian National Museum of American History in Washington, D.C., for all Americans to see.

Fort McHenry

Mr. Key then told me that under the excitement of the time he had written a song, and handed me a printed copy of "The Star-Spangled Banner." . . . The next morning he took it to Judge Nicholson to ask him what he thought of it, and he was so much pleased with it that he immediately sent it to the printer, and directed copies to be struck off in hand-bill form. In less than an hour after it was placed in the hands of the printer it was all over the town, and hailed with enthusiasm and at once took its place as a national song.

America won the War of 1812. Key's poem set to music became the national anthem of the United States in 1931.

No matter what nation wins or loses in any war that is fought on earth, the Bible teaches us the eternal truth that:

> God reigns over the nations,
> God sits on His holy throne.
> Psalm 47:8

Lesson Activities

- All Around the USA map: Find Baltimore, Chesapeake Bay, and Washington, D.C.

- Rhythms and Rhymes: Enjoy "The Star-Spangled Banner" on page 18.

- Student Workbook: Complete the Lesson 23 page.

- Literature for Units 5-8: *Toliver's Secret*

Review Questions

- What countries fought against each other in the War of 1812?

- What poem did Mary Pickersgill's flag inspire Francis Scott Key to write?

- What are some ways people can use their talents and skills to help their country?

Hands-On History Ideas

- See the Unit 8 Project instructions on page 170.

America's
First
School for the Deaf

Nine-year-old Alice Cogswell stood off by herself while the other children played. Anyone could see that none of the other children wanted her around. They didn't even seem to notice her. Thomas Gallaudet, a local minister, did notice her. He felt a special connection with the little girl. When he was a little boy, he had been left out, too. He had always been weak and sickly. He remembered how hard it was for him to keep up with the other children.

Thomas Gallaudet continued to watch the lonely little girl. One of Gallaudet's younger brothers, Teddy, was in the group of children playing. Gallaudet called Teddy over to him to ask about the girl. "That's the doctor's daughter," Teddy told him. "She's deaf and she can't talk. She doesn't even know her name is Alice."

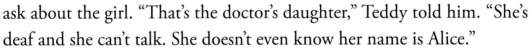

As the other children went on with their game, Gallaudet walked up to Alice. Many people in the United States thought that people who were deaf could not learn. Gallaudet felt sure that this was not true. He believed that even though Alice's ears could not hear, her mind could learn.

H-A-T

Thomas Gallaudet picked up a stick and wrote the letters H-A-T in the dirt. He took his hat and laid it on the ground above the letters. He pointed at his hat and at the word again and again. He hoped that Alice would understand the connection. At first she thought it was just a game. Thomas tapped the letters and touched his hat; Alice tapped her toes and wiggled her fingers.

For over an hour, Gallaudet kept trying. How could he help Alice see that his hat and the letters H-A-T went together? Finally it happened. All in a moment, Alice understood. She excitedly grabbed the hat and put it on her head. She pointed to the word in the dirt and then to the hat. Gallaudet could see her spirit soar. Alice picked up the stick and handed it to Thomas. She tapped her own shoulders with her fists. Thomas knew she was asking him a question. Thomas bent down to write the answer. He scratched the letters A-L-I-C-E in the dirt.

Hope for the Hopeless

Statue of Alice Cogswell in Hartford

Thomas Gallaudet told Alice's father what had happened. She had connected the hat with the letters H-A-T. Dr. Mason Cogswell was overjoyed. The Cogswells knew their daughter was intelligent. They had tried to teach her at home. They wanted to open her mind so that she could understand. They wanted to help her learn about all that was around her, but they didn't know how. The Cogswells had heard of schools for the deaf in Europe. They did not want to send their little girl so far away from their home in Hartford, Connecticut. Thomas Gallaudet gave them hope that Alice could learn without going far away.

A Hero

It was 1814. The United States and Great Britain were fighting the War of 1812. Men who went off to fight in battle became heroes. Nurses who tended the wounded became heroes. Thomas Gallaudet was not strong enough to fight, but he became a hero, too.

Gallaudet learned sign language from books Dr. Cogswell ordered from France. Gallaudet spent hours with Alice. Through him, Alice continued to learn. He patiently taught her one sign after another. Some of Gallaudet's younger siblings joined in the fun. They learned the new signs right along with Alice.

Dr. Cogswell gathered some wealthy men from Hartford for a meeting in his home. He invited Thomas Gallaudet to speak to them about his work with Alice. Gallaudet helped the men understand that deaf men, women, and children could learn. Gallaudet wanted to teach the deaf how to read, write, and communicate. More importantly, he wanted to teach them the Word of God. How could they ever learn about Jesus if there were no schools in America to teach them?

Some Hartford residents were not sure about the idea of teaching the deaf. Others, though, had watched Alice learn. They donated money to help the cause. With the money, Thomas Gallaudet went to Europe. He learned ways to teach the deaf. He met a young deaf Frenchman named Laurent Clerc. Gallaudet and Clerc became friends. Clerc agreed to come back to America with Gallaudet and help establish a school for deaf Americans.

Thomas Gallaudet

Laurent Clerc

American School for the Deaf

America's first school for the deaf opened in Hartford, Connecticut, in 1817. The first year, thirty-three deaf children and adults became students.

American School for the Deaf

President James Monroe

Stained glass window of
Thomas Gallaudet

American School for the Deaf

In the spring of 1818, President James Monroe visited Hartford and made a speech. President Monroe praised Thomas Gallaudet and the work of the school. Gallaudet, Alice, and several other students demonstrated sign language for President Monroe and the crowd. Monroe announced that the government would begin helping to pay for the education of citizens with disabilities. Soon more schools for deaf students opened in other states.

When Monroe visited Hartford, he wore a tricorner hat. Students of the school made up a sign for him. They formed the shape of his hat with their hands. Their sign became the sign language for the word "president." That sign is still used today.

Not long after the school opened, Gallaudet began to have special feelings for one of his students. Sophia Fowler was beautiful and brought a special light into Gallaudet's life. Gallaudet was concerned that Sophia might not want to marry him. His health was not good and he was eleven years older than she. Sophia was not sure Thomas should marry her. She was afraid that if they had a child, the baby might be deaf. As they talked about marriage, Gallaudet assured her that he believed they could solve any problems together. They married in 1821. They had eight children, all of whom could hear.

Thomas Gallaudet worked with the school in Hartford until 1830. After he resigned, he became a minister once again. He also wrote books.

A Longing Fulfilled

When Thomas Gallaudet was a little boy he was sickly, left out, and felt like he didn't measure up. He had often wondered what he might become someday. He liked to dream about what the future might hold. When he grew up and finished his education, he tried different jobs in different places. Nothing felt quite right. He longed for God to show him what He wanted him to do with his life. God answered that longing the day Alice Cogswell learned the word "hat." God showed Thomas Gallaudet what He wanted him to do, and Gallaudet did it well. The American School for the Deaf still operates in Hartford today.

As those who have been
chosen of God, holy and beloved,
put on a heart of compassion,
kindness, humility,
gentleness, and patience.
Colossians 3:12

Lesson Activities

- All Around the USA map: Find Hartford.
- Rhythms and Rhymes: Enjoy "Billy Boy" on page 19.
- Timeline: Look at pages 16-17.
- Literature for Units 5-8: *Toliver's Secret*

Review Questions

- Why did Thomas Gallaudet feel a connection with Alice when he first noticed her?
- How did people work together to establish America's first school for the deaf?
- How did Thomas Gallaudet make a difference for people in America who were deaf?

Unit Review

- Student Workbook: Complete the Lesson 24 / Unit 8 Review page.

Hands-On History Ideas

- Pretend that you can only communicate through sign language.
- Use building blocks to build a school for people with disabilities.

Unit 8 Project
The Star-Spangled Banner

Supplies

- 1 piece white poster board
- 1 ruler/yardstick
- pencil
- 1 sponge
- white paper
- cardstock
- pen
- scissors
- craft paint: red, blue, white
- 2 small paper plates

Directions

1. Mark an 11-inch by 11-inch square on the top left of the dull side of the poster board, as illustrated above.
2. Mark the remainder of the poster board in 15 even stripes. (Ours are 1 ⅜ inches.) If you have extra space, trim it from the bottom.
3. Make a star stencil by tracing the star above onto white paper. Cut out the star and trace it onto cardstock. Cut out the cardstock star.
4. Using the star stencil, trace the star with a pen on one side of the sponge.
5. Ask an adult to cut the star from the sponge and to cut two triangles from the remaining sponge.
6. Squirt red and blue craft paint onto a paper plate.
7. Dip one sponge into blue paint. Wipe off extra. Dab the sponge up and down (not a sweeping motion) to sponge-paint the square blue.
8. Dip the other sponge in red paint. Dab the sponge up and down to paint alternating stripes red. The top and bottom stripes are red. Tip: use the pointed end of your sponge to outline the stripe. Then fill in the rest of the stripe.
9. Let the paint dry completely.
10. Squirt white paint onto the second paper plate. Practice making stars on scrap paper to see how much paint you need on the sponge and how to gently press all corners down.
11. Make 15 stars on the blue square in five alternating rows of three, as shown.
12. Let dry completely.

Note: The original U.S. flag had thirteen stars and thirteen stripes. In 1794 Congress authorized a new design with fifteen stars and fifteen stripes to represent the fifteen states in the Union at the time. Three more states joined the Union before the War of 1812, but Congress did not authorize a new flag until 1818. At that time, Congress decided to go back to thirteen stripes and add only a star for each new state.

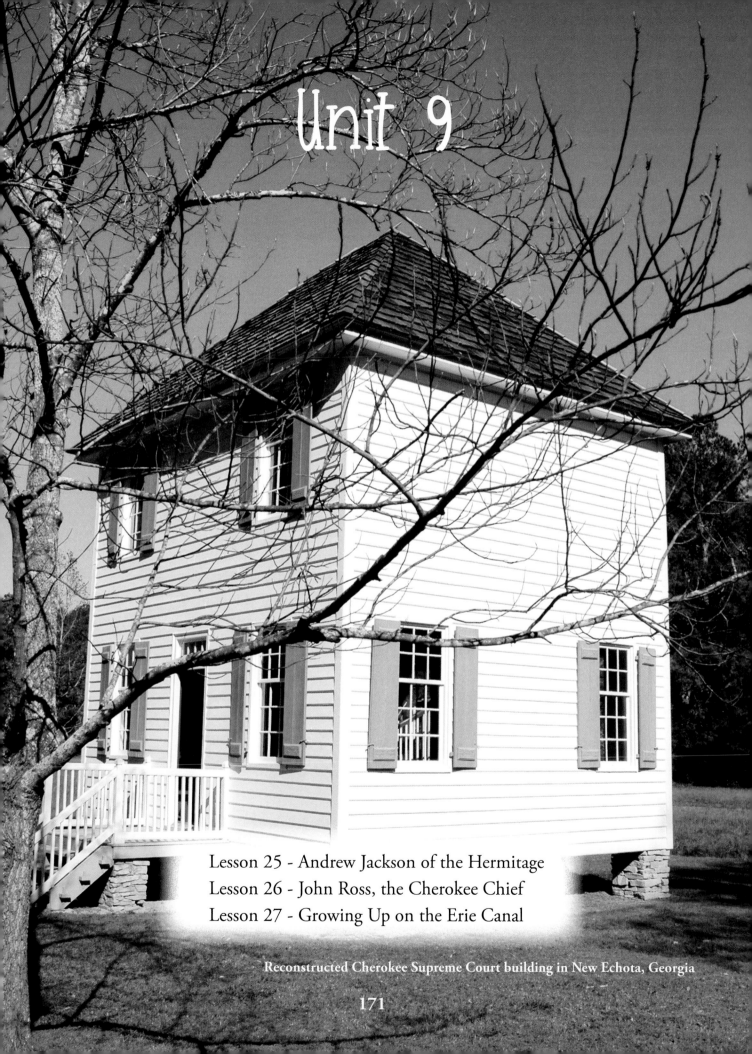

Unit 9

Reconstructed Cherokee Supreme Court building in New Echota, Georgia

Andrew Jackson
of the
Hermitage

Andrew and Elizabeth Jackson were weavers in the village of Boneybefore in Ireland. In May of 1765, Andrew, Elizabeth and their sons, Hugh and Robert, left their thatched-roof cottage. They traveled to the seacoast town of Larne to board a ship to America. Hugh was 2 years old. Robert was 6 months old.

Andrew Jackson was part of the Jackson clan from Scotland. In the early 1600s, England's King James I had encouraged Scottish Presbyterians to emigrate to Ireland. Now many of their descendants were leaving Ireland for the thirteen colonies in America.

Andrew, Elizabeth, and their sons settled in the Waxhaw area near the border between North Carolina and South Carolina. Early in 1767, while Andrew and Elizabeth waited for the birth of their third child, Andrew died. On March 15, Elizabeth gave birth to a third son. She named him Andrew after his father. One day he would become President of the United States.

Elizabeth and her sons moved in with relatives who had also emigrated from Ireland. Elizabeth became their housekeeper. She took her sons to church each Sunday. She managed her money well and was able to send Andrew to study with Presbyterian ministers.

Carrickfergus Castle was a short distance from the Jackson home in Boneybefore.

The Jacksons and the American Revolution

When soldiers fought battles in the American Revolution near their home, Hugh, Robert, and Andrew joined the fight against the British. Andrew was only thirteen years old.

Hugh died of heat stroke after a battle. The British captured Robert and Andrew. Robert caught smallpox. Elizabeth got the boys out of prison and took them home. Soon Robert died.

Andrew came down with smallpox, too. Elizabeth lovingly nursed Andrew back to health. Then she went to Charleston, South Carolina, to help other sick and wounded soldiers. She caught cholera there and died. At only fourteen years old, Andrew was alone.

Lawyer and Tennessean

Andrew Jackson was handsome, tall, and slim. His eyes were blue and his hair was red. At age seventeen, he began studying to become a lawyer. When Andrew was twenty-one years old, he got a job as a lawyer in Tennessee. He traveled across the Appalachian Mountains on the Wilderness Road that Daniel Boone and his thirty woodcutters had cleared just thirteen years before.

After a short time in Tennessee's oldest town of Jonesborough, Jackson moved to the small settlement of Nashville. The frontier town was only eight years old.

Andrew met and married Rachel Donelson. Her father was one of the founders of Nashville. Tennessee became a state in 1796. Andrew Jackson helped to write the state constitution. He became the first U.S. representative from Tennessee. He later served as a U.S. senator.

Charleston, South Carolina, in 1774

Scenes from Martin Station, a stop along the Wilderness Road

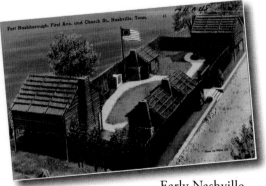

Early Nashville

Andrew and Rachel Jackson's
first home at the Hermitage

Enslaved Persons

In 1804 Andrew Jackson purchased a farm which he named the Hermitage. Andrew and his wife Rachel moved into the two-story log cabin already on the farm. In 1819 workers began building a brick mansion. An English gardener designed a beautiful garden. Two years later, Andrew and Rachel moved from the log cabin to the mansion. Workers removed the second story of the cabin. It became a home for enslaved persons.

The Hermitage was a working plantation. The main crop was cotton. Sadly, Andrew Jackson depended on slave labor. When Andrew Jackson purchased the Hermitage, he had nine enslaved persons. He continued to purchase more land. He eventually had 161 slaves. Though they worked in slavery, they used great skill. On these pages are the names of enslaved persons who lived and worked at the Hermitage, along with their jobs on the plantation and the kinds of tools they used. Masters often only recorded first names for their slaves.

House Servants
Billy   Charlotte   Hannah   Nancy
Nelly   Sarah   Louisa

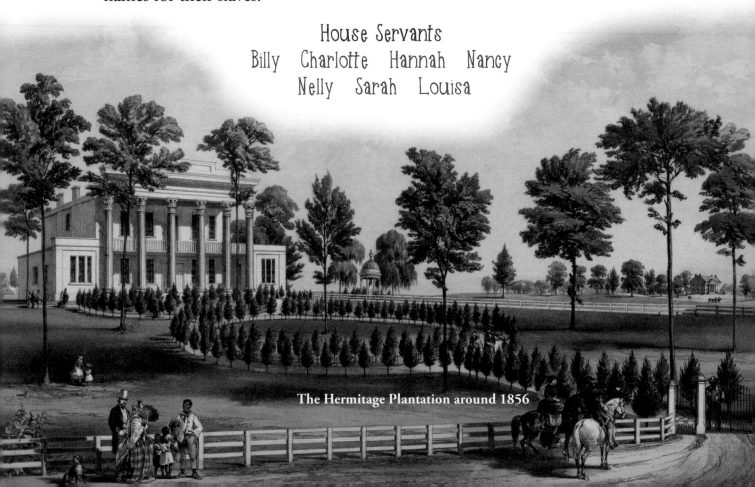

The Hermitage Plantation around 1856

and Their Work at the Hermitage

Spinner
Eliza

Carriage Driver
Charles

Hog Feeder
Smith

Cattle Feeder
Moses

Seamstress
Gracy

Blacksmith
Aaron

Washer
Jane

Weavers
Creasy
Gincy

Milker
Anny

Fiddler
Squire

Carpenters
Aaron
Ned

Cooks
Betty
Maria
Mary
Old Dick
Old Hannah

Horse Groomer
Dunwoody

Waggoner
Alfred

Gardener
Old Sampson

Children's Nurse
Louisa

Field Hands

Aggy   Augustus   Ben   Big Sampson   Byron   Campbell
Davis   Dick   Essex   Florida   George   Jenny   Littleton
Malinda   Morgan   Sam   Sally   Sylvia   William

This mural of the Battle of New Orleans is located in Washington, D.C.

General Jackson

Early in the War of 1812, President James Madison made Jackson the commander of a division of volunteer soldiers. Jackson's first assignment was to take 1,500 troops to New Orleans in case the British attacked the city.

General Jackson

Two months later the War Department ordered Jackson to send his soldiers home. Jackson was furious when the government did not give the men money to travel. He led them back to Tennessee himself and shared all their hardships. He let sick soldiers ride on his horses while he walked. The troops decided that Jackson was as tough as a hickory tree. For the rest of his life, his nickname was Old Hickory.

Jackson won a promotion to general after winning battles against the Red Sticks during the War of 1812. The Red Sticks were a group of Creek natives who attacked white settlers.

Jackson meets with Creek Chief Red Eagle in 1814.

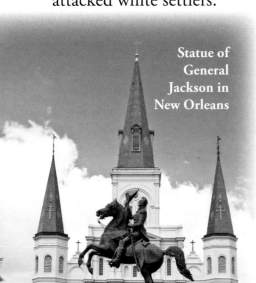

Statue of General Jackson in New Orleans

In December of 1814, General Jackson led his troops back to New Orleans. This time the British did attack. General Jackson and his untrained volunteers won easily over the well-trained British army in the Battle of New Orleans. He became a national hero.

Andrew and Rachel Jackson's Family

Andrew and Rachel Jackson helped to rear and educate several children. Some were Rachel's relatives. Rachel and Andrew adopted one of Rachel's nephews and named him Andrew Jackson Jr.

Three Creek children came to live at the Hermitage. One of them was Lyncoya, whose mother died during a battle between U.S. soldiers and the Red Sticks. Andrew wrote to Rachel about Lyncoya. He said the child reminded him of losing his own family as a child.

Rachel Jackson

President Andrew Jackson

In November of 1828, Andrew Jackson was elected as the seventh President of the United States. In December, his beloved Rachel died. She was buried in their garden on Christmas Eve. Jackson was heartbroken when he left the Hermitage in January to travel to Washington, D.C.

Americans thought of Jackson as the people's president. President Jackson was the first president who was not from Virginia or Massachusetts. He was the first president whose father and mother were both immigrants. Jackson was the first president to ride a train. He was the first and only president who helped the country pay back all of the money that it owed. He easily won a second term in 1832.

Rachel's tomb

Supporters greet President Jackson on his way to Washington. They celebrate at the White House after his inauguration.

President Jackson
in the White House

Ephesus Church

Hermitage Dining Room

Home to the Hermitage

Andrew Jackson came home to the Hermitage after his second term as president. He wrote many letters in his library, including letters to leaders in Washington. He visited Rachel's tomb each day.

Andrew Jackson Jr., his wife Sarah, and their children lived with President Jackson. Sarah's sister and her children also lived at the Hermitage. President Jackson spent happy hours in the back parlor with his family. In the evenings they gathered for devotionals.

Jackson and several neighbors had donated money to build a church. When the church started, the church had nine members. They named it Ephesus Church. Before Rachel died, Andrew promised her that he would become a church member. He joined Ephesus Church two years after coming home from Washington, D.C.

Hannah, an enslaved woman, greeted visitors at the door of the Hermitage. She served as the head of the household servants. Jackson entertained visitors in the front parlor with tales of his years in the army.

Entry Hall at the Hermitage

At 3:00 p.m. his family and guests gathered for a large meal in the formal dining room. Sometimes as many as twenty-five people ate at Jackson's table. Guests who stayed overnight included James K. Polk and Martin Van Buren, both of whom served as president after Jackson.

Andrew Jackson died in 1845, surrounded by his family. Hannah was in the room, as she had been when Rachel died 20 years before. Nearly 10,000 people attended Jackson's funeral. He was buried in the garden beside Rachel.

Some of the last words Andrew Jackson spoke on the afternoon when he died were these: "I hope to meet you all in Heaven, both black and white."

It is good that Andrew Jackson recognized God's love for every person with his dying words. However, Andrew Jackson never gave any of his slaves the freedom they deserved. The apostle Peter said:

> . . . in every nation the man
> who fears Him
> and does what is right
> is welcome to Him.
> Acts 10:35

Lesson Activities

- All Around the USA: Find Waxhaw, Charleston, Appalachian Mountains, Wilderness Road, Jonesborough, Nashville, New Orleans, and Washington, D.C.
- Rhythms and Rhymes: Enjoy "Turkey in the Straw" on pages 20-21.
- Student Workbook: Complete the Lesson 25 page.
- Literature for Units 5-9: *Toliver's Secret*.

Review Questions

- What was Andrew Jackson's nickname? How did he get it?
- What battle made Andrew Jackson a national hero?
- Who did Andrew Jackson depend on to run his Hermitage plantation?

Hands-On History Ideas

- Pretend you are President of the United States. Whom will you invite to visit the White House? What will you try to improve in the country?
- Use building blocks to build a fancy garden with fences, benches, gazebos, fountains, and any other features you wish to include.

John Ross
the
Cherokee Chief

Chief John Ross

One of the saddest events in American history began in 1838. President Andrew Jackson and the U.S. government forced the Cherokee to leave their homelands in Alabama, North Carolina, Georgia, and Tennessee. After years of trying to keep this from happening, Chief John Ross led his people west toward Indian Territory, which is now Oklahoma. Hundreds of Cherokee died on the way.

In English the event is called the Trail of Tears. In Cherokee it is *Nunna-da-ul-tsun-yi*. It means "the place where they cried."

Modern Cherokee demonstrates shooting with a blowgun.

Cherokee chief, 1762

The Real People

Hernando de Soto met members of the Cherokee nation in the 1500s, when he explored the area that would one day be the southeastern United States. Cherokee called themselves *Aniyunwiya*. The word means "the real people." They lived in villages in the southern Appalachian Mountains. The Cherokee spoke an Iroquois language. They may have migrated south from lands near the Great Lakes.

Great-Grandparents of Chief John Ross

In the 1700s, immigrants from Scotland and Ireland came into Cherokee lands to trade. William Shorey was a Scot who learned to speak the Cherokee language well. He came to Cherokee lands in what would one day become Tennessee. William married Ghigooie, a Cherokee woman. He and Ghigooie had three children. The oldest was their daughter Anne.

The Cherokee fought on the same side as the British during the French and Indian War. William Shorey worked as an interpreter at Fort Loudoun, a British fort in what became Tennessee.

Grandparents of Chief John Ross

John McDonald was born in the Scottish Highlands in 1747. John emigrated to America when he was 19. He also came across the Appalachian Mountains to trade with the Cherokee. There he met and married William and Ghigooie Shorey's daughter Anne. In 1770 Anne gave birth to their daughter Mollie. John McDonald opened a store where he traded with the Cherokee.

Fort Loudoun

Parents of Chief John Ross

Daniel Ross was born in Scotland in 1760. About 1770 he and his mother set sail for America. Mrs. Ross was a widow. She died during the trip. The orphaned Daniel arrived in the Maryland colony.

When Daniel grew up, he became a trader with the Cherokee. One day, as he traveled on a flatboat on the Tennessee River near the McDonald store, some Cherokee threatened to kill him. John McDonald saved his life. Daniel Ross settled near the McDonalds. He married John and Anne McDonald's daughter Mollie.

Daniel and Mollie Ross had nine children. They named their third child John after his grandfather John McDonald. John Ross' grandmother Anne and his mother Mollie taught him the traditions of the Cherokee. He wore Cherokee clothing and participated in Cherokee ceremonies.

John was homeschooled in his early years. His father provided his family with American and English newspapers and with many books and maps. He built a school on his property. He hired a tutor and invited other children to come there to study. Still later, he sent John to a boarding school.

John Ross' mother died while he was away at boarding school. He left school and moved back among his relatives. He spent much of his time at the home of his grandfather, John McDonald. John Ross cherished happy memories of his mother all his life and clung to her Cherokee teachings.

When John Ross grew up, he became a businessman, like his father and grandfather. He married Quatie, a Cherokee widow with one child. John and Quatie Ross had six children.

Ross' Landing

John Ross and a partner ran a warehouse along the Tennessee River. They sold goods to the Cherokee and to the U.S. government. John Ross built a place for flatboats to land. He also ran a ferry across the Tennessee River. This place became known as Ross' Landing.

John Ross the Soldier

We learned in the previous lesson that some Creek warriors formed a group called the Red Sticks. During the War of 1812, John Ross encouraged the Cherokee to fight with Andrew Jackson against the Red Sticks. Ross and other Cherokee warriors helped Jackson defeat them.

Brainerd Mission

In the early 1800s, Cherokee leaders agreed for missionaries to start a mission on Cherokee land. The missionaries named the mission school Brainerd Mission after David Brainerd. He had been a missionary to the Delaware tribe in the mid-1700s. The missionaries began teaching Cherokee children in 1817. Many famous Americans and Europeans visited the school. President James Monroe spent the night there in 1819.

Teachers at the Brainerd Mission taught in English. They studied the Bible with Cherokee children. They taught them hymns, prayer, reading, writing, arithmetic, grammar, and geography. They taught the boys how to raise livestock, how to take care of gardens, and how to do blacksmithing and carpentry. They taught Cherokee girls how to spin and weave and how to do chores at home. When older students learned their lessons, they helped to teach younger students.

John Ross' grandmother Anne frequently attended worship services at the mission. She became a believer in Jesus and a devoted member of the church.

Sequoyah and His Cherokee Syllabary

Sequoyah was another of the Cherokee who fought with General Jackson. He noticed that white soldiers could read orders, keep journals, and write letters home to their families. The Cherokee did not have writing. After the war, Sequoyah worked for many years to create a Cherokee syllabary. Each symbol represents a syllable. Thousands of Cherokee learned to read and write their native language.

Sequoyah

Samuel Worcester was a missionary at the Brainerd Mission. He used the new Cherokee writing symbols to translate much of the Bible into the Cherokee language. He set up a print shop and began the *Cherokee Phoenix*. It was America's first newspaper in a native language.

Nunna-da-ul-tsun-yi — The Trail of Tears

The Cherokee wrote a constitution similar to the U.S. Constitution and set up a government at New Echota, Georgia. In 1828 they elected John Ross to be chief of the Cherokee nation.

In 1830 the U.S. Congress passed a law stating that most native people living east of the Mississippi River had to move west of the Mississippi. Chief John Ross went to Washington, D.C., again and again trying to keep them from having to go. President Andrew Jackson was determined to force them to move west.

Routes of the Trail of Tears

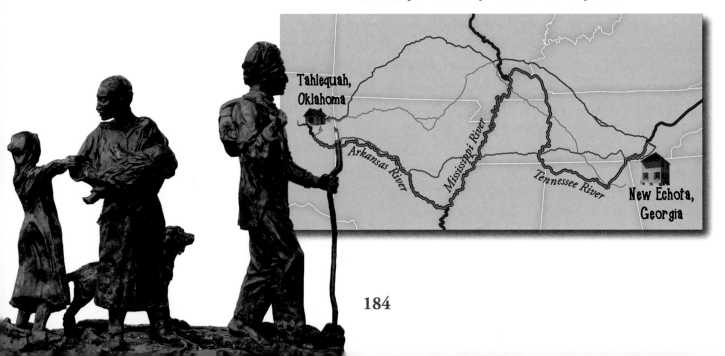

Thousands of Cherokee began the journey west in 1838. The map at left shows the four main routes they traveled. Chief Ross led the last group to leave. They traveled by boat along the route marked in orange. The journey was long and hard. Hundreds of people died on the way, including Chief Ross' wife Quatie.

After the Cherokee reached Oklahoma, they elected John Ross as their chief again. They established a capital city at Tahlequah. Ross helped the Cherokee write a new constitution. Ross served his people as their chief until he died at seventy-five years old in 1866.

Sequoyah's invention continues to have a lasting impact on the Cherokee people. This is the Lord's Prayer in Cherokee.

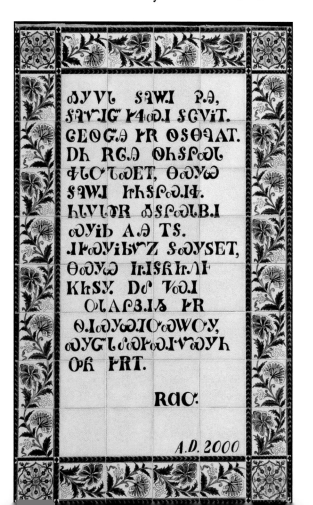

Lesson Activities

- All Around the USA map: Find Appalachian Mountains, Tennessee River, Ross' Landing, New Echota, Mississippi River, Washington, D.C., and Tahlequah.

- Rhythms and Rhymes: Enjoy "Amazing Grace" (Cherokee Version) on pages 22-23.

- Student Workbook: Complete the Lesson 26 page.

- Literature for Units 5-9: *Toliver's Secret*.

Review Questions

- John Ross' family background was a mix of Cherokee and people who moved to America from what country?

- How did a written language change life for the Cherokee?

- Why do you think Andrew Jackson and the United States government wanted native people to move west of the Mississippi?

Hands-On History Ideas

- See the Unit 9 Project instructions on pages 193-194.

Growing Up
on the
Erie Canal

Early in the 1800s, New York City became the largest city in the United States. New York Governor DeWitt Clinton had once been mayor of New York City. He believed that New York City would become a more important place if boats could travel between the city and Lake Erie.

The Hudson River begins in the Adirondack Mountains. It flows through New York state until it empties into the Atlantic Ocean at New York City harbor. The city of Albany is on the banks of the Hudson River. The city of Buffalo, New York, is on the shores of Lake Erie. Governor Clinton wanted to build a canal to connect Albany and Buffalo.

Many people made fun of Governor Clinton's idea. Some called the canal "Clinton's Ditch." Clinton kept working to get the project completed. The Erie Canal opened in 1825. Governor Clinton was right. New York City became the busiest port in the United States.

The Hudson River flows through the Adirondacks.

A canal boat tows a barge filled with coal.

Moving Goods and People

Canal boats were like today's tractor trailer trucks. They carried goods from one place to another. Some canal boats transported passengers, just like modern buses, trains, and planes.

A canal boat captain hired a steersman and two drivers. The captain and the steersman took turns driving the boat. The drivers walked on the land leading the horses or mules that towed the boat along the canal. They often whistled a tune while they walked.

Passenger canal boat

187

Home Sweet Home

Many canal boat captains lived on their boats with their families. Daddies did their work as boat captains. Mamas did the work that other mamas were doing in the houses they passed on the way. Children played, learned, and did their chores.

A canal boat had a cabin for the captain and his family. It had a caboose for the steersman and drivers and a stable for the mules or horses. The captain's cabin had furniture, toys, clothes, and other possessions just like houses on land. Bunks were often below deck. The sloshing water lulled the children to sleep.

Mamas worked to keep their cabins tidy and clean. They made them pretty with decorations and hung curtains at the windows. Some parents put shiny varnish on the floors. The parents of one little girl pressed her footprints into the varnish before it dried.

Parents hung an awning on the boat deck or on top of the cabin if it had a flat roof. This gave the family a shady spot. When the steersman took his turn steering the boat, the captain might take a nap under the awning while his wife sat sewing and his children played.

Canal Boat City

Sometimes canal boats came so close together that people stepped from one to another. They became like floating communities. When the boats came close, the parties began. A fiddler or accordion player made music while dancers danced in the moonlight on the clean white decks of the canal boats. Ladies also visited other ladies on their boats, just like ladies on land visited in their friends' houses.

Accordion

The Locks

The Erie Canal went through hilly countryside. Engineers had to design locks for the Erie Canal. A lock is like an elevator. A lock lifts or lowers a boat so that it can continue traveling on the canal. A locktender worked at each lock. Sometimes a child on a canal boat got to blow a tin horn to let the locktender know his family's boat was coming. The people living near locks planted beautiful flower beds for canal boat families to enjoy. Some locktenders handed the travelers bouquets as they went through the locks.

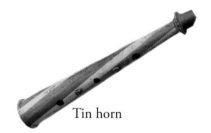
Tin horn

Historic and modern locks on the Erie Canal

Shopping Along the Canal

Merchants found creative ways to sell to canal families. When many boats came to a lock, families had time to get off the boat and shop at canal-side stores while they waited for their turn to get through the lock. These stores sold most of what they needed. People packed into the stores to buy everything from hay for the mules to silk for the ladies.

Shopping didn't stop when the boats started moving. Peddlers walked from boat to boat selling their wares. Small boats called "bum boats" brought goods out to the canal boats. They brought ice cream and sweets.

Cash register from a store along the Erie Canal

Farmers set up fruit and vegetable stands beside the canals. When a canal boat got close to a farmer's stand, someone on the boat called out an order. The farmer threw fruits and vegetables onto the boat. The buyer stuck coins into a potato and threw it back to the farmer. The boat didn't even have to stop. Other farmers used their own rowboats as a sort of bum boat. They rowed up beside the canal boat and sold the ladies fresh eggs, milk, and cream.

Don't Fall Off the Boat!

Mamas and daddies had to keep their children from falling into the water. Often they tied a rope or chain to the littlest children so they could easily pull them back on the boat if they fell in.

One time a little boy of about five fell into the canal. His daddy jumped in to save him. The daddy swam to shore with the little boy under his arm. They climbed up the bank and walked on the towpath to the next bridge and then climbed back onto the boat.

Even parents had trouble staying out of the water sometimes. If the water was rough, a daddy might have to crawl on his hands and knees to get across the deck to keep from falling into the water.

Learning and Playing

Canal children played boat, just like children on land play house. Children also enjoyed corn cob dolls, jacks, dominoes, and card games.

Canal boat parents taught their children reading, writing, arithmetic, and recitation. Children used chalk to write on slates. They read from the Bible and from *McGuffey's Readers*.

The Erie Canal froze in the winter. Canal boat families who had farms moved to their farms for the winter. Some of their children went to school for a few months.

Illustration from a *McGuffey's Reader*

Jacks and Dominoes

Children learning on a canal boat on the Erie Canal

"Little Chuck" on the Canal Boat

One day a canal boat mama prepared lunch for her family. Her little boy Chuck, who was about five years old, stood on a stool looking out the window. The mama kept hearing little splashes in the canal. When she went to get the silverware out of the drawer, she found it empty. Chuck had been busy throwing every spoon, knife, and fork overboard one at a time.

A joyful heart
makes a cheerful face,
But when the heart is sad,
the spirit is broken.
Proverbs 15:13

Lesson Activities

- All Around the USA map: Find New York City, Lake Erie, Adirondack Mountains, Hudson River, Albany, Buffalo, and the Erie Canal.

- Timeline: Look at pages 16-21. You may also wish to review the previous pages you have learned about.

- Literature for Units 5-9: *Toliver's Secret*.

Review Questions

- In what state was the Erie Canal built?

- How did canal boats move along the canal?

- What do you think would be fun about living on a canal boat?

Unit Review

- Student Workbook: Complete the Lesson 27 / Unit 9 Review page.

Hands-On History Ideas

- Pretend that you live on a canal boat. You can help steer the boat, take care of the horses or mules, do school and chores, have parties with other boat families, and shop along the shore or right from your boat.

- Use building blocks to build a canal boat.

Unit 9 Project
Hand-Woven Basket

Basket-making has been an important part of Cherokee culture for many generations.

Supplies

- 1 paper cup
- pencil
- scissors
- popsicle sticks
- white glue
- raffia, yarn, or narrow string (raffia is long strands of dried grass, available at craft stores)

Directions

1. Mark the paper cup in several places 1 ¼ inches from the bottom.

2. Cut down from the top of the cup to one of your marks, then cut around to make the cup 1 ¼ inches tall.

3. Glue popsicle sticks around the cup. Use a generous amount of glue and hold each stick in place for 10 seconds before moving to the next one. Sticks should be very close to each other but not as tight as possible.

continued

1. After gluing all the sticks, let dry for at least three hours.

2. Make a loop a couple of inches from one end of the raffia, yarn, or string.

3. Ease the loop down over one stick to the level of the cup. Gently tighten the loop.

4. Start weaving in and out between the sticks. Pull very gently to avoid pulling the stick off the cup. When you finish one row, weave the next row alternating from the previous row.

5. Frequently press the rows down toward the bottom to make the weaving tight.

6. You can make the basket all one color with one continuous piece of raffia, yarn, or string. You can also tie on new colors. If you need to add raffia, yarn, or string, leave a few inches at the end of the strand you are weaving. Tie on a new piece with a strong knot. Position the tied ends inside the basket as you weave.

10. Continue weaving as high as you can. Tie the end to the top of a stick.

11. Trim any ends of raffia, yarn, or string inside the basket, leaving ½ inch extra.

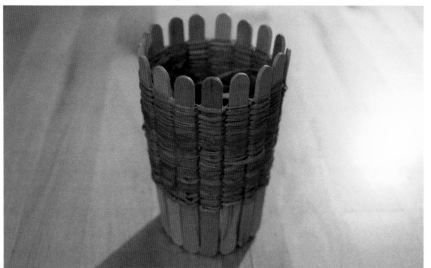

Unit 10

Cotton Mill in Lowell, Massachusetts

Caroline Ernst
and the
Settlement of Texas

Caroline Ernst tried to find a place to lie down and rest, but the ship was too crowded. Passengers and luggage were everywhere. Caroline felt that if a strong wind arose, they would all drown in the Gulf of Mexico. Caroline and the other passengers were all bound for Mexico.

Caroline was German. Two years earlier, when Caroline was ten, her family had emigrated to the United States. Now it was 1831 and they were emigrating again, this time to Mexico. Spain once ruled Mexico, just as Great Britain once ruled the colonies. Now Mexico was an independent country. The area we now know as Texas was a part of Mexico.

Pelican over the Gulf of Mexico

Stephen Austin is called "The Father of Texas." He led a group of settlers from the United States to Texas in 1822. Many families, including Caroline's, decided to follow.

The Mexican government welcomed new settlers to Texas. They wanted men to bring their families and build communities. The settlers were called Texians. A family could claim about 4,600 acres of land and pay only four cents an acre. In the United States, settlers paid about $1.25 an acre. Land in Texas was cheap!

Texas Countryside

Life for Caroline's Family

Life was hard for many of the new Texians. Caroline Ernst wrote about her family's experience in Texas:

[We lived in] a miserable little hut, covered with straw and having six sides, which were made out of moss. The roof was by no means water-proof, and we often held an umbrella over our bed when it rained at night, while the cows came and ate the moss. Of course, we suffered a great deal in the winter. My father had tried to build a chimney and fireplace out of logs and clay, but we were afraid to light a fire because of the extreme combustibility of our dwelling. So we had to shiver. Our shoes gave out, and we had to go barefoot in winter, for we did not know how to make moccasins. Our supply of clothes was also insufficient, and we had no spinning wheel, nor did we know how to spin and weave like the Americans. It was twenty-eight miles to San Felipe, and, besides, we had no money. When we could buy things, my first calico dress cost 50 cents per yard. No one can imagine what a degree of want there was of the merest necessities of life, and it is difficult for me now to understand how we managed to live and get along under the circumstances. Yet we did so in some way. We were really better supplied than our neighbors with household and farm utensils, but they knew better how to help themselves.

At first we had very little to eat. We ate nothing but corn bread at first. Later, we began to raise cow peas, and afterwards my father made a fine vegetable garden. My father always was a poor huntsman. At first, we grated our corn until my father hollowed out a log and we ground it, as in a mortar. We had no cooking-stove, of course, and baked our bread in the only skillet we possessed. The ripe corn was boiled until it was soft, then grated and baked. We lived in our doorless and windowless six-cornered pavilion about three years.

The Texas Revolution

Some of the Mexicans who lived in Texas did not welcome the new settlers. Stephen Austin formed a militia to defend his colony and to maintain peace.

Many Texians wanted Texas to become part of the United States. Others wanted it to become an independent country. The U.S. government tried to pressure Mexico into selling Texas to the United States. Mexico refused. More Texians than Mexicans lived in some parts of Texas. The Mexican government was afraid the Texians might turn against Mexico. The Mexican government began to limit the number of white Americans who could settle there. They encouraged more Mexicans to settle in Texas.

Stephen Austin and other Texians

Sometimes Texian settlers clashed with Mexican soldiers. In 1835 they fought a battle at Gonzales. This was the start of the Texas Revolution. On March 2, 1836, Texians declared Texas to be a separate country. One of the most famous battles of the revolution was the Battle of the Alamo. The Mexicans defeated the Texians in that battle.

The Alamo

The revolution ended at the Battle of San Jacinto. There the Texians defeated the Mexicans. The battle lasted only eighteen minutes. Texas became an independent country. Nine years later, in 1845, Texas became part of the United States.

Caroline Ernst wrote about her experience during the Texas Revolution:

When the war broke out, my father at first intended quietly to remain at his home. But the Mexicans had induced the Kickapoo Indians to revolt, and he was warned [about the danger]. We then set out with the intention of crossing the Sabine [River] and seeking safety in the [United] States. When we arrived at the Brazos [River], we found so many people assembled at the ferry that it would have been three days before the one small ferry-boat could have carried us over the stream. The roads were almost impassable. So my father pitched his camp in the middle of the Brazos [River] bottom near Brenham. Here we remained until after the battle of San Jacinto. After the war, times were hard. However, my father had buried a good many things and had in this way succeeded in keeping them from the Mexicans. He had placed two posts a considerable distance apart, and had buried his treasures just midway between them. The posts had both been pulled out and holes dug near them, but our things had not been found. Our house and garden had been left unharmed, though those of our neighbors had been destroyed.

Brazos River

People fight each other for many reasons. Jesus taught that no matter what other people do, we must love them and pray for them.

You have heard
that it was said,
"You shall love your neighbor
and hate your enemy."
But I say to you, love your
enemies and pray for those
who persecute you, so that you
may be sons of your Father
who is in heaven;
for He causes His sun to rise
on the evil and the good,
and sends rain on the righteous
and the unrighteous.
Matthew 5:43-45

Lesson Activities

- All Around the USA map: Find the Gulf of Mexico, the Alamo, San Jacinto, and the Brazos River.

- Rhythms and Rhymes: Enjoy "A Dress to Make" on pages 24-25.

- Student Workbook: Complete the Lesson 28 page.

- Literature for Units 10-12: *Freedom Crossing*

Review Questions

- When Caroline Ernst and her family settled in Texas, the land was a part of what country?

- What happened nine years after Texas became a country independent of Mexico?

- What are some reasons you can think of that people fight wars with each other?

Hands-On History Ideas

- Pretend that you are a member of the Ernst family. Travel to Texas and establish your family's farm as described in this lesson.

- Use building blocks to build a six-sided house.

Factory Girls at Lowell

Her friends talked of nothing else. At Lowell you can improve your mind. At Lowell you can be fashionable. At Lowell you can get rich! There was work for girls in the factories at Lowell. She and Father had talked it over. He wanted her on the farm. She tried to be content. Her older brothers had gone west. How could Father manage alone? But he owed money to the bank. They made so little from the farm. One day at breakfast, he said she could go.

She wore her best dress. She clutched her box of clothes. She thought of Father the whole trip. Other girls in the coach talked without stopping. None had ever been far from home. Nothing could be more exciting than Lowell, or more frightening! The coach stopped. She waited her turn to get out. On the coach steps, she stopped. The factories were enormous! Sidewalks swarmed with people. She stepped out. She looked up, then around. The other girls were not talking now. Starting tomorrow, they were factory girls.

Factory beside a canal in Lowell, Massachusetts

Cotton

Loom

Hands to Machines

In the early 1800s, most Americans lived on farms. They produced most of what they needed. They made a little money selling extra goods. People worked with their hands. Each handmade item required a great deal of time and work. For example, making cloth or "textiles" from cotton required several steps. People planted, weeded, watered, and harvested cotton. People removed seeds from cotton. People untangled the cotton fibers. People cleaned cotton. People spun cotton into thread with a spinning wheel. People wove thread into cloth with a loom. Then they made clothes from the cloth. These methods had barely changed in hundreds of years.

In the late 1700s and early 1800s, people invented many useful machines. Machines changed the way people made things. Machines made things more quickly and cheaply than people could make them by hand. Businessmen knew they could make a lot of money from machine-made goods. This brought an Industrial Revolution. "Industrial Revolution" sounds like a war. It was not a war. It was a revolutionary or enormous change in the way people worked and lived.

Spinning wheel

Hamilton Canal in Lowell, Massachusetts

Water Power at Pawtucket Falls

The Merrimack River flows through northeast Massachusetts. Pawtucket Falls on the Merrimack River falls thirty-two feet over rocks. The English settled this area soon after they settled Plymouth. John Eliot preached to native people there in 1646. In the early 1800s, the area was still quiet. Small farms surrounded a tiny village. The river was a good fishing spot. Then the Industrial Revolution swept in. Change came fast.

Land near Pawtucket Falls was a perfect place for factories. Many early machines used moving water for power. Beginning in the 1820s, companies built huge textile factories beside the Merrimack River. They also built canals to bring more water power to the mills.

Machines could perform every step of making cloth. Fluffy cotton went into the factory. Folded cloth came out. Companies built the town of Lowell around the factories. The factories needed people to run the machines. Factory owners found workers on New England's farms.

Mill in Lowell, Massachusetts

204

Machines and spools of thread inside a factory in Lowell

Farmers' Daughters

The daughter of a New England farmer helped her family in the house, kitchen, garden, barn, and fields. She had many skills. Her way of life had not changed much since the first English settlers came to America. Then factories arrived.

Textile companies sent agents into the countryside to recruit workers. Agents assured parents that their teenage and young adult daughters would be safe in Lowell. Farmers' daughters loved the prospect of money and adventure. They came to Lowell by the thousands. Most of them planned to work only a few years. They planned then to get married and manage homes like their mothers.

Life as a Factory Girl

Factory girls woke to the sound of a bell. They hurried to the factory at five a.m. They worked for ten to thirteen hours every day except Sunday. They stopped for a half hour at breakfast and again at lunch. Another bell signaled the end of the work day.

Factory girls lived in large houses the factories owned. Girls paid for their room and meals. Each house had a keeper. This woman was responsible for the house, the meals, and the girls' behavior. Keepers reported to factory managers. If a girl was wild, rowdy, or missed church too often, she could lose her job at the factory.

Farm in New England

Factory girls prided themselves on making the most of their time off. They read books, magazines, and newspapers. They discussed what they read. They could go to school in the evening. Girls could share the cost of renting a piano and paying a music teacher. In church, girls had an opportunity to worship God, learn, socialize, and help others.

Dining room in Lowell boarding house

Farmers' daughters enjoyed having money of their own. They spent some on candy and fancy clothes. They also built savings at Lowell's Savings Bank. Many factory girls worked for a specific reason. Some paid for a brother to go to college. Some helped parents pay debts. Some saved to help furnish a home after marriage.

Watching Lowell

Lowell became a famous place. People were curious about it. Lowell was a new way of life. What would happen to these factory girls? Was it respectable for girls to earn a living? Would they become slaves of the factory owners? Many presidents, leaders, and writers visited Lowell. They were amazed. The city was clean. The factory production was amazing. Most surprisingly, the factory girls seemed healthy and happy.

Textile companies made great wealth. By 1848 Lowell was the largest factory center in America. Lowell's factories produced 50,000 miles of cloth every year. This was enough cloth to go around the world twice.

Lowell around 1850

Change Comes Again

Other businessmen saw the success of Lowell. They built factories in other cities. Lowell's factories had competition. They had to lower prices to sell cloth. The factory girls had to work harder for less pay. They tried to protest, but factory owners did not listen. They had no need to keep factory girls happy. Plenty of people wanted their jobs. Factory girls began to leave Lowell.

In the 1840s, the country of Ireland faced a potato famine. Poor people were desperate to escape. Many came to Lowell and other factory towns in the United States. They needed jobs. Immigrants from many other nations followed the Irish. Factory owners treated them poorly. They paid them less. Whole families of immigrants had to work to make money for their households. They lived in crowded, run-down factory houses. Factory owners ran the machines faster. People got hurt on the job. Immigrants could not go back to the farm. The bright first chapter of life in Lowell had come to an end.

The Bible teaches employers to treat their workers fairly.

The laborer is worthy of his wages.
1 Timothy 5:18

Lesson Activities

- All Around the USA map: Find Lowell.
- Student Workbook: Complete the Lesson 29 page.
- Literature for Units 10-12: *Freedom Crossing*

Review Questions

- How did the Industrial Revolution change the way many things are made?
- Why do you think Lowell factory owners originally recruited New England farm girls?
- Who replaced factory girls when they started to leave their jobs in Lowell?

Hands-On History Ideas

- See the Unit 10 Project instructions on page 214.

Sailing to America
on the
"Norwegian *Mayflower*"

Pilgrims sailed to America on the *Mayflower* in 1620. They wanted a safe place to worship God the way they believed they should. Over 200 years later, in 1825, Norwegians left Norway. They sailed on a small sloop called the *Restauration*. They wanted a safe place to worship God, too.

Cleng Peerson Comes to America

In 1821 Cleng Peerson came to New York from Norway. He made a trip back home three years later. He told other Norwegians about America. Lars Larson was one of those who listened to Peerson. Larson was a Quaker. At the time, the Lutheran Church was the state church of Norway. The Norwegian government made life difficult for believers who were not part of the state church, including Quakers. Larson and others decided to go to America. Cleng Peerson returned to America to find land for these new immigrants.

Lutheran church in Norway

The *Restauration* Arrives in America

In 1825 Lars Larson, his wife, and members of five other families went together to purchase the *Restauration*. They loaded it with iron. They planned to sell the iron and the sloop when they got to America. A sloop is a small ship with only one mast. The Pilgrim's *Mayflower* was also a small ship, but the *Mayflower* was more than four times bigger than the *Restauration*!

Counting the crew, fifty-two people set sail from Stavanger, Norway, in early July. They arrived in New York City harbor fourteen weeks later. Now they numbered fifty-three. Mrs. Larson had a baby during the trip across the Atlantic Ocean.

Hearing about the tiny *Restauration's* long voyage shocked people living in New York City. A New York City newspaper told about the boldness of the captain to try such a trip. It mentioned that all of the passengers arrived in good health. The newspaper reported that the Norwegians had come to America to escape persecution. It said that more Norwegians would be coming.

Stavanger, Norway

Trouble in New York City Harbor

The Norwegian immigrants were surprised to learn that they had disobeyed an American law. They had far too many passengers for a ship that size. American officials seized the *Restauration*. They charged the immigrants a fine of $3,150.

Lars Larson, the ship captain, and another immigrant asked officials for mercy. On November 15, 1825, President John Quincy Adams wrote out a pardon for the immigrants so they would not have to pay the fine. This group of Norwegian immigrants came to be called the "Sloopers."

Settling in America

Cleng Peerson met his fellow Norwegians when they got off the ship. By the time President Adams pardoned them, many had already traveled to the land Peerson found for them. They settled along Lake Ontario in the northwest corner of New York state. Lars Larson's wife and baby went ahead with the other travelers.

Ice skates

Larson stayed in New York City to sell the ship and its cargo of iron. Afterward, he set out to join his family. When he reached Albany, the new Erie Canal was frozen. Larson skated on the frozen canal most of the way from Albany to where his wife and baby waited.

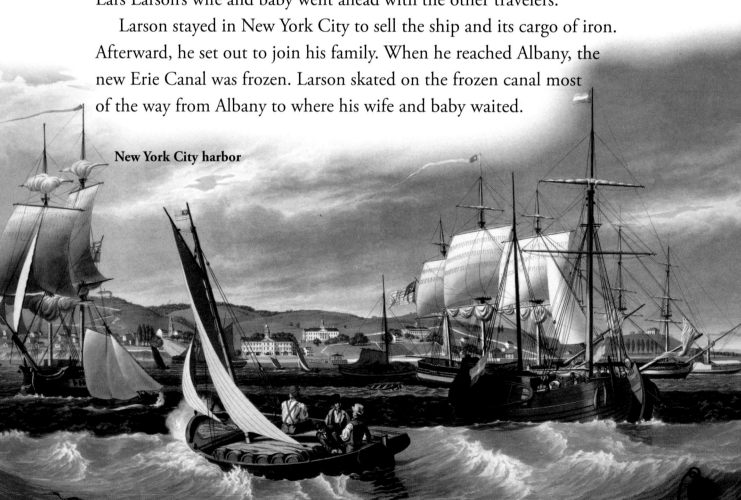

New York City harbor

Moving Farther West

Most of the Sloopers later moved to Illinois, where Cleng Peerson found better land. Between 1825 and 1847, Peerson helped Norwegians settle in New York, Indiana, Illinois, Wisconsin, Minnesota, Iowa, and Missouri. Some people call Cleng Peerson the "father of Norwegian immigration to the United States." Others call him the "Norwegian Daniel Boone."

Lars Larson had been a ship builder in Norway. He and his family did not move to Illinois with the other Sloopers. They settled in Rochester, New York, where he built canal boats. Many Norwegian immigrants enjoyed the hospitality of the Larson family as they made their way to their new homes farther west.

Norwegian Lutherans in America

Norwegian individuals and families continued to come to America. They often settled in communities with other Norwegian immigrants. So many people left Norway that officials became concerned. In 1845 Norway passed a law giving all Christians freedom of religion.

Norwegians who were Lutherans also immigrated to America. After they arrived, they longed for Lutheran churches like those they were part of back in Norway.

In June of 1853, Vilhem Koren was finishing his studies in Norway to become a minister. He heard about the needs in Iowa. In July, he became an ordained Lutheran minister. In August, he married Elisabeth Hysing. Vilhem was 26 years old. Elisabeth was 21.

Journey from Norway to Iowa

Vilhem and Elisabeth Koren left Norway on September 5, 1853, just seventeen days after their wedding. They sailed first to Kiel, Germany. Then they traveled by train to Hamburg, Germany. Vilhem and Elisabeth sailed away from Hamburg on September 15. They arrived in New York City on November 20. Vilhelm and Elisabeth stayed for a while with a family from Denmark. They enjoyed being tourists in New York City.

In late November, the young couple began a three-week journey to Iowa. Transportation was very different from the way it is now. The Korens faced a long and complicated journey. First they traveled by train to Toledo, Ohio. In Toledo they took a steamboat across the Maumee Bay of Lake Erie. Then they traveled by train until they reached Chicago.

In Chicago, Vilhem and Elisabeth boarded an elegant steamship which carried them on Lake Michigan to Milwaukee, Wisconsin. From Milwaukee, the Korens traveled to Milton, Wisconsin, on a train that had only one car.

From Milton, the Korens first rode in a lumber wagon. On a cold day in the middle of December, a minister drove them in his buggy to the home of another Lutheran minister.

From there, a blacksmith transported the Korens for several days by wagon. One day they were surprised to see two wagons filled with native people who wore red face paint and feathers.

Before arriving at the settlement that would be their new home, two French ferrymen carried them across the icy Wisconsin River in a canoe. They crossed the frozen Mississippi River in a buggy. A Scotsman transported them in another wagon.

The Egge cabin on page 213 and the artifacts on pages 210-212 are from the collection of the Vesterheim Norwegian-American Museum in Decorah, Iowa.

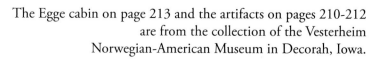

This is the home that Erik and Helene Egge shared with Vilhem and Elisabeth Koren.

A Tiny Log Cabin in Iowa

Finally, Vilhem and Elisabeth reached the Iowa settlement where they would live for the rest of their lives. They had to wait many months before they could move into their own parsonage.

Meanwhile, fellow Norwegian immigrants Erik and Helene Egge and their two children welcomed Vilhem and Elisabeth to share their fourteen-foot by sixteen-foot log cabin. Four days after they arrived, they celebrated a Norwegian Christmas.

Sixty-one years later, in 1914, Elisabeth Koren wrote these words: "With gratitude I look back on my long life here in this land . . . ." Paul wrote to the Christians in Colossae:

Let the peace of Christ
rule in your hearts,
to which indeed you were called
in one body; and be thankful.
Colossians 3:15

213

Lesson Activities

- All Around the USA map: Find New York City, Lake Ontario, Erie Canal, Albany, Rochester, Toledo, Chicago, Lake Michigan, Milwaukee, and Iowa.

- Rhythms and Rhymes: Enjoy "America" on page 26.

- Timeline: Look at pages 18-20.

- Literature for Units 10-12: *Freedom Crossing*

Review Questions

- Why did American officials seize the *Restauration* and tell the Norwegians they had to pay a large fine?

- Why do you think Cleng Peerson is called the "Norwegian Daniel Boone"?

- Why do you think Vilhem and Elisabeth Koren were willing to make such a difficult journey to get to Iowa?

Unit Review

- Student Workbook: Complete the Lesson 30 / Unit 10 Review page.

Hands-On History Ideas

- Pretend that you are taking a long, complicated journey using many different types of transportation.

- Use building blocks to build a settlement of Norwegian immigrants. Include a church.

Unit 10 Project
By Hand, By Machine

Supplies

- white or colored paper
- ruler
- colored pencils, crayons, or markers
- stapler

Look at machines around your house. Think about anything in your house that uses batteries or plugs into the wall, such as a stove, a camera, or a washing machine. How did people cook food, create pictures, and wash clothes before those machines were invented?

Directions

1. Choose 5 to 10 machines you see around your house.
2. Think about how people did the job now performed by a machine before the machine was invented.
3. Prepare a page for each machine you chose. Use a ruler to draw a line down the middle of the page.
4. On the left side, draw the way people performed the task by hand.
5. On the right side of the page, draw the machine that performs the task now.
6. Make a cover that says "By Hand, By Machine." Staple all the pages together to make a book.

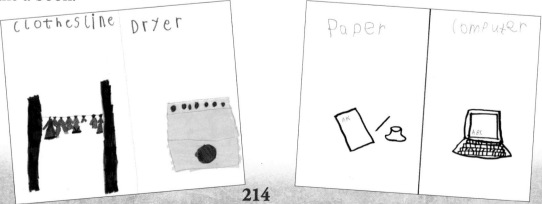

Unit 11

215

The Applegate Family
and the
Oregon Trail

What would you think if your parents told you that you are going to leave your house and almost everything in it? You are moving two thousand miles away to a place you have never even seen a picture of. The journey will be an adventure! You will get to see new and exciting places. Your family will have a fresh start in a brand new place. The journey will also be a challenge. You have heard that native people might attack. You wonder if you will be able to find enough food and water and firewood. It will take four to six months to reach your destination. What do you think? Do you want to go?

About 500,000 men, women, and children—like you—made this journey on the Oregon Trail in the middle of the 1800s.

Oregon Trail display at Scotts Bluff
National Monument, Nebraska

The Applegate Family Heads West

Charles
Applegate

Lindsay
Applegate

Jesse Applegate
(drawn by his nephew)

In 1843 brothers Charles, Lindsay, and Jesse Applegate moved their families from Missouri far west to Oregon Country. The Applegates joined a group of about one thousand people. The group gathered in Independence, Missouri. This was the first large group to travel on the Oregon Trail. They left behind their homes and farms. They left many friends and relatives.

Not long after they began their journey, the group realized they had too many wagons and animals to stay together. They divided into two smaller wagon trains. The Applegates became part of the group with large herds of cattle. This group was called the "Cow Column." They kept a tight schedule to ensure they made good progress on their journey.

A Day With the Cow Column

The men took turns staying awake at night. Their job was to make sure everyone was safe and the animals did not get away.

The men on duty at 4:00 a.m. fired their rifles as a signal that it was time to get up. There were sixty wagons and five thousand animals in the Cow Column. It took a great deal of time to get everything ready to start a day's journey! They had to prepare and eat breakfast. They had to take down their tents and herd their animals into place.

217

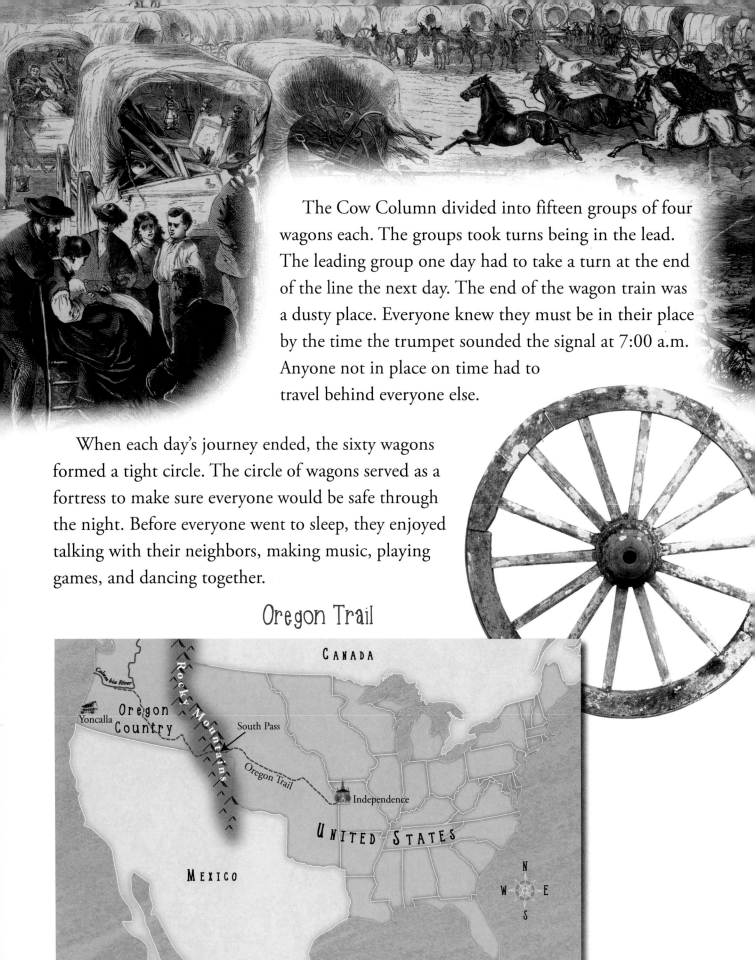

The Cow Column divided into fifteen groups of four wagons each. The groups took turns being in the lead. The leading group one day had to take a turn at the end of the line the next day. The end of the wagon train was a dusty place. Everyone knew they must be in their place by the time the trumpet sounded the signal at 7:00 a.m. Anyone not in place on time had to travel behind everyone else.

When each day's journey ended, the sixty wagons formed a tight circle. The circle of wagons served as a fortress to make sure everyone would be safe through the night. Before everyone went to sleep, they enjoyed talking with their neighbors, making music, playing games, and dancing together.

Oregon Trail

CANADA

Columbia River

Rocky Mountains

Oregon Country

Yoncalla

South Pass

Oregon Trail

Independence

UNITED STATES

MEXICO

N
W · E
S

Across the Mountains

As the Cow Column traveled west, it seemed the prairie would never end. Mile after mile stretched out in front of them. The cows plodded on and the wagon wheels creaked. Finally the prairie did end, and the Rocky Mountains rose up before them.

The Rocky Mountains (or Rockies) stretch from Canada to New Mexico. In most places the Rocky Mountains tower high into the sky. By following the Oregon Trail, the Cow Column crossed the Rockies at South Pass. South Pass is one place in the Rockies where travelers hardly notice they are going through a mountain range at all. When the Cow Column crossed South Pass, they were about halfway to Oregon.

Near the end of the Oregon Trail, the Cow Column came to the banks of the Columbia River. They had no choice but to make the dangerous crossing. Some members of the Cow Column drowned in the crossing.

The Applegate Family in Oregon

The Applegates finally reached Oregon. Jesse Applegate helped establish a government to provide law and order. New settlers continued to come west in a steady stream.

Columbia River in Oregon

Chief Halo

Applegate House

Bluegrass band at a modern-day Applegate House festival

A few years after they arrived, Jesse and Lindsay Applegate joined a group of men to explore the area. They established a safer route for travelers on the Oregon Trail. They did not want people to have to cross the dangerous Columbia River. This route was later called Applegate Trail.

Some settlers in Oregon Country were cruel to the native people who were already living there. The Applegate family, however, made friends with them. The United States government tried to force all the native people to move to a reservation of land they had assigned to them. Chief Halo of the Yoncalla Kalapuya tribe refused to go. The Applegates offered for Chief Halo and his family to live on their land. The Applegates later built a house for the chief and his family.

Applegate House

In 1852 Charles Applegate began building a two-story house for his family in the settlement of Yoncalla. The house took four years to build. It wasn't too hard for Charles to get the wood, brick, and sandstone he needed. The glass for the windows was a different story.

There weren't any glass factories in Oregon. There was no railroad to bring glass from the factories in the East. The glass had to travel by boat. It traveled south through the Atlantic Ocean and around the tip of South America into the Pacific Ocean. It then sailed far north to Oregon Country.

Once the glass arrived, Charles and his sons traveled nearly forty miles to the town of Scottsburg to bring the glass home. The Applegates traveled a long way to get to Oregon, but their route was short compared to the journey their windows made to get there!

The Legacy of the Applegates

The house that Charles Applegate built is one of the oldest houses in Oregon today. The Applegate family has owned it continuously ever since Charles Applegate built it. The house is now used to host events that teach about traditional arts and the customs of both the Kalapuya and the settlers who joined them in Oregon Country.

The legacy of the Applegate family and the role they played in settling Oregon lives on today. In addition to having a trail named after them, they have a river, a lake, a valley, a mountain, and a town named in their honor.

A good name is to be
more desired than great wealth,
Favor is better
than silver and gold.
Proverbs 22:1

Applegate Lake in Oregon

Lesson Activities

- Rhythms and Rhymes: Enjoy "Skip to My Lou" on page 27.

- Student Workbook: Complete the Lesson 31 page.

- Literature for Units 10-12: *Freedom Crossing*

Review Questions

- Why do you think a family would have wanted to move to Oregon?

- Why did the men in a wagon train take turns staying awake at night?

- What do you think would be hard about traveling on the Oregon Trail?

Hands-On History

- Pretend that you are traveling on the Oregon Trail! What could your wagon be? Perhaps your bed or the couch. What will you need to take with you? Make sure you're ready by the time you hear the trumpet!

- Use building blocks to build a wagon train.

The Trist Family
and the
Mexican War

As the carriage wheels turned on the drive to Monticello, teenage Nicholas Trist caught sight of the grand mansion. Beautiful farmland rolled out in every direction. This was the home of Thomas Jefferson! Former President Jefferson was a friend of Nicholas' grandmother. Jefferson had invited Nicholas to come to Monticello and study law. Jefferson's mansion was exquisite. His bustling farm was full of life. His granddaughter Virginia was charming and beautiful. Nicholas was soon in love. He asked for permission to marry Virginia. Both his mother and her mother thought the couple were too young. After six years of waiting, Nicholas and Virginia finally became husband and wife in 1824.

Trist became Thomas Jefferson's personal secretary. The two grew to be close friends. They enjoyed spending time together as they walked and rode horses side-by-side. After Thomas Jefferson died, Trist helped to manage his home and land.

Monticello

The Trist Family Grows

Virginia Trist gave birth to Pattie in 1826. Two years later she gave birth to their second baby. They named their little boy Thomas Jefferson Trist. They called him Jeff for short. Jeff was a happy and healthy baby, but Nicholas and Virginia's hearts were broken the day they discovered that their little boy was deaf.

Soon after Jeff was born, Nicholas Trist took a new job in Washington, D.C. He worked for the United States government as chief clerk in the State Department. People who work for the State Department are responsible for taking care of official government business with other countries. Virginia, Pattie, and Jeff moved to Washington the next year to join Nicholas. While they lived in Washington, Virginia gave birth to another little boy named Browse.

As little Jeff grew up he developed his own form of sign language to communicate with his family. His parents felt that they could not teach their little boy everything they wanted him to know. They decided to put him in a school for the deaf in Philadelphia. Jeff and other deaf children lived at the school. They learned many skills. They learned how to read and write. They learned how to communicate through sign language.

Washington, D.C.

Philadelphia

The Trist Family in Cuba

Nicholas Trist worked closely with President Andrew Jackson. Jackson described Trist as a man of integrity and honor. Trist believed in doing what was right, even when it was hard. In 1833 Jackson appointed Trist to serve as United States consul to Cuba. Trist's job was to make sure any Americans who lived in Cuba were safe. He also helped keep a good relationship between Cuba and the United States.

Most people in Cuba speak Spanish. Trist learned Spanish while he lived there. Trist also learned about Spanish ways and customs. Trist did not know it at the time, but this knowledge would be very important a few years later.

After Trist had lived in Cuba for two years, Virginia, Pattie, and Browse joined him. Jeff wrote in a letter that he wanted to come to Cuba as well. Trist arranged for Jeff to travel to Cuba. He stayed for a few months so the family could all be together, at least for a short time.

After his visit to Cuba, Jeff returned to the school for the deaf in Philadelphia. Virginia took Pattie and Browse to France so they could attend school there. Jeff was able to visit them in France for a few months.

Cuban countryside

Two years later, Virginia, Pattie, and Browse returned to Cuba. Trist lost his job as consul, but the family continued to live in Cuba. They owned a small farm and sold milk and vegetables in the nearby city of Havana.

Jeff did well in his studies at the school for the deaf, but he missed his family. The family stayed in touch by writing many letters back and forth. His parents sent him gifts, such as a copy of the book *Robinson Crusoe*. As he grew up, Jeff became interested in politics. He also became a skilled artist.

Havana, Cuba

President
James K. Polk

Nicholas Trist

The Mexican War

In 1845 the Trist family left Cuba and moved back to the United States. Trist went back to work for the State Department, this time under President James K. Polk. Also in 1845, Texas became part of the United States. The next year, the United States went to war with Mexico. The United States and Mexico disagreed about where the border between Texas and Mexico should be. Both countries wanted more land. President Polk hoped to gain all the land from Texas to the Pacific Ocean, which then belonged to Mexico. Some Americans, including the president, even wanted all of Mexico to become part of the United States.

Trist in Mexico

In 1847 President James K. Polk chose Nicholas Trist to travel to Mexico. Trist's job was to work out a peace treaty with the Mexican government to end the war. Since Trist spoke Spanish and was familiar with Spanish customs, he seemed like a good choice. Before long, President Polk was sorry he had chosen Trist. He was concerned that Trist would not push hard enough to get the most land possible from Mexico. Polk sent a message to Trist and told him to stop his work on the treaty and come home.

U.S. troops in Mexico

Disputed Land During the Mexican War

Trist was getting ready to leave Mexico City when a friend stopped by to visit. The friend convinced Trist to stay in Mexico and continue working for peace. To go against a president's order was a bold and daring thing to do. Trist knew this decision could mean the end of his political career. He did it anyway because he believed it was right. Trist believed it would be wrong for the United States to continue fighting against Mexico.

Trist worked out a treaty with the Mexican government to end the fighting. According to the treaty, the United States would pay Mexico for the land between Texas and the Pacific Ocean. The border between Texas and Mexico would be a river, the Rio Grande.

When the treaty reached President Polk for his approval, he was not happy. Still, he decided that the best thing to do was to go along with it. When the United States Senate approved the treaty, the Mexican War was officially over. Polk was furious with Trist for disobeying his orders and fired him from his job.

After the War

Through the years, the Trist family had often struggled to have enough money. Now that Trist did not have his job, they struggled all over again. Sometimes doing what you believe to be right makes things hard.

A few years after the Mexican War ended, Jeff Trist became a teacher at the school for the deaf in Philadelphia which he had attended as a child. Three years later, Jeff married Ellen Lyman, who was also deaf. Thomas Gallaudet performed their wedding ceremony. Jeff was known as being intelligent, refined, and a faithful teacher. He had strong morals and was called "a true Christian in his daily walk." Like his father, Jeff knew that it was important to do what is right.

Let us not lose heart
in doing good,
for in due time we will reap
if we do not grow weary.
Galatians 6:9

Lesson Activities

- All Around the USA map: Find Monticello, Washington, D.C., Philadelphia, and the Rio Grande.

- Student Workbook: Complete the Lesson 32 page.

- Literature for Units 10-12: *Freedom Crossing*

Review Questions

- Why did Jeff Trist live in a different place from his family?

- How did Nicholas Trist's knowledge of Spanish help him after he left Cuba?

- Why did Nicholas Trist decide to disobey President Polk's order?

Hands-On History

- Pretend that you have a small farm in Cuba. Take care of your family, animals, and crops. You can also sell milk and vegetables at a market.

- Use building blocks to build Monticello, home of Thomas Jefferson (pictured on page 222).

Bill Wilson
and His
Gold Nugget

On a January day in 1848, James Marshall was at work as usual. He was overseeing the construction of a sawmill for General John Sutter in California. As Marshall walked along the bank of the stream at the construction site, he saw something glittering on the ground. He didn't think much about the shiny object at first and walked on. Then he saw another glittering object. He wondered if he should take the trouble to investigate. After debating with himself two or three times, he bent down and picked it up. He was astonished. It appeared to be pure gold. When he showed the workmen what he had found, some of them laughed. They thought he was crazy! Surely it couldn't be real gold. Marshall didn't let their doubt stop him. He gathered up twenty or thirty more pieces he found nearby. He wrapped them in a rag, mounted his horse, and rode off to the office of John Sutter, who owned the land.

James Marshall
at Sutter's Mill, c. 1850

When Marshall arrived, he told General Sutter he had some important and interesting news for him. He asked if they could speak privately. General Sutter led Marshall into a private room, but he forgot to lock the door. Just as Marshall pulled his precious rag out of his pocket, a clerk opened the door into the room. General Sutter later remembered, "how quick Mr. M. put the yellow metal in his pocket again can hardly be described." As soon as the clerk was gone again, Marshall made sure the door was locked before he showed General Sutter what was in his pocket.

General John Sutter

At first John Sutter wasn't sure the pieces in James Marshall's rag were really gold. He read the long article about gold in his encyclopedia. He performed some simple experiments. Then he was convinced. It was gold!

The next day, General Sutter visited the construction site and spoke to the men working for him on the mill. He asked them to keep this discovery a secret for just six weeks. He had some business he needed to take care of before word started to spread. His men promised, but they soon broke their promise.

California Gold Rush

News of the discovery at Sutter's Mill spread quickly. The next year, thousands of men rushed to California. They came from all corners of the United States and from other countries around the world. They hoped to find gold and make a fortune.

People traveled from as far away as Chile, China, France, Germany, Ireland, Mexico, and Turkey. The year was 1849, and those searching for gold were called '49ers.

Gold nuggets

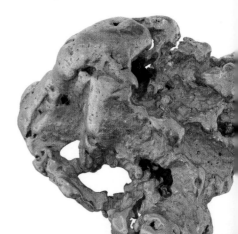

Some pioneers who had recently traveled west on the Oregon Trail quickly headed south down the Applegate Trail in hopes of getting rich. Lindsay Applegate was one of those pioneers. He made it to California ahead of the big rush and found $6,000 worth of gold.

Even though they were anxious to get their hands on the gold in California, people in the eastern United States did not have a quick way to get there. They could travel over land on the Oregon Trail, or they could travel by boat around the southern tip of South America. Both trips could take up to six months. Some people took a shortcut through Panama. After they took a boat to Panama, '49ers hired a mule or a horse and traveled through the jungle. Many of them died of disease. If they made it through the jungle, they got on another boat and sailed north to California.

People wanted a quicker and easier route. Before long some private American companies decided to build a railroad across Panama. This helped people reach California much faster.

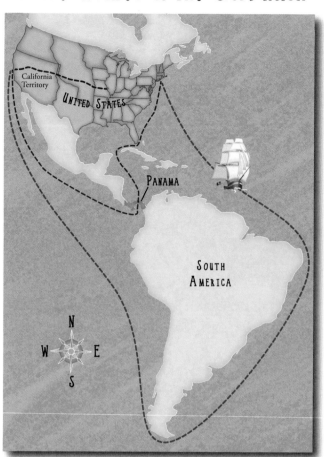

Travel Routes of the Gold Rush

Panama jungle

Bill Wilson's Nugget

Women and children were a rare sight in the gold mining camps. Bill Wilson was one of the few '49ers who brought his wife with him. On Christmas day in 1849, Wilson's wife gave birth to a twelve-pound baby boy in their mining camp on California's Canyon Creek. One of Wilson's fellow miners decided to play a joke on the other '49ers in the area. He spread the news that Bill Wilson had found a twelve-pound nugget and that it was the most handsome nugget ever seen. Every miner in the camp wanted to see this amazing find. They quickly began to line up at the Wilson cabin.

Bill Wilson was in on the joke himself. He took the men, just a few at a time, into his cabin. He proudly showed them his twelve-pound nugget, the best and the biggest ever found on Canyon Creek!

The miners loved the joke, and they loved seeing a real baby. They hadn't seen one in a long time. As the men left the cabin, they told the other men waiting outside that Wilson's nugget was indeed the finest they had ever seen.

California mining camp, c. 1850

Panning for gold, 1849

Modern reenactment of a
'49ers wagon train in California

News of Wilson's nugget kept
spreading. Men continued to line up
all day and far into the night to get a
glimpse for themselves. Two or three
days after the fine nugget arrived, the
miners were still coming. Some traveled
from other camps as far as ten miles
away.

On the day of the little Wilson baby's
birth, his daddy still found time to pan
for gold—and what a find he made
that day! To pan for gold, '49ers filled
a pan with river gravel, or some other
rocks they thought might contain gold.
They added some water and swished
the mixture around in the pan. Gold is
a heavy metal, so if there was any gold
in the pan, it stayed in the bottom. The
water and other materials sloshed over
the sides of the pan and washed away.
The day Bill Wilson's twelve-pound
nugget arrived at his cabin, he found
$3,000 worth of gold nuggets in his pan!

Even after everyone knew what Bill Wilson's twelve-pound nugget really was, miners still loved to stop by to see the baby. The Canyon Creek miners were proud of the fact that they had a baby in their camp. They had a beautiful ring made for the baby's mother, using pure gold they had found themselves.

The End of the Gold Rush

By 1855 the California Gold Rush was pretty much over. While a few people struck it rich, most people did not. After their panning days were over, some '49ers went back home. Others made a new home for themselves in California.

Since the days of the Bible, people have valued gold. The Bible makes it clear that even though gold is special, there are things that are much more important than gold:

How much better it is
to get wisdom than gold!
And to get understanding
is to be chosen above silver.
Proverbs 16:16

Gold mining pan

Lesson Activities

- All Around the USA map: Find Sutter's Mill.

- Rhythms and Rhymes: Enjoy "The First Baby In Camp" on page 28.

- Timeline: Look at pages 22-23.

- Literature for Units 10-12: *Freedom Crossing*

Review Questions

- Why do you think General Sutter wanted his workers to keep the discovery of gold a secret?

- Describe the different ways people traveled to California to find gold.

- Why do you think most miners did not bring their families with them?

Unit Review

- Student Workbook: Complete the Lesson 33 / Unit 11 Review page.

Hands-On History

- See the Unit 11 Project instructions on page 234.

Unit 11 Project
James Marshall Finds Gold!

Supplies

- construction paper in these colors: black, blue, brown, gray, and gold or yellow
- pencil
- glue stick
- scissors
- small shoes to trace

Directions

1. Draw a wavy line diagonally from one corner to another corner of the blue paper. Cut along the wavy line.

2. Glue one part of the blue paper onto the brown paper to make a "stream" and "bank."

3. Trace a pair of shoes on the black paper. Cut them out and glue them on the brown paper to make James Marshall's "footprints." It's okay if the footprints hang off the edge of the paper.

4. Tear round and oval-shaped "rocks" from the gray and yellow paper. Make most of them gray and just a few yellow. Glue them along the edge of the stream.

Unit 12

Kansas Prairie

235

Amos Lawrence and the Fight Against Slavery

Anthony Burns left the clothing store where he worked in Boston, Massachusetts. He headed home as usual. Burns had once been a slave. He had escaped slavery and now lived in the fine city of Boston. He could stand tall. He was a free man with a job of his own choosing. He earned money for his work. How good to be free!

Suddenly everything changed. Some men grabbed Burns and carried him off to the courthouse. His former master had discovered where he was and had him arrested. He'd been found. He had awakened that morning a free man, and now he was a captive once again. According to the law, Burns had no rights to defend his freedom.

Boston

Boston Slave Riot of 1854

Boston was filled with abolitionists. Abolitionists were people who worked to stop slavery. When the abolitionists heard that Anthony Burns had been taken prisoner, they were furious. They wanted to set him free. Some were in favor of working for his release peacefully. Others wanted to be violent. Many of these violent men formed an angry mob and stormed the courthouse. They carried a battering ram, axes, and other weapons. They broke into the building, but officials stopped the riot. The abolitionists were not able to free Burns. The event became known as the Boston Slave Riot of 1854.

The mayor of Boston posted notices all over the city that said:

> Under the excitement that now pervades the city, you are respectfully requested to cooperate with the Municipal Authorities in the maintenance of peace and good order. The laws must be obeyed, let the consequences be what they may.

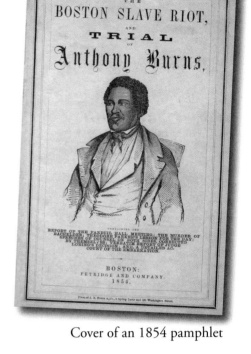

Cover of an 1854 pamphlet

Free Anthony Burns!

From his prison cell, Anthony Burns sent a request to the ministers of the churches in Boston. He asked them to pray that he could once again enjoy the blessings of liberty.

A judge decided that Burns must return to slavery. Officials took Burns from the courthouse to a nearby ship. The ship would take him back to Virginia. Tens of thousands of people gathered on the streets to watch Burns pass. Many soldiers stood along the streets to make sure there was not another riot.

Handcuffs

Scenes from the life of Anthony Burns (clockwise from lower left)

Many abolitionists refused to give up. They raised $1,300 and bought Anthony Burns' freedom. Burns returned to Boston, attended college, and became a minister.

A Nation Divided

The United States was divided between states that allowed slavery and states that didn't allow slavery. Slavery was illegal in Northern states. Southern states allowed slavery. Kansas and Nebraska became new United States territories in 1854. According to law, the legislature in each territory had the right to vote on whether or not slavery would be allowed there. In 1861 the Nebraska legislature voted against slavery. The decision in Kansas was more complicated. Many people from the eastern United States moved into Kansas. Some were for slavery, and some were against it. Everyone hoped that their own group would have the larger number of voters. Each side wanted to have the most votes in the Kansas territory legislature. The legislature would decide whether Kansas would be a free state or a slave state.

Fighting Against Slavery

Amos Lawrence lived in Boston. Lawrence was outraged when Anthony Burns was arrested. After Burns' arrest, Lawrence wrote a letter to the mayor of Boston. Lawrence said that he would prefer to see the courthouse torn down "rather than that the fugitive now confined there be returned to slavery."

Anthony Burns and the procession down State Street

Lawrence, Kansas

Lawrence wrote a letter to his brother. He said:

The newspapers will give you an account of the slave excitement here. I tell you it was high times. [Anthony Burns] was a good-looking fellow and well dressed; and as he marched down State Street in the procession, cavalry and artillery with cannon and United States troops were before and behind him; but he held his head up and marched like a man.

Amos Lawrence knew that slavery was evil. He decided to do something to fight against it. Lawrence had plenty of money to help the cause. His family had made a fortune through their business that manufactured and sold cloth. Lawrence used his money to help abolitionists move to Kansas. As a way to thank Amos Lawrence for his help, the settlers named one of the new communities in Kansas "Lawrence."

Bleeding Kansas

Sadly, the slavery debate in Kansas soon became violent. Because of the fighting, the territory became known as Bleeding Kansas. Amos Lawrence and his brothers helped pay for rifles for the citizens of Lawrence, Kansas, to defend themselves. In 1856 a group of angry men from Missouri attacked the town of Lawrence. The attackers wanted Kansas to become a slave state.

After all the violence and protest, the abolitionists won. In 1861 Kansas became a part of the United States as a free state. Slavery was now officially against the law there. Two years later, pro-slavery men attacked Lawrence again. They killed at least 150 men and boys and burned many of the buildings. The people of Lawrence did not give up. They rebuilt their town.

"Border Ruffians" from Missouri who promoted slavery in Kansas

240

The Debate

In Boston, in Kansas, and in places all across the country, people continued to argue and fight about slavery. Should it be allowed anywhere? What laws should states decide for themselves? What laws should the federal government decide? Eventually the debate over slavery and states' rights led to the Civil War.

The Bible teaches us that the way of peace is best.

Deceit is in the heart
of those who devise evil,
But counselors of peace have joy.
Proverbs 12:20

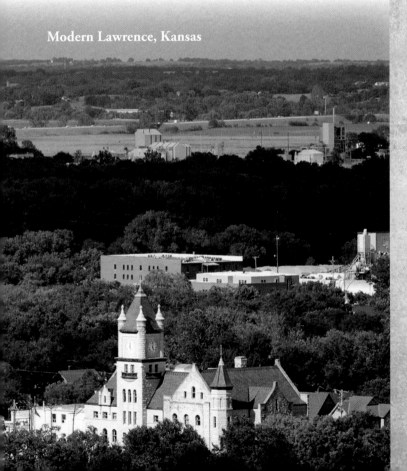
Modern Lawrence, Kansas

Lesson Activities

- All Around the USA map: Find Boston and Lawrence.

- Rhythms and Rhymes: Enjoy "Nobody Knows the Trouble I've Seen" on page 29.

- Student Workbook: Complete the Lesson 34 page.

- Literature for Units 10-12: *Freedom Crossing*

Review Questions

- Why was Anthony Burns arrested?

- What do you think was the best way for people to protest Anthony Burns' arrest and try to set him free?

- How did Amos Lawrence use his money to help Kansas become a free state?

Hands-On History Ideas

- Pretend that you know a slave and you are working to raise money to buy his or her freedom. What will you do to raise money? How will you get others to help?

- Use building blocks to build a store or home for a new settler in Lawrence, Kansas.

Sojourner Truth and Her Almighty Friend

Isabella lay on the scratchy straw that covered the floor of the cellar. In the rooms above her, the guests in her master's hotel slept in comfort. It was impossible for Isabella to get comfortable. The boards under the straw were loose. The mud and water below the boards gave off a horrible smell. Isabella felt like a horse, lying on the straw under her coarse blanket. Her master did not think his slaves needed the same comforts as white people. He considered them only a little better than animals. Still, Isabella's parents said they were fortunate. They told Isabella that compared to others, their master was kind to his slaves.

Isabella's Family

Isabella had a little brother named Peter. She did not know how many older brothers and sisters she had. She had never even met all of them. Isabella often found her mother crying. Isabella asked her mother what made her cry. "Oh, my child," her mother would answer, "I am thinking of your brothers and sisters that have been sold away from me." She often heard her parents speak of the day when their master sold her five-year-old brother and three-year-old sister together. Isabella had been a baby at the time. Her brother had been excited when he saw a horse-drawn sleigh pull up in front of their master's house. Then he saw his sister shut and locked into the sleigh box. He realized what was happening. He ran into the house and hid under a bed. He was soon found and forced into the sleigh with his sister. Then they were gone.

Isabella's parents spent hours talking of their children and recalling their cherished memories. How their hearts ached for them. At nighttime Isabella's mother pointed to the stars and said, "Those are the same stars, and that is the same moon, that look down upon your brothers and sisters, and which they see as they look up to them, though they are ever so far away from us, and each other."

After a long day of work, Isabella's mother sat down with her two children who were still with her. She spoke words which Isabella came to treasure. "My children," she would say, "there is a God, who hears and sees you. He lives in the sky. When you are beaten, or cruelly treated, or fall into any trouble, you must ask help of Him, and He will always hear and help you."

Pitchfork

Sold

After their master died, his heirs decided what to do with his slaves. They sold Isabella and Peter and most of the other slaves at a slave auction. They decided to give Isabella's father his freedom, however, because he was weak and unwell. They didn't think anyone would want to buy and care for him. They set Isabella's mother free so that she could take care of her husband. Isabella's parents continued to live in the cellar under the hotel.

Isabella was nine years old when a new master bought her at a slave auction for one hundred dollars. Isabella later recalled that her new master and mistress gave her "plenty to eat, and also a plenty of whippings." Through all her hardships, Isabella remembered her mother's teachings. She took all her trials and afflictions to God.

Isabella was bought and sold two more times. After she grew up she fell in love with a slave owned by another master. Isabella's master would not allow them to get married. Instead Isabella's master forced her to marry one of his own slaves. Isabella and her husband had five children. When Isabella worked in the field, she put her smallest baby in a basket. She tied a rope to each handle and hung the basket in a tree. One of her other children gently rocked the basket while Isabella worked.

Whip

244

Freedom

Isabella's master, Mr. Dumont, promised to grant her freedom on July 4, 1827. When the day came, however, he refused to let her go. Isabella decided to leave anyway. Early one morning, she took her infant daughter and set off on foot. Isabella and her daughter ended up at the home of a Mr. and Mrs. Van Wagener. The Van Wageners hired Isabella to work for them. Before long, Isabella's old master found her. He insisted she return with him. Isabella refused. Mr. Van Wagener did not believe in buying and selling slaves, but he offered Mr. Dumont money to pay for Isabella's services to his household. Mr. Dumont accepted the money and left.

Isabella was used to calling the white men for whom she worked "Master." Mr. Van Wagener did not want her to call him master. She was not his slave and he was not her master. "There is but one Master," Mr. Van Wagener told her, "and He who is your Master is my Master."

Runaway slave mother and child

The Van Wageners took good care of Isabella and made sure she was comfortable. She was so comfortable that she began to forget about her God in heaven. After a few months passed, Isabella one day felt God reveal Himself to her. She realized how she had forgotten about Him and failed to be faithful to Him. She felt terrible that she had forgotten God, whom she called her Almighty Friend. Isabella became a new person and her heart filled with joy and gladness.

I Sell the Shadow to Support the Substance.
SOJOURNER TRUTH.

Sojourner Truth

Isabella eventually changed her name to Sojourner Truth. She decided to travel the world and tell others about Jesus. She wanted to teach people about treating others right. She did not let the fact that she never learned to read or write hold her back. She made a powerful impact on society. She spoke on topics such as slavery, women's rights, the rights of free blacks, and prison reform. One of her grandsons who had learned to read and write traveled with her. He assisted her on her speaking tours. She earned money by selling portraits of herself. She also earned money through the sale of a book about her life.

I SELL THE SHADOW TO SUPPORT THE SUBSTANCE.

SOJOURNER TRUTH.

Years later, Sojourner Truth visited Mr. Dumont, one of her former masters. She discovered that he had a changed heart. Mr. Dumont had come to see that "slavery was the wickedest thing in the world, the greatest curse the earth had ever felt." Sojourner Truth fervently thanked the Lord that she had lived to hear her master say such blessed words. She rejoiced that her former master had become her brother in Christ.

There is neither Jew nor Greek, there is neither slave nor free man, there is neither male nor female; for you are all one in Christ Jesus. Galatians 3:28

Lesson Activities

- Student Workbook: Complete the Lesson 35 page.
- Literature for Units 10-12: *Freedom Crossing*

Review Questions

- Why did Isabella not know how many older brothers and sisters she had?
- Why is slavery wrong?
- What did Sojourner Truth discover when she visited her former master, Mr. Dumont?

Hands-On History Ideas

- Pretend that you hire a runaway slave to work for you as the Van Wageners hired Isabella. How will you help the runaway slave get used to living as a free person? What will you do when his or her master shows up at your house?
- Use building blocks to build a basket for a baby.

Liberty Hill
on the
Underground Railroad

Arnold Gragston clutched the oars tightly in his hands. He rowed hard against the current of the Ohio River. He needed to reach the other side as fast as he could. It was hard work. It was cold. The current was strong. Arnold was trembling, desperately hoping his master would not discover what he was doing. It was a dark night. He couldn't see the girl in the boat with him, but he could feel her eyes looking at him. He knew how desperate she was to escape slavery in Kentucky. In Ohio, on the other side of the river, she would be free. Arnold was a slave himself, but his master was good to him. He had no desire to run away.

Arnold and the girl did not dare even to whisper to each other. Arnold knew that if his master or any slave master discovered what he was doing, they would "tear him up."

Arnold felt sure that someone would find out, but he kept rowing toward the other side anyway. Arnold didn't know exactly where he should let the girl off. Suddenly Arnold spotted a tall light on a high hill that overlooked the Ohio River. He rowed toward it. Someone had told him about that light. It meant help and safety. It meant hope for runaway slaves.

When Arnold reached the Ohio shore, two men were waiting. Arnold began to tremble all over again. He felt certain they were going to capture him. He was sure he was about to die. He prayed to God. To his great relief, he discovered that the men were not there to capture him. They were waiting to help the girl! They even asked Arnold if he was hungry and offered to get him something to eat.

That was Arnold's first experience rowing a slave to freedom, but it was not his last. Over the next four years, he rowed as many as two or three hundred runaway slaves across the Ohio River. Arnold said, "It took me a long time to get over my scared feeling, but I finally did, and I soon found myself going back across the river, with two and three people, and sometimes a whole boatload. I got so I used to make three and four trips a month."

Arnold never received any payment or gifts to thank him for his service. He didn't want any. He only wanted to help others gain their freedom. Arnold let each of the runaways out on the north side of the river. As he rowed back to the southern side, the runaways quickly climbed one hundred wooden steps up Liberty Hill. At the top they reached the home of John and Jean Rankin.

Fugitive Slave Act

In 1850 the United States government passed the Fugitive Slave Act. This law said that the government would help slave masters recapture their runaway slaves. The law said that anyone who helped runaway slaves could be punished. Runaway slaves knew that even if they managed to reach a Northern state where slavery was illegal, they might get caught. They might be sent back to the South. Because of this, many runaway slaves traveled all the way to Canada where they could truly be free.

Ohio River

Runaway slave

The Rankin House On Liberty Hill

The Rankin house

The Rankin house in Ripley, Ohio, was one of many stations, or safe houses, on the Underground Railroad. The Underground Railroad was not a real railroad. It had no trains or train tracks or depots. Instead it was a secret network of people. The people helped runaway slaves escape to freedom.

For many runaway slaves who crossed the Ohio River, the Rankin house was their first stop on the Underground Railroad. John and Jean and their thirteen children worked together to provide the runaways with food and shelter. When the runaways were ready to move on to the next safe house, one of the Rankin sons often led them there on horseback.

Scene from *Uncle Tom's Cabin*

The Rankin family may have helped as many as two thousand slaves on their way to freedom. Sometimes they hid as many as twenty or thirty slaves at once. According to reports, not one of the slaves the Rankins helped was ever caught.

One of the slaves who stopped at the Rankin house for shelter was a mother who crossed the partly-frozen Ohio River carrying her two-year-old child. An author named Harriet Beecher Stowe heard the story of how this woman reached Ohio. She included the story in her book *Uncle Tom's Cabin*. Mrs. Stowe wrote this book to show America the evils of slavery. Her writing convinced many Americans that slavery must be stopped.

A Great Risk

It was expensive and dangerous to help runaway slaves. The Rankin family was willing to take the risk. They were committed to helping slaves gain their freedom. They believed it was the right thing to do. These two quotes from John Rankin describe his feelings about working on the Underground Railroad:

I have been attacked at midnight with fire and weapons of death, and nothing but the good providence of God has preserved my property from flames and myself and family from violence and death.

My house has been the door of freedom to many human beings, but while there was a hazard of life and property, there was much happiness in giving safety to the trembling fugitives.

Greater love
has no one than this,
that one lay down his life
for his friends.
John 15:13

Lesson Activities

- All Around the USA map: Find Ohio River and Ripley.

- Rhythms and Rhymes: Enjoy "Get Off the Track!" on pages 30-31.

- Timeline: Look at pages 22-25. You may also wish to review the previous pages you have learned about.

- Literature for Units 10-12: *Freedom Crossing*

Review Questions

- What were ways that people helped runaway slaves on the Underground Railroad?

- Why did Harriet Beecher Stowe write the book *Uncle Tom's Cabin*?

- Why was John Rankin willing to put his family and property at risk to help escaping slaves?

Unit Review

- Student Workbook: Complete the Lesson 36 / Unit 12 Review page.

Hands-On History Ideas

- See the Unit 12 Project instructions on pages 255-256.

Unit 12 Project
Underground Railroad Safe House

Supplies

- construction paper: 1 red, 1 black, 1 brown, 2 white
- scissors
- glue stick
- ruler
- pen
- colored pencils

Directions

1. Cut a rectangle from brown paper for a door. Glue to the bottom middle of the red paper.

2. Cut the piece of black paper in half longways. Cut triangles off two corners to make a roof shape.

3. Trace the black paper roof shape onto one piece of white paper. Cut the same shape from the white paper.

4. Glue the black roof onto the top of the red paper.

continued

5. Draw four rectangular windows in the house and one in the attic.

6. Cut the top, right, and bottom sides of each window and door. You can gently fold the paper over to make a snip to begin cutting, as shown. Do not cut the left-side. This will allow the windows and door to open and close.

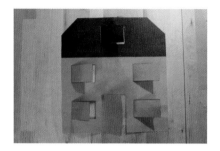 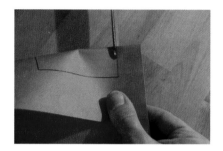

7. Turn the house over. Place glue everywhere except on the windows and door. Glue the white piece of paper to the red paper. Glue the white roof shape to the roof.

8. Add details to the outside of the house as you wish.

9. (Not pictured) Inside the door and windows, draw things that would be helpful to escaping slaves, such as kind people, food, candles, quilts, beds, new clothing, and hiding places.

Unit 13

"Reading the Emancipation Proclamation" by H. W. Herrick, 1864

257

From Log Cabins to the White House

In December of 1808, Thomas and Nancy Hanks Lincoln moved into a one-room log cabin on Sinking Spring Farm near Hodgen's Mill in Kentucky. In February of 1809, their toddler daughter Sarah turned two years old. A few days later, on Sunday, February 12, Nancy gave birth to a baby boy. She and Thomas named their baby Abraham in honor of Thomas' father. Their son would grow up to become one of the most honored presidents in United States history.

Thomas and Nancy Lincoln

Thomas Lincoln was born in Virginia during the American Revolution. His parents were Abraham and Bathsheba Lincoln. After Abraham received land in Kentucky to pay him for his service in the Continental Army, he moved his family there. Thomas's father died when Thomas was eight years old. His mother moved her children to what is now Washington County in Kentucky. Thomas grew up there and learned how to be a carpenter.

Thomas met and married Nancy Hanks. Nancy was born in what is now West Virginia. Her parents died when she was young. Nancy moved to Kentucky and lived with her Uncle Richard and Aunt Rachel. Aunt Rachel taught Nancy how to spin and sew, and how to do other homemaking skills. Thomas and Nancy were married at her aunt and uncle's home in Kentucky.

Replica of Abraham Lincoln's birthplace in Hodgenville, Kentucky

Abraham, his parents, and sister Sarah listen to the ideas of travelers on the turnpike road near their home in Kentucky.

The Lincolns on Knob Creek

When Abraham Lincoln was two years old, his pioneer family moved ten miles away from Sinking Spring to Knob Creek. As a young boy, Abraham helped his father on the farm. He carried water and gathered firewood. He picked berries on the hills, fished in the stream, and helped plant the garden. Sometimes he took corn to Hodgen's Mill for it to be ground into cornmeal.

Abraham also loved to be close to his mother and watch her face while she read the Bible. Nancy taught her children that learning is important. When Sarah started going to school, she took her little brother Abraham with her. They only had opportunities to go to school for short periods of time.

The Lincolns lived near a turnpike road that went from Louisville, Kentucky, to Nashville, Tennessee. Young Abraham met and learned from many kinds of people who traveled that road.

The Lincolns in Indiana

When Abraham was seven years old, his family moved to a settlement near Little Pigeon Creek in Indiana. There they lived in their third log cabin. Nancy and Abraham helped Thomas clear and farm the land.

In the fall of 1818, many people in the settlement got sick with a disease called "milk sickness." Nancy helped take care of her sick neighbors. After she drank milk from a cow belonging to a neighbor, Nancy got sick, too. She died two weeks later. After their mother died, eleven-year-old Sarah took over the housekeeping. She took care of her little brother. Abraham and Sarah were close companions.

Thomas went back to Kentucky the next year to find a new wife. He proposed to Sarah Bush Johnston. She was a widow he had known before. Sarah agreed to marry Thomas. He returned to Indiana with his new wife and her three children.

Statue of young Abraham Lincoln in Indiana

Sarah became a loving step-mother to Sarah and Abraham. She encouraged Abraham to learn and made their home a good place for him to study. There along Little Pigeon Creek, Abraham Lincoln grew to be a man.

Abraham Lincoln in New Salem, Illinois

Thomas and Sarah Lincoln and their children moved to Illinois when Abraham was twenty-one years old. The next year, Abraham moved west to New Salem and began life on his own.

Abraham Lincoln carried with him the teachings and example of his parents. He later described his mother as "a noble woman, affectionate, good, kind." A Lincoln family member described Thomas as "one of the best men that ever lived" and said that he was "good humored, patient, and kind." One family member said, "Abe got his honesty and his clean notions of living and kind heart from his father."

In New Salem, Abraham tried many jobs. He worked in stores. He served as postmaster. He tried land surveying. He also studied to become a lawyer. Lincoln became involved in politics. The first time he ran for office, he finished eighth among thirteen candidates. Later he was elected to the Illinois legislature. He served for eight years.

The Lincolns in Springfield, Illinois

In 1836 Abraham Lincoln received a license to be a lawyer. The next year, he packed up his belongings in two saddlebags and moved to Springfield. He shared a rented room with a local store owner. He became a law partner with John Todd Stuart.

Two years later, Mary Todd moved to Springfield to live with her older sister Elizabeth and Elizabeth's husband. Mary was also a cousin of John Todd Stuart. Abraham met Mary at a ball.

Three years later, minister Charles Dresser performed their wedding ceremony at his home. Abraham was thirty-three; Mary was twenty-three. The Lincolns rented a room in the Globe Tavern rooming house. The next year in their rented room, Mary gave birth to their firstborn son, Robert Todd Lincoln.

Old Illinois State Capitol in Springfield

Abraham Lincoln

Mary Todd Lincoln

Statue of Abraham, Mary, and Tad Lincoln in Springfield

261

Lincoln returns to his home in Springfield after campaigning for president.

Mary, Willie, Robert, Tad, and Abraham Lincoln

The Lincolns purchased Charles Dresser's home, at left, in 1844. A second son, Edward Baker Lincoln, was born in 1846. The family called him Eddie. Abraham was soon elected to the U.S. House of Representatives. He served one two-year term. Eddie Lincoln died in 1850, when he was almost four years old. He probably had tuberculosis. A third son, William Wallace Lincoln, was born later that year. The family called him Willie. The Lincolns had a fourth son in 1853. They named him Thomas after Abraham Lincoln's father. The family called him Tad.

The Lincolns in Washington, D.C.

By 1860 trouble between Northern and Southern states had become much worse. Lincoln ran for president that year and won. The day before his birthday in 1861, Lincoln gave a farewell address at the Springfield train station. Abraham, Mary, Willie, and Tad then took a twelve-day train ride to Washington, D.C. Robert was away at boarding school.

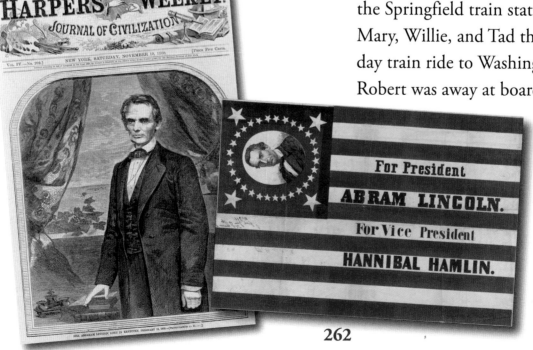

Newspaper reporting Lincoln's election as the sixteenth president and a campaign flag from the 1860 campaign

262

The Lincolns' time in Washington was a tragic time. During the weeks between election day in November and Lincoln's inauguration in March, seven Southern states seceded from the United States. To secede means to withdraw. In April Southern soldiers fired on Fort Sumter in South Carolina. Fort Sumter was a U.S. Army fort. Four more states soon seceded. The country was divided in two and fought a terrible Civil War.

In 1862, Willie Lincoln became ill and died in the White House, likely of typhoid fever.

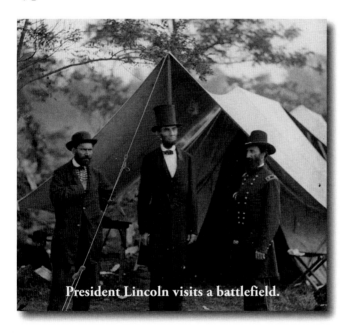
President Lincoln visits a battlefield.

The war dragged on, while the Lincoln family and the country longed for peace. The book of Hebrews teaches Christians to:

Pursue peace with all men.
Hebrews 12:14

Lesson Activities

- All Around the USA map: Find Hodgen's Mill, Louisville, Nashville, Little Pigeon Creek, New Salem, Springfield, Washington, D.C., and Fort Sumter.

- Turn the page to see the map of Union and Confederate states.

- Rhythms and Rhymes: Enjoy "Old Sister Phoebe" on page 32.

- Student Workbook: Complete the Lesson 37 page.

- Literature for Units 13-15: *Farmer Boy*

Review Questions

- In what kind of places did Abraham Lincoln grow up?

- What did Southern states do right before and right after Abraham Lincoln became president?

- What two sides fought each other in the Civil War?

Hands-On History Ideas

- See the Unit 13 Project instructions on page 278.

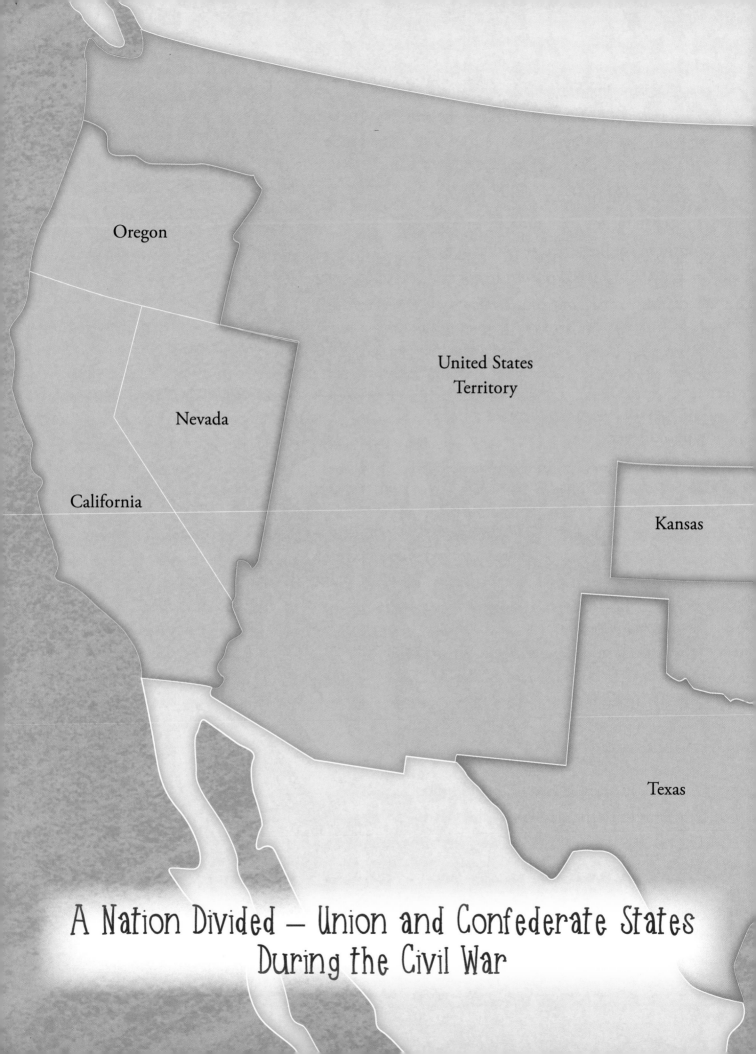

Oregon

Nevada

California

United States
Territory

Kansas

Texas

A Nation Divided — Union and Confederate States
During the Civil War

A Northern Father and a Southern Mother

In 1850 Theodore Roosevelt Sr. from New York City traveled south for a vacation. He traveled with Hilborne and Susan West, his friends from Philadelphia. Theodore loved Susan's tales about her childhood on a Georgia plantation. He wanted to see it for himself.

In Georgia, Theodore met Martha Bulloch. She was Susan's beautiful half-sister. Everyone called her Mittie. Theodore and Mittie met again when she visited Susan and Hilborne in Philadelphia. Theodore and Mittie fell in love. Theodore wrote a letter to Mittie's widowed mother and asked for permission to marry her daughter. Mittie traveled to New York City to meet Theodore's parents.

In December of 1853, Theodore and his parents traveled to Georgia for the wedding. The young couple were married in the dining room of Bulloch Hall three days before Christmas.

Bulloch Hall and nearby countryside

The Roosevelt and Bulloch Families

Mittie and Theodore had both grown up in wealthy families. Mittie's father had owned a plantation and thirty-three slaves. He had been a partner in a cotton mill.

Mittie Roosevelt

The Bullochs were a Southern family. The first of Mittie's Bulloch ancestors to arrive in America came from Scotland in 1728. Mittie's great-grandfather was one of the Georgia colony's representatives to the Continental Congress. He fought in the Revolutionary War.

The Roosevelts were a Northern family. The ancestors of Theodore's mother Margaret were Quakers. They had come to Pennsylvania with William Penn. Theodore's father Cornelius was from a long line of Manhattan Roosevelts. The Roosevelts had come to America from the Netherlands. Six generations had been born on Manhattan Island. Cornelius was the first Roosevelt to become a millionaire. Theodore worked in his father's glass business.

At Home in New York City

When newlyweds Theodore and Mittie arrived in New York City, they stayed with Cornelius and Margaret at first. Soon they moved into a new five-story home on 20th Street. Cornelius gave them the home as a wedding present. Theodore and Mittie Roosevelt had four children. Their first child, Anna, was born in 1855. They called her Bamie. Two years after Bamie was born, Mittie's mother and Mittie's sister (also named Anna) moved from Georgia to live with Theodore and Mittie. Theodore Jr. was born in 1858, Elliott in 1860, and Corinne in 1861. Theodore Jr. would grow up to be the twenty-sixth President of the United States.

Roosevelt Parlor

Theodore Sr. and Mittie Roosevelt were affectionate parents in a loving family. Corinne said that Bamie was "like a second mother." Corinne described her parents and the three younger children in this way:

In those days we were Teedie, Ellie, and Conie, and we had the most lovely mother, and the most manly, able, and delightful father . . . .

Theodore Sr. and Bamie   Theodore Jr.   Elliott   Corinne   Mittie

Learning at Home

Aunt Anna begged to be the children's first tutor. She wanted to thank Mr. Roosevelt for welcoming her and her mother into their home. Aunt Anna and Mittie taught the children in the family nursery. After he grew up, Theodore Jr. wrote this about those times:

She and my mother used to entertain us by the hour with tales of life on the Georgia plantations; of hunting fox, deer, and wildcat; of the . . . horses, Boone and Crockett . . . .

The Roosevelt children had evening prayers with their mother. Each day before breakfast, their father called them to gather with him on the sofa for morning prayers.

Roosevelt Nursery

Theodore Jr. later described his father as the "most wise and loving father that ever lived." He also wrote:

> I never knew any one who got greater joy out of living than did my father, or any one who more whole-heartedly performed every duty; and no one whom I have ever met approached his combination of enjoyment of life and performance of duty.

Roosevelt Library

Theodore Roosevelt Sr. spent one day of every week visiting the poor in their homes. He helped to start museums and a hospital. Some boys in New York City worked as newsboys. They sold newspapers on the sidewalks. Some newsboys had no place to sleep. Mr. Roosevelt helped to start the Newsboys Lodging House. He visited there each Sunday night. He took his children along so they could help the boys, too.

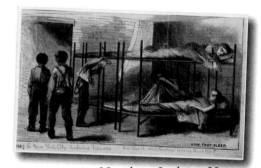

Newsboys Lodging House

Mittie's Home State Joins the Confederacy

Mittie's home state of Georgia was one of the Southern states that seceded from the Union and formed the Confederate States of America. Two of Mittie's brothers joined the Confederate Navy.

Mittie's family owned slaves, but Theodore Sr.'s father Cornelius believed that slavery should end. The Bullochs treated their slaves better than many plantation owners did. Grandmamma Bulloch had taught one of her slaves to read, even though it was against the law to do so.

When Mittie was a girl, she and her mother made visits to the enslaved persons in their cabins. The Bullochs had close relationships with some of their slaves and loved them, but they did not give them their freedom.

Theodore Roosevelt Sr. Helps the Union

People called the states that remained in the United States the Union. Theodore Sr. wanted to join the Union Army, but he knew that it would be very hard on Mittie for him to fight against her brothers.

Theodore Sr. decided to help the Union in other ways. He assisted sick and wounded soldiers. He helped soldiers who had been wounded to find jobs. He rode on horseback from one Army camp to another to encourage Union soldiers to send part of their Army pay back home to help their families.

Theodore Roosevelt Sr. spent many months in Washington, D.C. President and Mrs. Lincoln enjoyed his company. They invited him to parties at the White House. Once Theodore Sr. took Bamie with him to Washington. She got to sit on President Lincoln's knee.

Theodore Sr. was away from home for almost two years. While he was gone, Mittie, her sister Anna, and their mother sent packages to relatives in the South.

Mittie Roosevelt

Theodore Roosevelt Sr.

Letter Theodore Roosevelt Sr. wrote to Bamie and Theodore from Washington, D.C., in 1861

President and Mrs. Lincoln greet guests at a White House ball.

Theodore and Mittie Roosevelt did not let their different opinions about the Civil War affect how they treated one another. They stayed close. They wrote loving letters to each other while Theodore Sr. was away. Mittie did not complain about her loneliness. She wrote about the home life that she knew her husband missed so much. In one letter, he wrote to her:

I know you will not regret having me do what is right, and I do not believe you will love me any the less for it.

Your Loving Husband Who Wants Very Much to See You.

The Civil War divided many families, but the Roosevelts did not let that happen to them. The book of Romans helps Christians know what to do when people have different opinions and when they mistreat one another.

Never pay back evil for evil
to anyone. Respect what is right
in the sight of all men. If possible,
so far as it depends on you,
be at peace with all men.
Romans 12:17-18

Lesson Activities

- All Around the USA map: Find New York City, Philadelphia, Bulloch Hall, Washington, D.C.

- Rhythms and Rhymes: Enjoy "Tramp! Tramp! Tramp!" on pages 33-34.

- Student Workbook: Complete the Lesson 38 page.

- Literature for Units 13-15: *Farmer Boy*

Review Questions

- How were Theodore Roosevelt Sr. and Mittie's Roosevelt's family backgrounds similar? How were they different?

- How did the Roosevelt family help people in the North and in the South during the Civil War?

- Why do you think Theodore and Mittie Roosevelt were able to get along even though they disagreed about the Civil War?

Hands-On History Ideas

- Pretend that you are in Washington, D.C., during the Civil War. You can visit the Lincolns and help sick and wounded Union soldiers.

- Use building blocks to build a fancy room like the rooms in the Roosevelts' house.

America Returns to Peace

People living in the North believed that the Civil War would be over quickly. People in the South thought so, too, but the war dragged on. By the end of 1862, the Union Army had conquered several areas inside the Confederate states. Both sides were tired of hardships. Many Northerners were not sure why they were fighting. Slavery was one of the main issues Northerners and Southerners disagreed about. However, slavery was still legal everywhere it had been legal before the war began.

The Emancipation Proclamation

President Lincoln decided that Northerners would believe in the war if they believed they were fighting to make slaves free. On January 1, 1863, President Lincoln issued the Emancipation Proclamation. The document said that slaves were now free—but only in some places. It said that slaves were free everywhere in the South, except in the parts of the Confederate states where the Union Army was in charge. Slavery stayed legal in the Union states of Delaware, Kentucky, Maryland, and Missouri.

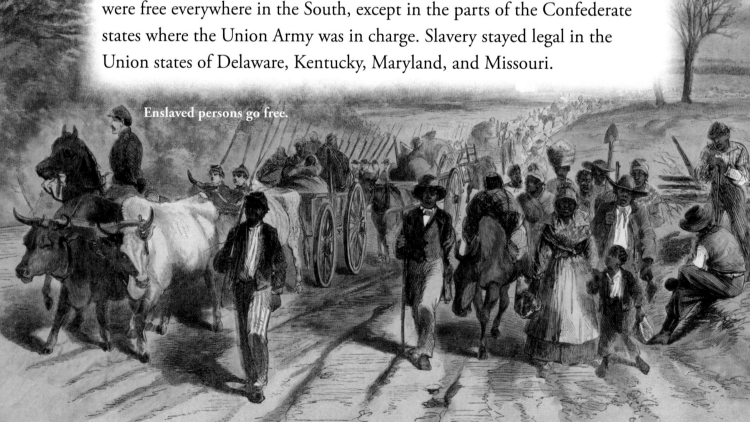

Enslaved persons go free.

General Sherman and his troops burn Atlanta.

The Emancipation Proclamation also said that black men could join the Union Army and the Union Navy. Theodore Roosevelt Sr. helped the first black men who joined the Union Army. He also helped black soldiers have the equipment they needed.

President Lincoln gave this photograph to Theodore Roosevelt Sr.

Sherman's Troops March Through Georgia

The Union and Confederate armies continued to fight throughout 1863 and into 1864. In September of 1864, General William Tecumseh Sherman and his Union troops captured and burned Atlanta, Georgia. Then they marched through Georgia to the city of Savannah. They ruined farms. They destroyed homes. The soldiers took what they wanted from the plantation mansions, including Bulloch Hall, family home of Mittie Roosevelt.

General Sherman leads Union troops through Georgia.

273

E. W. Evans' Story

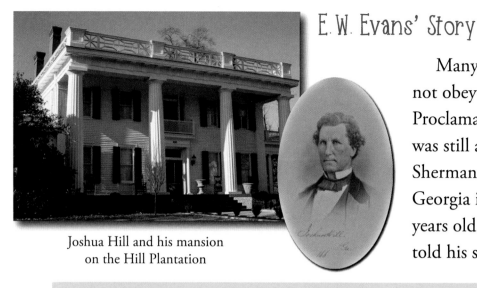

Joshua Hill and his mansion
on the Hill Plantation

Many slave owners did not obey the Emancipation Proclamation. E. W. Evans was still a slave when General Sherman marched through Georgia in 1864. He was nine years old. Many years later, he told his story in his own words:

My parents were slaves on the plantation of [Joshua] Hill, a slave owner in Madison, Georgia. I was born on May 21, 1855. . . . I was a small boy when Sherman left here at the fall of Atlanta. He came through Madison on his march to the sea and we children hung out on the front fence from early morning 'til late in the evening, watching the soldiers go by. It took most of the day.

My master was a Senator from Georgia . . . . His wife, our mistress, had charge of the slaves and plantation. She never seemed to like the idea of having slaves.

The next week after Sherman passed through Madison, Miss Emily called the five women that were on the place and told them to stay around the house and attend to things as they had always done until their husbands came back. She said they were free and could go wherever they wanted to . . . .

She meant that they could rent from her if they wanted to. In that number of women was my mother, Ellen, who worked as a seamstress for Mrs. Hill. The other women were Aunt Lizzie and Aunt Dinah, the washer-women, Aunt Liza . . . a seamstress to help my mother, and Aunt Caroline . . . the nurse for Miss Emily's children.

Union forces destroy a Georgia railroad.

274

I never worked as a slave because I wasn't old enough. In 1864, when I was about nine years old, they sent me on a trial visit to the plantation to give me an idea of what I had to do someday.

The place I'm talking about, when I was sent for the tryout, was on the outskirts of town. It was a house where they sent children out old enough to work for a sort of training. I guess you'd call it the training period. When the children were near ten years old they had this week's trial to get them used to the work they'd have to do when they reached ten years. At the age of ten years they were then sent to the field to work. They'd chop, hoe, pick cotton . . . and pull fodder, corn, or anything else to be done on the plantation. I stayed at the place a whole week and was brought home on Saturday . . . .

Well, this was just before Sherman's march from Atlanta to the sea and I never got a chance to go to the plantation to work again, for Miss Emily freed all on her place and soon after that we were emancipated.

The soldiers I mentioned while ago that passed with Sherman carried provisions, hams, shoulders, meal, flour . . . and other food. They had their cooks and other servants. I remember seeing a woman in that crowd of servants. She had a baby in her arms. She hollered at us children and said, "You children get off that fence and go learn your ABC's." I thought she was crazy telling us that . . . for we had never been allowed to learn anything at all like reading and writing. I learned but it was after surrender and I was over ten years old.

Former enslaved persons march with Sherman and his troops.

Confederate General Lee surrenders to Union General Grant at Appomattox Court House, Virginia.

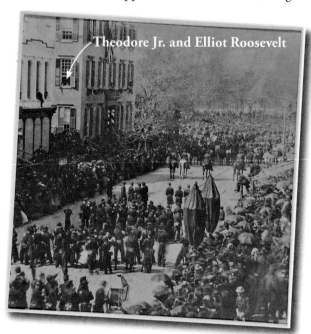

Theodore Jr. and Elliot Roosevelt

Lincoln's funeral procession through New York City

The End of the Civil War

President Abraham Lincoln ran for a second term as president in 1864. He was re-elected. Lincoln was inaugurated on March 4, 1865. A few weeks later, on April 9th, Confederate General Robert E. Lee and his army surrendered to Union General Ulysses S. Grant at Appomattox Court House in Virginia.

Five days later, President and Mrs. Lincoln attended a play at Ford's Theater in Washington, D.C. John Wilkes Booth was an actor and a Southerner. He was bitter about the Civil War. Booth shot President Lincoln, while he was watching the play. President Lincoln died the next morning at a nearby hotel. Vice President Andrew Johnson took the presidential oath and became the seventeenth President of the United States.

After a funeral in the White House, Lincoln's body lay in state at the United States Capitol. Then the President's body was taken in a processional to several cities before it was taken to Springfield, Illinois, to be buried there. In New York City, the funeral procession passed the home of Cornelius and Margaret Roosevelt, parents of Theodore Roosevelt Sr. In the picture at center left, find two boys looking out the side window on the second story. They are Theodore Jr. and Elliott Roosevelt.

276

Remembering Lincoln's Words

Two years before Lincoln died, he traveled to a Civil War battlefield at Gettysburg, Pennsylvania. There he spoke encouraging words about America's future. In this Gettysburg Address, Lincoln concluded with these words:

We here highly resolve that these dead shall not have died in vain, that this nation under God, shall have a new birth of freedom and that government of the people, by the people, for the people shall not perish from the earth.

See that no one repays another with evil for evil, but always seek after that which is good for one another and for all people.
1 Thessalonians 5:15

Lincoln Memorial in Washington, D.C.

Lesson Activities

- All Around the USA map: Find Atlanta, Savannah, Bulloch Hall, Madison, Appomattox Court House, Washington, D.C., Springfield, New York City, and Gettysburg.

- Timeline: Look at pages 26-27.

- Literature for Units 13-15: *Farmer Boy*

Review Questions

- What did the Emancipation Proclamation change?

- Which side won the Civil War?

- What happened to Abraham Lincoln soon after Confederate General Lee surrendered to Union General Grant?

Unit Review

- Student Workbook: Complete the Lesson 39 / Unit 13 Review page.

Hands-On History Ideas

- Pretend you are traveling around the South telling slaves the news of the Emancipation Proclamation.

- Use building blocks to build a new home for E. W. Evans and his family after they were freed from slavery.

Unit 13 Project
Abraham Lincoln's Log Cabin Game

Supplies

- 40 popsicle sticks
- black marker
- black construction paper
- ruler
- 4 pennies
- 4 sheets blue construction paper
- crayons, colored pencils, or markers
- 2 dice

Directions

1. Abraham Lincoln served in each of these roles. Write one role and the corresponding number on each of ten popsicle sticks. Write them as shown in the picture. Four need to be toward the left side and six need to be toward the right side.
   - 1. Son
   - 2. Brother
   - 3. Stepson
   - 4. Storekeeper
   - 5. Illinois legislator
   - 6. Lawyer
   - 7. Husband
   - 8. Father
   - 9. U.S. Congressman
   - 10. President
2. Repeat three times to make three more sets of ten sticks.
3. Cut four 1-inch squares from black construction paper (windows).
4. Cut four 1-inch by 2-inch rectangles from black construction paper (doors).
5. Cut two 5-inch squares of black construction paper. Draw a line from one corner to another corner of both squares. Cut along the lines to make four triangles (roofs).
6. Draw trees, grass, flowers, and sky on each sheet of blue construction paper as desired. Leave enough space in the picture for the cabin.

To Play (4 players)

The first player to assemble a complete log cabin scene is the winner.

1. Give each player a background scene (the picture on blue paper).
2. Spread all the popsicle sticks, black shapes, and pennies in the center of the playing area.
3. On each turn, player rolls dice. Player takes/gives according to roll:
   - Player can take a stick from the center that matches each number rolled or a stick from the center that matches the total of the two dice. (Example: With a roll of 3 and 6, player can take stick #6 and stick #3, or take stick #9.)
   - When dice roll totals 11 (5 and 6), player can take any two items from the center.
   - Double 1s, 2s, 3s, and 4s: player can choose any item needed from the center.
   - Double 5s: Player can take item of choice from center or from another player.
   - Double 6s: Player must give one of his/her items to any other player. The other player gets to choose the item.

278

Unit 14

Mrs. Page
and
Reconstruction

Mrs. Page looked around her home near Lexington, North Carolina. Once it had been a grand place. Once there was food in the kitchen and dishes on the table. Once she lived in comfort and plenty. Then the Civil War came right to her doorstep. Union troops had invaded her plantation. They had nearly destroyed the home she loved. There wasn't a chair left. Her garden was in ruins. She still had one large iron pot, but there were no forks, spoons, cups, or plates. That did not matter too much, though. She hardly had any food to eat, anyway.

A Southern street in ruins after the Civil War

Now the war was over. The South had lost. Facing defeat was hard. Perhaps now things could return to normal, though it would take a long time. It would be a new kind of normal. The world Mrs. Page knew before the war had been turned completely upside down.

Life After the Civil War

Mrs. Page's neighbors were also adjusting. A few still had cotton and tobacco that the Union Army had somehow overlooked during the war. With so little cotton and tobacco around, it sold for a high price.

Some days Mrs. Page and her neighbors saw a Confederate soldier making the long walk home from his last battlefield. His clothes might be completely ragged. He might not have shoes on his feet. Mrs. Page and her neighbors were happy to invite such a soldier to stay for the night. Some soldiers preferred to stay in the barn. They felt unworthy of the grand home—or rather the home that had been grand before the war. Sometimes a soldier came inside anyway and shared what little food there was. Some even joined in some jolly music and dancing after dinner. For even in the midst of hard times, Southerners could still have fun.

One day a neighbor of Mrs. Page asked her to share some food. The neighbor had nothing to eat. Mrs. Page did not have much, but she sent the last of her pork. She also sent a dry and crusty bread called hardtack. Her servant Frank had managed to get it from some Union soldiers. Frank had been Mrs. Page's slave before the war. He was free now, but he was a faithful friend who loved Mrs. Page. After the war he chose to stay with her and continue to work for her.

Cotton

Tobacco

Union soldier with cases of hardtack

A Starvation Party

Mrs. Page decided a have a party. She was determined to have some fun, even if she and those around her were perfectly miserable. The Southerners gave this kind of party a special name: a starvation party. If they were going to nearly starve, they might as well do it together. And they might as well have fun.

Mrs. Page invited ten ladies to her starvation party. They all walked to her house. There were no longer any carriages in the neighborhood to ride. Before the war, all these ladies had enjoyed elegant food and fine entertainment. Mrs. Page wondered what she would set before them now.

According to an account written about the party, Mrs. Page and her guests sat on rough benches at a "bare, mutilated table." Mrs. Drane, one of the guests, sat at the head of the table to serve. "The menu consisted of a pudding of cornmeal and dried whortleberries sweetened with sorghum . . . . The pudding, filling half of a large gourd, was placed in front of Mrs. Drane, and she, using hardtack as spoon, dipped it up, depositing it daintily on other hardtack which answered for plates and saucers." The ladies drank from cups made of folded newspapers. They had to drink quickly before the liquid soaked through.

Mrs. Page's starvation party was a success. Her guests "assured their hostess that they had rarely attended a more delightful feast."

Dried whortleberries

Gourd

Richmond, Virginia, in
ruins after the Civil War

**Former slaves
hiding in Louisiana**

Picking Up the Pieces

The time after the Civil War is called Reconstruction. The United States had to be reconstructed, or put back together. The Southern states had seceded, or withdrawn, from the United States. Now the government had to figure out how to let those states be part of the country again. Slowly one state after another rejoined the Union. In 1866 Tennessee became the first to rejoin. Georgia became the last in 1870. Union troops remained in the South until 1877.

The United States passed three amendments to the U.S. Constitution. One ended slavery in all states. One made all persons born in the United States citizens. One made male citizens eligible to vote regardless of their skin color or whether they had once been enslaved. Sadly some states passed laws that limited the freedom of former enslaved people.

People who had been slaves had to figure out how to live as free people. Some former slaves left the South to look for better opportunities in the North and the West. Others decided to stay in the South and work for their former masters. Sometimes this arrangement worked well, but often the former masters did not pay the former slaves fairly. It was almost as if they were still living in slavery.

Former slaves endured prejudice in many ways. Some whites were angry about the end of slavery. They threatened the former slaves. Sometimes they hurt or even killed them. Some former slaves had to hide to stay safe.

Carpetbag

Carpetbaggers

Many men who served in the United States government wanted to punish the South after the Civil War. They wanted to prevent anyone who had helped the Confederacy from serving in the government. They made a requirement that anyone who was going to serve in the government had to promise they had never helped or comforted a Confederate. The requirement was so strict that even if a person had given a cup of water to a Confederate soldier, he was not allowed to serve in the government. There were not many people in the South who could honestly say they had never helped a Confederate.

Some people from the North took advantage of this situation. They moved to the South so that they could get elected to serve in the government or make a profit. Many were dishonest and selfish. These men were called carpetbaggers. The name came from the suitcases made out of carpet the men sometimes carried.

Helpers

Not everyone in the North wanted to take advantage of people in the South. Many wanted to help. In many places before the Civil War, it was illegal to teach a slave to read and write. After the Civil War, many former slaves were hungry to learn. Many men and women in the North and the South helped make that happen. They opened schools and colleges for former slaves. Sometimes three generations of a former slave family—grandparents, parents, and children—all learned together how to read and write.

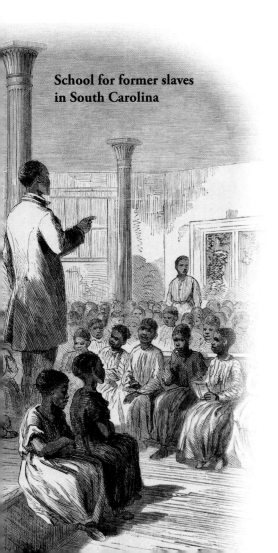

School for former slaves in South Carolina

284

At one school for former slaves in South Carolina, the students were so eager to learn that when the school let out for a vacation, they felt they were being punished. They didn't want a break from school because they wanted to keep learning!

Throughout history, selfish people have made life harder for others. Kind people have made life better for others. Jesus taught that when we serve others and provide for their needs, it is the same as doing those things for Jesus Himself.

I was hungry,
and you gave Me something
to eat; I was thirsty, and you
gave Me something to drink;
I was a stranger,
and you invited Me in;
naked, and you clothed Me;
I was sick, and you visited Me;
I was in prison,
and you came to Me. . . .
Truly I say to you, to the extent
that you did it to one of these
brothers of Mine,
even the least of them,
you did it to Me.
Matthew 25:35, 36, 40

Lesson Activities

- Rhythms and Rhymes: Enjoy "Grandfather's Clock" on pages 35-36.

- Student Workbook: Complete the Lesson 40 page.

- Literature for Units 13-15: *Farmer Boy*

Review Questions

- What were some ways Reconstruction was a hard time for people who lived in the South?

- What did people in the South have to promise to be able to serve in government?

- Why do you think former slaves were eager to learn to read and write?

Hands-On History Ideas

- See the Unit 14 Project instructions on pages 299-300.

Hiram Revels
in the
United States Senate

On a February day in 1870, long lines of people streamed into the United States Capitol building in Washington, D.C. They climbed the stairs to the Senate galleries. In the galleries, visitors could watch the United States Senate in action. A newspaper reported that day "there was not an inch of standing or sitting room in the galleries, so densely were they packed." Everyone wanted to watch. Something important was about to happen. When the moment came, those who had seats stood up with the rest of the crowd "that they might miss no word or lose no glimpse." Everyone's eyes rested on Hiram Revels, the tall and dignified man from Mississippi. They watched as he became the first black senator of the United States.

United States Capitol

Not all of the senators were happy about Revels being a senator. Some did not think he would do a good job because the color of his skin was different from theirs.

A Servant to Others

Hiram Revels was born in North Carolina in 1827, many years before the Civil War began. He and his ancestors, as far back as he knew, had always been free. He did not know what it was like to be a slave himself, but he did know about the hardships and suffering of his people.

When Revels grew up, he moved to the North and attended school in Indiana and Ohio. He was one of only a few black men in the country who attended college before the Civil War. Revels became a teacher and minister. He traveled and worked in several states in the North and the South. While in Missouri, authorities arrested him and sent him to jail. His crime was preaching the gospel to black people. In his travels, he did not encourage slaves to run away from their masters. However, if he encountered a slave who was already running away, he helped the slave to escape.

After the Civil War began, Revels helped recruit black soldiers to fight for the Union. He served in the Union Army as a chaplain. A chaplain is a minister who travels with soldiers to teach and encourage them spiritually.

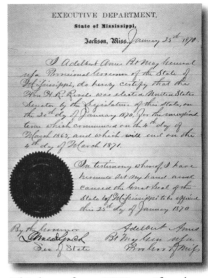

This letter from 1870 certifies that Hiram Revels was elected to the United States Senate.

Union soldier

287

Messy Politics

President Andrew Johnson

After the Civil War, Hiram Revels became involved in politics. Politics were messy after the Civil War. Congress wanted to punish the Southern states. President Andrew Johnson did not agree with Congress. Congress did not agree with President Johnson.

In 1867 Congress passed new laws that limited what a president could do. The new laws went against the Constitution. President Johnson wanted to obey the Constitution, so he did not obey the new laws. Because he disobeyed them, the House of Representatives impeached Johnson. To impeach a government official is to accuse him of doing something wrong. According to the Constitution, after a person is impeached, the Senate must hold a trial and vote on whether or not the person is guilty. If he is found guilty, he can no longer serve in his elected office. When the Senate voted on President Johnson, they found him not guilty. That meant he could serve out the rest of his presidential term.

Impeachment trial of President Andrew Johnson in the United States Senate chamber

Old Mississippi State Capitol

Hiram Revels

Revels In Washington

Hiram Revels was elected to the Mississippi state senate in 1869. The most important job for the new state senators and representatives was to choose two men to go to Washington, D.C. These men would represent Mississippi as United States senators. Revels had gained the respect and attention of his fellow state senators when he led a prayer on the opening day of the Mississippi state senate. When the time came to select two men for the United States Senate, they chose Revels to be one of them.

While he was a senator, Hiram Revels tried to help the other senators see how poorly people treated blacks all over the United States. Even though all Americans in the country were now free, blacks were still not treated equally with whites. Revels was concerned that things were getting worse.

289

Illustration of black man being forced off a railroad car

Revels talked against railroad and steamship companies treating people differently based on the color of their skin. He told the Senate he did not agree with having separate schools for white children and black children. Some people thought that if black children attended the same schools as white children, the schools would be "seriously damaged." Revels assured the senators that this was not true. He encouraged them to visit a school that welcomed all children. He said they would "find the schools in as prosperous and flourishing a condition as any to be found in any part of the world."

1881 illustration of influential black Americans Blanche Kelso Bruce, Frederick Douglass, and Hiram Revels

Even though Revels and many others worked against prejudice and segregation, black Americans would continue to struggle for many years to gain equal rights with white Americans.

The Revels Family

Hiram Revels was deeply devoted to his wife and their six daughters. When he arrived in Washington to become a senator, the first thing he did was write a letter to his wife back in Mississippi. He was careful about the influences in his girls' lives. He loved them and cared about them as a father should.

The Revels Family

Just as a father has compassion
on his children,
so the Lord has compassion
on those who fear Him.
Psalm 103:13

Lesson Activities

- All Around the USA map: Find Washington, D.C. and Mississippi.
- Student Workbook: Complete the Lesson 41 page.
- Literature for Units 13-15: *Farmer Boy*

Review Questions

- What does it mean to impeach a government official?
- Why do you think some people treat other people unkindly because of the color of their skin?
- What are some ways mentioned in this lesson that black people were treated unfairly?

Hands-On History Ideas

- Pretend that you are one of the people who watch Hiram Revels become a senator. Do you live in Washington, D.C., or did you travel a long way to come? How do you get to the Capitol? How old are you? Did you bring your family? Will you have a picnic lunch after the big event?
- Use building blocks to build the U.S. Capitol building shown on page 286.

John Driggs
and the
People of Alaska

People told Secretary of State William Seward, "You're crazy!" Others called his idea "Seward's Folly." "What is America supposed to do with 'Seward's Icebox'?" people asked with a chuckle. Why would the United States of America waste $7.2 million on "President Johnson's Polar Bear Garden"?

Alaska

The U.S. Purchases Alaska

Before the Civil War, Russia offered to sell Alaska to the United States. The Russian government needed money. They had watched the United States take over more and more land in North America. Russia was concerned that the United States might try to fight a war with Russia to gain Alaska. Russia decided to offer to sell the land to the U.S. When Russia made the offer, the United States was dealing with its own problems about slavery and states' rights. The Civil War began. The U.S. was not ready to buy more land. The people in the land it already owned were trying to figure out how to get along. After the war was over, Russia made the offer again. Secretary of State William Seward thought it was a wonderful idea. He saw great possibilities in the purchase. He encouraged Congress and President Andrew Johnson to agree to the deal. They bought Alaska in 1867, two years after the end of the Civil War.

This 1867 newspaper shows a cartoon of William Seward pushing a wheelbarrow with a huge chunk of ice labeled "Russian America."

Polar bears in Alaska

Gold miners in Alaska, 1897

Seven million dollars might sound like a great deal of money, but Alaska is a big place. The land only cost the United States about two cents per acre. A few Americans decided to go to Alaska and see what the land had to offer. In the late 1800s, word spread that Alaska had gold. People rushed to Alaska just as the '49ers had rushed to California before the Civil War. In addition to gold mining, settlers made money on furs and fish. Over the years, people have also made money on whale oil, copper, timber, platinum, zinc, lead, and petroleum in Alaska. The territory became a state in 1959. It is now one of the richest states in the country.

Native Alaskans

When the Russians settled in Alaska in the 1700s, there were already thousands of people living there. The Russians were often cruel to these native groups. They made some natives their slaves and killed others. After the United States bought the land, the U.S. government sent soldiers to occupy the territory. Not all Americans treated the native people well. The government did not consider the native people citizens. Native Alaskans could not vote. For many years the U.S. government tried to make the native groups in Alaska and all across America abandon their traditional cultures and lifestyles.

Totem pole in Alaska

While many people mistreated the native Alaskans, others loved them and respected their culture. One of these people was Dr. John Driggs. Driggs arrived in Alaska in 1890. He went to serve native Alaskans as a doctor, teacher, and minister. When he first arrived he made a tent for himself using boxes and barrels. He used a piece of canvas for a roof. After a while, carpenters from a nearby whaling ship built him a little house.

Inupash people lived in a village about a mile away. The Inupash enjoyed making music on drums and one-string fiddles. They used these instruments to accompany singing and dancing. They passed down their stories, legends, and songs from one generation to the next. They freely shared many of their songs, but others they carefully guarded as treasured secrets. Dr. Driggs described the tradition of the secret songs:

> When a father is about to pass away, he will call his son and impart to him the song as a legacy. No one else is allowed to be present on such an occasion, it being regarded in the same solemn light as a dying parent's blessing. The son in his turn, when he has grown old, and is about ready to take leave of the world, will impart the song to the next one in line of inheritance. These heirlooms have descended through families from one generation to another for an immense length of time.

Inupash people

Native Alaskan baskets

Tooloogigra and Webukside

For many centuries, all around the world, people groups have passed down stories to their children and grandchildren. Some of these stories are similar to stories in the Bible. For example, many cultures have a story about a flood that covered the whole earth. Where have you learned about that? The people who tell these stories might not know about God. Perhaps many generations back their ancestors did know about God. Over time, perhaps people changed the stories. Perhaps they remembered some of the characters, but forgot about God.

As Dr. Driggs spent time with the Inupash, he learned many of their traditional stories. These people did not know about Jesus. But one of their stories was strikingly similar to the story of the true Savior. This story told of Tooloogigra, a great and good spirit who once lived on earth as a human. When Tooloogigra had finished his time on earth, he went up into the sky. People on earth watched him until he had faded from sight. The Inupash believed that one day the world would come to an end on Webukside, or Judgment Day.

The Inupash believed that on Webukside, Tooloogigra would judge all people. The wicked would be rejected and consumed with fire. Those who had lived good lives would go to a new home where they would live forever. There they would be free from all cares, sorrows, and suffering.

Russia

Alaska

Arctic Circle

Canada

United States

Mexico

United States Territory — 1867

Dr. Driggs and others shared the true story of Jesus with the native Alaskan people. After he had spent many years in Alaska, Driggs wrote,

Should one take a trip through the Arctic portion of Inupash land, it is doubtful if he would meet with very many really non-Christians, for the people are now accepting the Nazarene as their great good spirit. The workers in the field truly taking an interest in the people and trying to benefit their condition have been few, but the people themselves have spread the teachings they have received, and the seed has fallen on fertile ground. It is true there is yet much of the old superstition of the past, but it has had its day and is gradually lessening its hold on the people.

The Nazarene that Driggs wrote of is Jesus of Nazareth, the one and only Son of God,

. . . who desires all men to be saved and to come to the knowledge of the truth.
1 Timothy 2:4

Lesson Activities

- Rhythms and Rhymes: Enjoy "The Sourdough" on page 37.
- Timeline: Look at pages 28-31.
- Literature for Units 13-15: *Farmer Boy*

Review Questions

- Why do you think some people thought it was crazy to buy Alaska?
- What country sold the land of Alaska to the United States?
- Why do you think John Driggs wanted to move to Alaska?

Unit Review

- Student Workbook: Complete the Lesson 42 / Unit 14 Review page.

Hands-On History Ideas

- Pretend that you live in Alaska as a teacher, minister, or doctor (or all three) with the Inupash people. What kind of house will you have? How will you serve your neighbors?
- Use building blocks to build a little house for John Driggs in Alaska.

Unit 14 Project
Starvation Party

Celebrate like Mrs. Page and her friends! We have substituted graham crackers for the hardtack (you can thank us later!). First, make a folded cup for each person.

Supplies

- Food-safe paper (waxed paper or parchment paper) cut in 9-inch squares

Directions

1. Fold square in half diagonally.

2. With paper folded, face point away from you. Fold left corner over to right side.

3. Fold right corner up to left side.

4. Fold top layer of top corner down.

5. Turn over. Fold top corner down.

6. Spread open at the top.

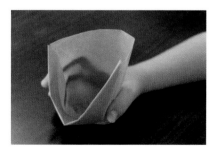

7. Add a little water and drink quickly before it soaks through!

continued

Adult supervision and involvement is required for making the cornmeal mush.

Ingredients

- ½ cup cornmeal
- ½ cup water
- 1 ½ cups additional water
- ¼ teaspoon salt
- ⅓ cup dried fruit (such as cranberries or raisins, or whortleberries, if you have them!)
- 2 to 3 tablespoons molasses (or ¼ cup sorghum, honey, or maple syrup)
- graham crackers

Directions

1. In a small bowl, stir together cornmeal and ½ cup water with a whisk.
2. Place 1 ½ cups water and ¼ teaspoon salt in a small saucepan. Bring to a boil.
3. Slowly add the cornmeal and water mixture to saucepan, stirring as you go.
4. Turn heat to low. Cook for five minutes, stirring frequently (see consistency in photo).
5. Stir in dried fruit and sweetener.
6. Turn stove off. Cover and let sit ten minutes.
7. Serve on graham crackers!

Unit 15

Nebraska Settlers (photo by Solomon Butcher)

Clara Barton
and Her
Heart for Helping

Clara was a shy and fearful little girl. She was afraid of thunder and afraid of strangers. She did not have many friends, but she was close to her brothers and sisters. They were all much older than she.

Clara loved to learn. Her siblings taught her many skills. Her sisters Dorothy and Sally taught her how to read. Her brother David taught her how to ride a horse when she was five. Her brother Stephen taught her math. When she was older he taught her how to weave cloth. Her father had once been a soldier. Clara listened breathlessly to his stories of war. The two of them acted out some of the stories. Her father taught her the difference between a colonel, a captain, and a sergeant.

Birthplace of Clara Barton

BIRTHPLACE OF
CLARA BARTON
FOUNDER OF THE
AMERICAN RED CROSS

When Clara was eleven years old, her brother David fell from a barn roof on their Massachusetts farm. It took him two years to recover. His little sister Clara tenderly cared for him day after day until he was well.

Clara became a teacher when she grew up. She later moved to Washington, D.C. There she got a job with the United States government. It was unusual for a woman to work for the government at this time in history. Clara Barton did her job well.

Then the Civil War began. Barton wanted to do something to help. She took supplies to Union soldiers staying in the Capitol building in Washington, D.C. She recognized some of the men. She had taught them in school when they were boys. Barton wanted the soldiers to have the things they needed, such as food, clothing, and blankets. She also wanted to help keep their spirits up. She read to them, listened to them, and prayed with them. As Clara Barton thought about the soldiers on the battlefields, she knew they needed her help, too.

For the next several years, Barton followed the soldiers from one battlefield to another. She remembered the war stories her father told her when she was little. Those stories helped prepare her for serving the soldiers.

Barton risked her life to help care for the wounded men. She served as a nurse and a cook. She comforted the hurting men. Someone once wrote a letter about her to President Abraham Lincoln. The man described Barton as "one of the most useful, devoted, valuable ladies in the country."

Union soldiers in front of the U.S. Capitol building

Wounded Union soldiers on the battlefield

Office of Correspondence with the Friends of the
Missing Men of the United States Army,

Washington, D. C., July 17, 1865.

Dear Madam:

Your communication of July 5
is received, and the name of
Thos Jeffer. Payntarr
will be placed upon my rolls. It will
constitute my most earnest endeavor to
bring these rolls within the notice of
returned soldiers everywhere.

Be assured that as soon as any
information of interest to yourself is
gained, it will be most promptly and
cheerfully forwarded to you.

Very sincerely, yours,

Clara Barton

**Letter from Clara Barton
about missing soldiers**

**Interior of one of Clara Barton's rented rooms where she operated the Missing Soldiers Office
(Today part of the Clara Barton Missing Soldiers Office Museum in Washington, D.C.)**

The Civil War finally ended. Many soldiers returned home, but many others had died in the war. Many families did not know what had happened to the soldiers they loved. They wondered if their loved one might be a prisoner somewhere. Some received news that their soldier had died, but no one knew where he was buried. Clara Barton set up the Missing Soldiers Office. Families from all over the country sent letters to the office, asking about soldiers they loved. Sometimes Barton and her helpers had information they could share with the families. Other times they had to write the family and tell them they didn't know anything about their soldier. In the years after the war, the Missing Soldiers Office received and answered over 63,000 letters.

Clara Barton

When Clara Barton finished her work with the Missing Soldiers Office, she was tired. She traveled to Europe to rest. While in Switzerland, she learned about a group called the Red Cross. The Red Cross helped sick and wounded soldiers during wartime. It was an international organization, which meant that different countries were part of it. Even though she was in Europe to rest, Barton started working with the Red Cross. France was in the middle of a war. Barton helped the French soldiers just as she had helped American soldiers a few years before.

Original sign for the
Missing Soldiers Office

When Barton returned to the United States, she worked to set up a Red Cross organization. For the United States to become part of the International Red Cross, the president had to agree to it. President Chester A. Arthur agreed for the U.S. to join the International Red Cross in 1881.

Later the Red Cross decided to do more than help soldiers during wartime. They began to help people when there were floods, earthquakes, fires, tornadoes, and other disasters. The Red Cross organizations in America and around the world still help people who face disasters.

Children in schools across America studied about Clara Barton in their history classes while she was still alive. Many children wrote letters to her. They asked her to write about what she did before her work in the Civil War and with the Red Cross. A few years before she died, Barton wrote a book especially for children about her own childhood. The book begins with a letter in which Barton told the children:

Five-year-old
Red Cross volunteer

Early Red Cross office

. . . because of my love for you, I have dedicated this little book to you. I have made it small, that you may the more easily read it. I have done it in the hope that it may give you pleasure, and in the wish that, when you shall be women and men, you may each remember, as I do, that you were once a child, full of childish thoughts and action, but of whom it was said, "Suffer them to come unto Me, and forbid them not, for of such is the Kingdom of Heaven."

Clara Barton dedicated her life to serving others. She did not want her life to be easy. She did not want to live in comfort when she knew that people were suffering. She worked hard to make a difference in America and in the world. She knew that her strength to serve others came from God.

. . . whoever serves is to do so as one who is serving by the strength which God supplies; so that in all things God may be glorified through Jesus Christ . . . .
1 Peter 4:11

Lesson Activities

- All Around the USA map: Find Washington, D.C.
- Student Workbook: Complete the Lesson 43 page.
- Literature for Units 13-15: *Farmer Boy*

Review Questions

- What is one way Clara's childhood experiences helped prepare her for her future?
- What need after the Civil War caused Clara Barton to start the Missing Soldiers' Office?
- What was the original purpose of the Red Cross?

Hands-On History Ideas

- Pretend that you are helping to bring supplies to soldiers and helping sick and wounded soldiers.
- Use building blocks to build a hospital for wounded soldiers.

Dugouts
and
Soddies

J. D. Strong and John Morrison took the road leading out of town. They had directions to a home where they could find shelter. They had just arrived in Custer County, Nebraska. They came to start farms of their own.

They followed a path leading away from the main road. The path got smaller, then disappeared. Night settled in. Up and down hills of grass, they wandered for hours. They were new to this wilderness. They were lost. Finally, up ahead, they saw shadows. Horses! Cows! Horses and cows meant people must be close by. Ah, see that ahead? A fencepost! Surely a fence would lead them somewhere.

J. D. eased up to the post. He waved his hands on either side to find the fence wires in the dark. No wires? Just a fencepost on a hill? He put his hand on top of the post. It felt warm. The "fencepost" was a stovepipe! He was standing on someone's roof! It was a dugout, a house dug into a hill.

J. D. stepped carefully in the dark. He looked for the door. Suddenly he rolled right through the dugout's window. Crash!

Dugouts

He landed on a pile of dishes. He heard shouts, "Get out!" and "Get a light!" and "Get the gun!" Thankfully J. D. and John were able to explain. J. D. had only broken a few things. They had found shelter. They had entered the life of homesteaders on the Nebraska prairie.

The Homestead Act

By the mid-1800s, the government of the United States owned a great deal of land. It was better for the country if people used the land for something. Sometimes the government gave land to soldiers as payment for their service. The government also tried to sell land to citizens. Few people could buy government land because of the high price.

Congress passed the Homestead Act in 1862. Beginning January 1, 1863, the government made 160-acre homesteads available to people willing to work the land. To apply for a homestead, you had to be at least twenty-one or the head of a family. You had to be a citizen or have plans to become a citizen of the United States.

The government did not give away the land. People earned it. The Homestead Act required homesteaders to:

- File an application and pay $10.
- Build a house on the homestead.
- Farm and improve the land.
- Live on the homestead for five years.

News about the Homestead Act spread around the world. Many immigrants came to America for a farm of their own. The Homestead Act opened new opportunities for poor young men, for single women, for freed slaves, and for families looking for a fresh start.

South Dakota dugout

Inside a dugout

Homesteaders

309

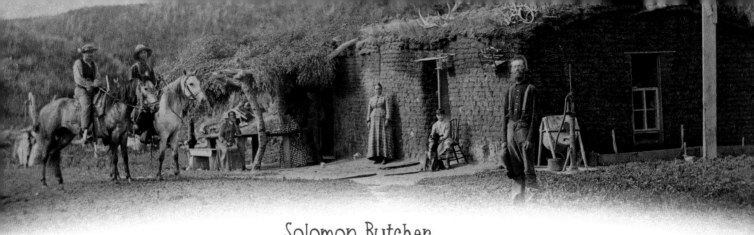

Solomon Butcher

In 1880 Solomon Butcher was twenty-four years old. His father surprised him with news. He was going to take a homestead in Nebraska. Solomon was ready for a new adventure. Solomon, his brother, and his brother-in-law went along. They traveled to Nebraska by covered wagon. The journey from Illinois to Nebraska was seven hundred miles. It took them seven weeks. They chose claims in Custer County. For shelter, they dug a hole in the ground and used their wagon cover for a roof. Next they built a sod house.

Many homesteaders built a sod house or "soddy." The materials were free and available. Sod is the top layer of dirt with grass growing in it. Homesteaders used plows to cut a few inches down into the sod. They turned the sod over in long strips. They cut the strips into bricks. Thick grass roots held the bricks of dirt together. Each brick weighed about fifty pounds! Homesteaders cut and stacked thousands of sod bricks to build even a tiny soddy. Solomon Butcher said building a sod house wore out "his hands and his patience." Most sod houses had only one room. Windows and doors were often just a hole covered by a blanket.

Solomon Butcher soon decided that homesteading life was not for him. He lasted only two weeks living in a dugout on his own claim. His land went back to the government. But he loved the Nebraska prairie and the people who lived there.

Solomon married in 1882. He and his wife set up a photography business. People did not have much money to buy portraits. Solomon also worked at different times as a teacher, a postmaster, and his father's farmhand to support his family.

Homesteading History

In 1886 Solomon Butcher had a new idea. He started working on a book of the history of Custer County, Nebraska. Nebraska and the surrounding states were changing fast. The Homestead Act was bringing many new people. The wild prairie was turning into farms. Towns were springing up with stores, schools, and churches. Railroads were changing everyday life.

Solomon Butcher visited homesteaders. He wrote down their stories. He went from farm to farm taking pictures. Families dressed up in their best clothes. They posed proudly in front of their dugouts and soddies.

J. D. Strong gave Solomon Butcher the story of his late-night roll into the dugout for his book, *Pioneer History of Custer County*. Solomon Butcher honored the lives and work of his homesteading neighbors by taking their pictures and telling their stories. Solomon Butcher photographed the Nebraska families on these pages and the next two pages.

Proving Up

The steps for earning a homestead claim were a challenge. Half of the homestead land that people claimed later returned to the government. Winters were long and difficult on the plains. Life on a homestead was lonely. Supplies were expensive and hard to get. Floods, drought, and grasshoppers ruined crops. People got sick or injured and could not work. Some people, like Solomon Butcher, tried homesteading and did not like it. Some tried their best yet failed.

Amazingly, millions of people succeeded in claiming their own piece of America. After five years of hard work, homesteaders would return to the land office to "prove up." They turned in papers to prove they had completed all the steps.

Successful homesteaders received a patent. The patent was a certificate proving that they owned their land. Many people proudly displayed their patent on a wall in their home.

The Homestead Act continued as law for 123 years, from 1863 to 1986. Four million Americans applied for homesteads. People claimed about eight percent of America through the Homestead Act. These 270,000,000 acres of land are spread through thirty states. In Nebraska, homesteaders claimed almost half of the land in the state. Homesteaders passed down land to their children's children's children. Their example of courage, diligence, and perseverance are even more valuable than the land.

Poor is he who works
with a negligent hand,
But the hand of the diligent
makes rich.
Proverbs 10:4

Lesson Activities

- All Around the USA map: Find Custer County.

- Rhythms and Rhymes: Enjoy "Weevily Wheat" on page 38.

- Student Workbook: Complete the Lesson 44 page.

- Literature for Units 13-15: *Farmer Boy*

Review Questions

- How did the Homestead Act distribute land that the United States government owned?

- What character traits do you think were necessary to succeed as a homesteader?

- What do you think would be hard about being a homesteader?

Hands-On History Ideas

- Pretend that you are a homesteader. You will need to choose your homestead, file your claim, build a house, and work the land. Maybe you'll find time for a little rest and fun!

- Use building blocks to build a dugout or a soddy.

Riding the Rails
with
Owney

At the Albany, New York, Post Office in 1888, you could bring your dog to work. One of Albany's postal workers had a puppy named Owney. Owney liked to trot to the post office beside his master. Owney loved the mail, especially the mail bags. He liked to watch postal workers sort the mail and lock the mail bags. Before long, Owney's master left his post office job. Owney loved the mail more than his master! He stayed at the Albany Post Office. One day Owney followed the mail bags right onto a train and took a ride. He was hooked! Owney became a traveling mail dog.

The Railway Mail Service crisscrossed the country to carry the mail. Owney rode along. He hopped on the train when he wanted to. He hopped off the train when he wanted to, whether it was Massachusetts, Kentucky, or California.

Owney

Owney visited local post offices. Postal workers shared their lunch with him. They also took Owney visiting around town. Owney often curled up to sleep on a pile of mail bags. Sometimes he stayed overnight in hotels with traveling postal workers. Owney even guarded the mail! He grew fierce if anyone without a postal uniform tried to touch the mail bags. After his brief stops, Owney would follow the mail bags to another railway mail car. Off for a ride to another post office!

Owney visited almost every state in the country. He became America's most famous dog. Newspapers in small towns and large cities published articles about Owney's visits. Thousands of postal workers across America considered scruffy little Owney to be their own dog. Owney made friends across the country one train ride at a time.

Owney with a mail carrier from Albany, New York

Missouri newspaper featuring Owney

315

Railroads Connect the Country

During the 1800s, American railroad companies built thousands of miles of railroad track. Railroads linked more and more cities and towns. Railroad companies completed the Transcontinental Railroad in 1869. Trains could now travel across the entire country, all the way from east to west.

Workers on a bridge of the Transcontinental Railroad

Railroads brought many changes to American life. Railroads moved everything faster. With railroads, people in small towns could get supplies more easily. Food traveled on refrigerated railroad cars beginning in the 1840s. Farmers could ship meat, grain, vegetables, and fruit to more customers. People in New York City could buy fresh California produce! Railroads made travel safer and cheaper. More people were able to take trips for fun. America's beautiful and historic places became popular destinations. Trains replaced covered wagons as the way pioneers reached homesteads in the West. Trains allowed family members to visit loved ones who lived far away.

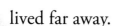

Happy 100th Birthday, America

The United States of America began in Philadelphia in 1776 with the Declaration of Independence. In 1876 Philadelphia hosted the Centennial Exhibition. Railroads made it possible for Americans from all over the country to attend.

Railroad Jobs

Railroads created many new jobs for Americans. Surveyors and civil engineers found the best route to lay railroad track. Many workers found jobs building railroads. After railroads were complete, workers had to repair them, too! Factory workers built many different types of train cars. Conductors were in charge of the operation of a train. An engineer's job was to make the train go. The fireman fed the engine with wood or coal to keep it running. Can you guess what the brakeman did?

Passenger trains carried people. Cooks prepared meals for passengers. Waiters served in the dining car. Maids cleaned sleeper cars. Porters carried luggage. Train stations had a station master and workers to handle tickets and baggage. Dispatchers planned what trains would travel on which track. Guards worked to keep trains safe. Trains also carried postal workers.

Railroads Move the Mail

Railroads changed the way mail traveled from one city to another. The goal of the United States Postal Service is to get mail safely and quickly to the right person. America had a postal service before the Declaration of Independence. Benjamin Franklin became America's first postmaster in 1775.

Railroad workers having fun

Railroad dining car advertisement

317

At first, mail traveled by horse, wagon, and ship. People complained that the mail moved too slowly. Railroads moved the mail faster. Bags of mail could travel from city to city by train.

In 1862 postal worker William A. Davis had an idea to speed things up even more. He set up a mini-post office in a train car. Postal workers could

sort the mail right in the train as it sped down the track. When the train reached the next station, the mail was sorted and ready. The Railway Post Office quickly became the main way mail traveled. Railway Postal Clerks crisscrossed the country delivering mail to every state. Sometimes Owney came along to help!

Most Railway Postal Clerks loved their job. It was not an easy job, but it was exciting. Clerks had to work fast. They had to sort the mail before they reached the next station.

Clerks had to be intelligent. Clerks took a difficult test twice a year. They had to have many post offices and postal routes memorized. They had to be steady. They worked on their feet while the train pitched and swayed along the track. Clerks had to be agreeable. Sorting bins and bags of mail made for a crowded workspace. Clerks worked in close quarters and became close friends.

Railway Postal Clerks had to be brave. Trains crashed frequently in the 1800s. Clerks were also in danger of fire. Mail cars were filled with paper. Gas lamps lit the work area. They caught fire easily. Clerks also had to be prepared for robberies. Thieves knew that mail contained valuables like money and gold.

Inside a Railway Mail Train

Owney with Railway Postal Clerks

Railway Postal Clerks had to be coordinated, too! Trains did not normally stop at most small-town stations. Clerks threw or kicked a town's mail bag off the train as it sped by. Railway Postal Clerks also picked up mail without stopping! The mail bag waited on a hook by the train track. At just the right moment, a Railway Postal Clerk put a long hook out the train window and grabbed the bag as the train sped past.

Bringing People Together

Trains connected a Florida orange farmer with a grocer in Illinois. Trains connected an Oregon family with grandparents in Florida. Trains took letters across the country in a few days. Trains brought a scruffy mutt to the post office to share lunch. Trains changed America by bringing people together.

Owney

Whatever you do, do your work heartily, as for the Lord rather than for men.
Colossians 3:23

Lesson Activities

- All Around the USA map: Find Albany.
- Look at the Happy 100th Birthday, America map on the inside of the back cover.
- Rhythms and Rhymes: Enjoy "I've Been Working On the Railroad" on page 39.
- Timeline: Look at pages 26-31.
- Literature for Units 13-15: *Farmer Boy*

Review Questions

- What is one way that railroads changed life in America?
- What was completed in 1869 that connected America all the way from the East Coast to the West Coast?
- What railroad job do you think would be the most fun? Why?

Unit Review

- Student Workbook: Complete the Lesson 45 / Unit 15 Review page.

Hands-On History Ideas

- See the Unit 15 Project instructions on pages 321-322.

Unit 15 Project
Owney Sock Puppet

Supplies

- white adult sock
- 2 clothespins
- craft or fabric glue
- 1 ¼ inch circle cut from cardboard
- markers: black, brown
- white paper
- pen

- scissors
- scraps of felt: red, black, brown
- 2 google eyes (or eyes made from two tiny circles of black paper glued to two small circles of white paper)
- small envelope
- old letter with postage stamp

Directions

1. Place sock on hand and arm.

2. Tuck in end of sock to shape a mouth. Place clothespins on sides of the mouth as shown.

3. Slowly pull sock from hand, turning it inside out. Leave the clothespins in place. Carefully squeeze open one clothespin through the sock, leaving it in place. Squeeze craft glue where the clothespin was pinching. Let clothespin pinch down over glue. Repeat on other side. Let dry one hour. (This will keep the mouth shape on the puppet.)

4. Turn sock right side out. Remove clothespins.

5. Write "OWNEY" on cardboard circle. Place sock on hand and arm. Use brown marker to draw a collar. Glue circle on front of collar. Let dry a few minutes.

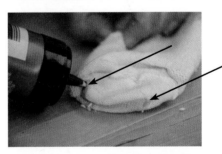

continued

321

6. Mark where eye spots, ears, nose, and tongue should be. (Marks for nose and tongue are not visible in photo.)

7. Trace the patterns for ears, spots, nose, and tongue on white paper. Cut out. Trace onto felt of the appropriate color. Cut out.

8. Stuff the foot part of the sock with crumpled paper.

9. Glue on the felt pieces and eyes. Use plenty of glue.

10. Let dry overnight. Remove crumpled paper.

11. Carefully remove a stamp from an old letter. Glue it to a new envelope. Address the envelope "Owney the Postal Dog, Albany, New York."

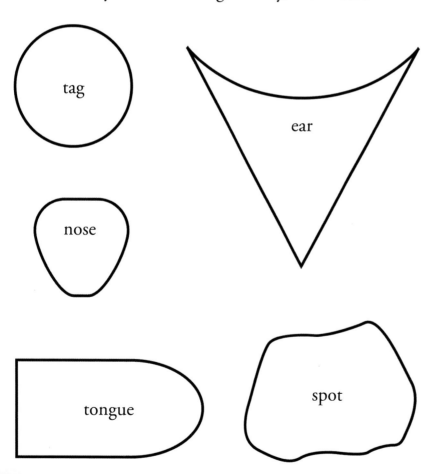

tag

ear

nose

tongue

spot

Sources

General Sources

American Heritage
American Red Cross
Brooklyn Daily Eagle
C-SPAN
Canadian Encyclopedia
Christian History
Dictionary of Canadian Biography
Encyclopedia Britannica
Encyclopedia of Alabama
Encyclopedia of Arkansas History and Culture
Encyclopedia Virginia
ExplorePAhistory.com
Colorado Encyclopedia
Iowa Pathways
National Public Radio
New Georgia Encyclopedia
The New York Times
NorwayHeritage.com
Ohio History Central
Oregon Encyclopedia
Public Broadcasting Service
SAH Archipedia
Society of Jesuits
Tennessee Encyclopedia
Union Pacific
The Virtual Museum of the City of San Francisco
The Washington Post

Academic Sources

American Social History Project, Center for Media and
    Learning, City University of New York
American Society of Mechanical Engineers
Boston University School of Theology
British Library
Center for Lowell History, University of Massachusetts
    Lowell Library
Eastern Illinois University
Economic History Association

George Mason University Antonin Scalia Law School
Hargrett Rare Book & Manuscript Library, University
    of Georgia Libraries
The Harvard Gazette
Harvard University
Jesus College Cambridge
Journal of the Southwest
Journal of Sierra Nevada History & Biography
Lillian Goldman Law Library at Yale Law School
Miller Center, University of Virginia
Nicholas Philip Trist Papers #2104, Southern Historical
    Collection, The Wilson Library, University of North
    Carolina at Chapel Hill.
North Carolina State University ArchaeInteractive
Pennsylvania History: A Journal of Mid-Atlantic Studies
Penn State University Libraries
Roy Rosenzweig Center for History and New Media,
    George Mason University
Special Collections Department, University of Virginia
    Library
Theodore Roosevelt Center at Dickinson State
    University
Tsongas Industrial History Center, University of
    Massachusetts Lowell
University of Arizona Libraries

Government Agencies

Cherokee Nation
Haudenosaunee Confederacy
Library of Congress
MuseumLink Illinois
NASA
National Archives and Records Administration
National Endowment for the Humanities
National Park Service
Smithsonian Institution
U. S. House of Representatives
U. S. Postal Service
U. S. Senate
U. S. State Department

Historial Sites and Organizations

Cane Ridge Meeting House
Carrickfergus History
Clara Barton Missing Soldiers Office Museum
Conrad Weiser Homestead
Crow Canyon Archaeological Center
Grouseland Foundation
Hermitage
Historical Society of Pennsylvania
Historical Society of Washington D.C.
Hudson River Valley Institute
Indiana Historical Society
Lowell Historical Society
Manitou Cliff Dwellings
Mariners' Museum & Park
Massachusetts Historical Society
Mount Vernon Ladies' Association
Natick Historical Society
National Abolition Hall of Fame and Museum
National Underground Railroad Freedom Center
New England Historic Genealogical Society
New England Historical Society
Norsk Museum
Norwegian-American Historical Association
Old South Meeting House
Paul Revere Memorial Association
Phillis Wheatley Historical Society
Pilgrim Hall Museum
Plimoth Plantation
Royal Museums Greenwich
San Joaquin County Historical Society and Museum
Society for the Preservation of Hudson Valley
	Vernacular Architecture
Sojourner Truth Institute
Tennessee Daughters of the American Revolution
Texas State Historical Association
Thomas Jefferson Foundation, Inc.
U. S. Lighthouse Society
White House Historical Association
Wisconsin Historical Society
Wyckoff House Museum

Books and Websites

Boston slave riot, and trial of Anthony Burns: Containing the report of the Faneuil Hall meeting, the murder of Batchelder, Theodore Parker's lesson for the day, speeches of counsel on both sides, corrected by themselves, verbatim report of Judge Loring's decision, and, a detailed account of the embarkation. Fetridge and Company, 1854.

Armstrong, Zella. *The History of Hamilton County and Chattanooga, Tennessee.* The Lookout Publishing Company, 1931. Reprinted 1993 by The Overmountain Press.

Avary, Myrta Lockett. *Dixie After the War: An Exposition of Social Conditions Existing in the South, During the Twelve Years Succeeding the Fall of Richmond.* Doubleday, Page & Company, 1906.

Barton, Clara. *The Story of My Childhood.* Baker & Taylor, 1907.

Bennett, William Porter. *The First Baby in Camp: A Full Account of the Scenes and Adventures During the Pioneer Days of '49.* California: Rancher Publishing Company, 1893.

Blegen, Theodore Christian. *Land of Their Choice: The Immigrants Write Home.* University of Minnesota Press, 1955.

Blegen, Theodore Christian. *Norwegian Migration to America, 1825-1860.* Ardent Media, 1931.

Burton, Alma Holman. *The story of Patrick Henry, for young readers.* Werner School Book Company, 1898.

Butcher, Solomon D. *Pioneer History of Custer County.* Solomon D. Butcher and Ephraim S. Finch, 1904.

Crew, H.W. *Centennial History of the City of Washington, D.C.* United Brethren Publishing House/H.W. Crew, Dayton, Ohio, 1892.

Dahn, Denise. "The illustrated story of Pieter Claesen Wyckoff." March 12, 2013. http://www.dahndesign.com/2013/03/12/the-illustrated-story-of-pieter-claesen-wyckoff/ Accessed April 15, 2018.

Dickinson, Henry Winram, *Robert Fulton, Engineer and Artist* John Lane, 1913.

Drake, Francis S. *Tea Leaves, Being a Collection of Letters and Documents relating to the shipment of Tea to the American Colonies in the year 1773, by the East India Tea Company. (With an introduction, notes, and biographical notices of the Boston Tea Party)* A.O. Crane, 1884.

Driggs, John. *Short Sketches from Oldest America.* George W. Jacobs & Company, 1905.

Hawkes, James. *A Retrospect of the Boston Tea Party with a Memoir by George R. T. Hewes.* S. S. Bliss, 1834.

Hensley, William L. Iggiagruk. "Why Russia gave up Alaska, America's gateway to the Arctic." The Conversation, March 29, 2017. https://theconversation.com/why-russia-gave-up-alaska-americas-gateway-to-the-arctic-74675?xid=PS_smithsonian. Accessed April 10, 2018.

Hill, Rev. George. "Two Ulster Heroes in America: President Andrew Jackson and General Sir Edward Pakenham." *Ulster Journal of Archaeology*, 2nd Series, Vol. III, No. 4. July 1897.

Hinueber, Caroline. "Life of German Pioneers in Early Texas." *The Quarterly of the Texas State Historical Association*, April and October 1898.

Hoffman Beasley, Maurine, Holly Cowan Shulman, and Henry R. Beasley. *The Eleanor Roosevelt Encyclopedia*. Greenwood Publishing Group, 2001.

Lawrence, William. *Life of Amos A. Lawrence, with extracts from his diary and correspondence*. Boston: Houghton, Mifflin, 1888.

Lawson, Elizabeth. *The Gentleman from Mississippi: Our First Negro Congressman, Hiram R. Revels*. 1960.

Mahin, Dean B. *Olive Branch and Sword: The United States and Mexico, 1845-1848*. Jefferson, NC: McFarland & Company, 1997.

Miles, Henry A., Lowell, *As It Was, And As It Is*. Merrill and Haywood, 1846.

Moulton, Gary E. John Ross, *Cherokee Chief*. University of Georgia Press, 1978.

Neimark, Anne E. *A Deaf Child Listened*. William Morrow and Company, 1983.

Ohrt, Wallace. *Defiant Peacemaker: Nicholas Trist in the Mexican War*. Texas A&M University Press, 1998.

Reigart, J. Franklin, *The Life of Robert Fulton* C.G. Henderson and Co., 1856.

Robinson, Harriet H., *Loom and Spindle, Or Life Among the Early Mill Girls*, Thomas Y. Crowell and Company, 1898.

Robison, John Kelly. "Agriculture and economy at Acoma Pueblo, 1598-1821." 1992. Graduate Student Theses, Dissertations, & Professional Papers. 1489.

Roosevelt Robinson, Corinne. *My Brother Theodore Roosevelt*. Charles Scribners's Sons, 1921.

Roosevelt, Theodore. *Theodore Roosevelt: An Autobiography*. Charles Scribner's Sons, 1920.

Stack, Debbie J. and Donald A. Wilson, editors. *Always Know Your Pal: Children on the Erie Canal*. Erie Canal Museum, 1993.

Starkey, Dinah. *Atlas of Exploration*. HarperCollins Publishers, 1999.

Steele, Rev. Ashbel. *Chief of the Pilgrims: or The Life and Time of William Brewster, Ruling Elder of the Pilgrim Company that Founded New Plymouth, the Parent Colony of New England, in 1620*. J. B. Lippincott and Co., 1857.

Sterlacci, Francesca and Joanne Arbuckle. *Historical Dictionary of the Fashion Industry*. Rowman & Littlefield, 2017.

Sutcliffe, Alice Crary, *Robert Fulton and the "Clermont,"* The Century Co., 1909.

Sweetser, Kate Dickinson. *Ten American Girls From History*. Harper & Brothers Publishers, 1917.

Thurston, Robert Henry, *Robert Fulton: His Life and Its Results* Dodd, Mead, and Co., 1891.

Truth, Sojourner. *The Narrative of Sojourner Truth*. Dictated by Sojourner Truth, edited by Olive Gilbert, 1850

Tyler, Moses Coit. *Patrick Henry*. The Riverside Press, 1915.

Weiser, C. Z. *The Life of (John) Conrad Weiser, the German Pioneer, Patriot, and Patron of two Races*. Daniel Miller, 1876.

Wheatley, *Phillis and Margaretta Matilda Odell. Memoir and Poems of Phillis Wheatley: A Native African and a Slave*. Geo. W. Light, 1834.

Image Credits

Original Maps by Nathaniel McCurdy
Unit Project Photos by Bethany Poore
Blue watercolor background by Pakhnyushchy / Shutterstock.com

Images marked with one of these codes are used with the permission of a Creative Commons License. See the websites listed for details.

CC BY 2.0   creativecommons.org/licenses/by/2.0/
CC BY-SA 2.0   creativecommons.org/licenses/by-sa/2.0/
CC BY-ND 2.0   creativecommons.org/licenses/by-nd/2.0/
CC BY-SA 3.0   creativecommons.org/licenses/by-sa/3.0/

title Wikimedia Commons
i   Library of Congress
iii   HarshLight / Flickr / CC BY 2.0
iv   Library of Congress
xi   *Benjamin West and His Cat Grimalkin*: Simon & Schuster; *Toliver's Secret*: Penguin Random House; *Freedom Crossing*: Scholastic; *Farmer Boy*: HarperCollins; *Mountain Born*: BJU Press; *Emily's Runaway Imagination*: HarperCollins; The Year of Miss Agnes: Scholastic; *Katy*: Notgrass History
1   Edward. S Custis / Library of Congress
2   Mary Evelyn McCurdy
3   Noah: Vladimir Wrangel / Shutterstock.com; Tower: FuzzyLogicKate / Shutterstock.com
4   Globes: Robert F. Balazik / Shutterstock.com; Desert: LOVE_CHOTE / Shutterstock.com
5   Top: Library of Congress; Middle: Igumnova Irina / Shutterstock.com; Polar Bears: Aleksandr Kutskii / Shutterstock.com
6   Gates Frontiers Fund Colorado Collection, Carol M. Highsmith Archive, Library of Congress, Prints and Photographs Division
7   Leif Eriksson: Ivan Marc / Shutterstock.com; Boat: Svetlana Mikhalevich / Shutterstock.com
8   Robert F. Balazik / Shutterstock.com
10   Nagel Photography / Shutterstock.com
11   Ruins: Charlene Notgrass; Macaws: Vladimir Melnik / Shutterstock.com
12   Bandelier: sumikophoto / Shutterstock.com; Mesa Verde: Nagel Photography / Shutterstock.com; Acoma buildings: Library of Congress; Acoma pueblo landscape: Ralf Broskvar / Shutterstock.com

13   Enchanted mesa: Ralf Broskva / Shutterstock.com; Kiva ladder: aceshot1 / Shutterstock.com; Portraits: Edward S. Custis / Library of Congress
14   Pottery: Charlene Notgrass; Acoma girls: Edward S. Custis / Library of Congress
16   Andrea Izzotti / Shutterstock.com
17   Spices: MikeDotta / Shutterstock.com; Stamp: neftali / Shutterstock.com; Supplies: alredosaz / Shutterstock.com
18   Stamp: neftali / Shutterstock.com; Tower: Stu22 / Shutterstock.com
19   Boats at top: New York Public Library; Ponce de Leon / Library of Congress; de Soto: New York Public Library; Necklace and Design: National Park Service; Timucua Pot: Nikki Montoya Taylor / Shutterstock.com
20   Landscape: National Park Service; March: Library of Congress
23   Suchan / Shutterstock.com
24   Joseph Sohm / Shutterstock.com
25   Amsterdam: Olena Z / Shutterstock.com; James: Everett Historical / Shutterstock.com
26   Windmill: JeniFoto / Shutterstock.com; Ship: Joseph Sohm / Shutterstock.com
27   Architect of the Capitol
28   Washing day: Digital Commonwealth Massachusetts Collections Online; Plimouth Plantation: Michael Sean O'Leary / Shutterstock.com
30   Johannes Vingboons / Library of Congress
31   Sunset: Andrey Bocharov / Shutterstock.com; Hudson: Everett Historical / Shutterstock.com
32   New Netherland: Jean Leon Gerome Ferris / Library of Congress; Bucket: inxti / Shutterstock.com

33 Map: Library of Congress; Rake: Aksenova Natalya / Shutterstock.com

34 Wyckoff house: H.L.I.T. / Flickr / CC BY 2.0; Before Dutch: Manhattan Island Art and Picture Collection, New York Public Library; Today: pisaphotography / Shutterstock.com

36 BeeRu / Shutterstock.com

37 Internet Archive Book Images

38 Lobster; Alex Staroseltsev; Oysters: JIANG HONGYAN; Clams: zcw; Corn: Maks Narodenko; Grouse: Eurospiders; Duck: Ademortuus; Squirrel: IrinaK; Deer: James Pierce / All from Shutterstock.com

39 Charlene Notgrass

40 Dan Logan / Shutterstock.com

41 Bay Psalm Book: New York Public Library; Genesis: Public Domain; Church and Grave: Daderot / Wikimedia Commons

42 Public Domain

45 Currier & Ives / Library of Congress

46 Victor Moussa / Shutterstock.com

47 Village: Wikimedia Commons; Tee Yee Neen Ho Ga Row: New York Public Library; Bread: Wikimedia Commons; Collar: The Children's Museum of Indianapolis / Wikimedia Commons / CC BY-SA 3.0; Doll: Sarah Stierch / Flickr / CC BY 2.0

48 Hunter: Wikimedia Commons; Longhouse: Rabsanity / Shutterstock.com

49 Portrait: Wikimedia Commons; Valley: CJ Hanevy / Shutterstock.com

50 Shikellamy: Philadelphia Museum of Art; Letter: New York Public Library; Trading: Wikimedia Commons; Wampum: Daderot / Wikimedia Commons

51 Smallbones / Wikimedia Commons

52 Morphart Creation / Shutterstock.com

53 Oglethorpe: New York Public Library; St. Simon's: Natalie Maynor / Flickr / CC BY 2.0

54 Wikimedia Commons

55 Wikimedia Commons

56 Public Domain

59 Stephen B. Goodwin / Shutterstock.com

60 Morphart Creation / Shutterstock.com

61 Abenaki: Wikimedia Commons; Fur: table Gus Garcia / Shutterstock.com

62 Verrazano: Wikimedia Commons; Pelt drying: Tony Moran / Shutterstock.com; Advertisement: Peter S. Duval / Library of Congress; Hats: Everett Historical / Shutterstock.com

63 Stained glass: jorisvo / Shutterstock.com; Louis XIV: Wikimedia Commons; Statue: Charlene Notgrass

64 meunierd / Shutterstock.com

66 Voyageurs: Illustrated London News / Library of Congress; Canoe: Maria Dryfhout / Shutterstock.com

69 Franz Xaver Hadermann / Library of Congress

70 CO Leong / Shutterstock.com

71 Hewes: The Miriam and Ira D. Wallach Division of Art, The New York Public Library; Malcom: Francois Godefroy / Library of Congress

72 King George: Sir Joshua Reynolds / Library of Congress; Boston: Franz Xaver Habermann / Library of Congress

73 Zack Frank / Shutterstock.com

74 Photo: chrisukphoto / Shutterstock.com; Drawing: Library of Congress

76 The Miriam and Ira D. Wallach Division of Art, The New York Public Library

77 Philadelphia: New York Public Library; Patrick Henry: George Bagby Matthews / Library of Congress

78 Philadelphia: The Miriam and Ira D. Wallach Division of Art, The New York Public Library; Poster: Everett Historical / Shutterstock.com

79 St. John's: Detroit Photographic Co. / Library of Congress; Speech: Currier & Ives / Library of Congress

80 The Miriam and Ira D. Wallach Division of Art, The New York Public Library

82 Theodore R. Davis / Library of Congress

83 Boston: The Miriam and Ira D. Wallach Division of Art, The New York Public Library; Pot: Kachalkina Veronika / Shutterstock.com

84 Primer: Public Domain; Boston: Franz Xaver Habermann / Library of Congress

85 Wheatley: The Miriam and Ira D. Wallach Division of Art, The New York Public Library; Quill: DioGen / Shutterstock.com; Parchment: photolinc / Shutterstock.com

86 Washington: The Miriam and Ira D. Wallach Division of Art, The New York Public Library; Parchment: photolinc / Shutterstock.com; Signature: Manuscripts and Archives Division, The New York Public Library

87 Jorge Salcedo / Shutterstock.com

89 Everett Historical / Shutterstock.com

90 Currier & Ives / Library of Congress

91 New York Public Library

92 John Singleton Copley / Wikimedia Commons

93 Newspaper: Library of Congress; Boston: Library of Congress; Pitcher: Los Angeles County Museum of Art (www.lacma.org)

94 Church: LEE SNIDER PHOTO IMAGES / Shutterstock.com; Statue: Charlene Notgrass

96 Library of Congress

97 Declaration: Architect of the Capitol; Reading: *Harper's Weekly* / Library of Congress; Statue: New York Public Library

98 Engraving: Library of Congress; Photo: Olivier Le Queinec / Shutterstock.com

99 Bridge: Zack Frank / Shutterstock.com; Committee: Library of Congress

100 Hancock: Library of Congress; Flag: David Smart / Shutterstock.com; Army: Library of Congress

101 Everett Historical / Shutterstock.com

102 Madison: Steve Heap / Shutterstock.com; Jefferson: Lucian Milasan / Shutterstock.com

103 Bust: Nagel Photography / Shutterstock.com; Gazebo: Jeffrey M. Frank / Shutterstock.com; Montpelier Andriy Blokhin / Shutterstock.com

104 College: New York Public Library; Madison: Library of Congress

105 Carol M. Highsmith Archive / Library of Congress

106 Hall: Pigprox / Shutterstock.com; Chair: Joseph Sohm / Shutterstock.com; Madison: Everett - Art / Shutterstock.com

109 Library of Congress

110 National Gallery of Art

111 Washington Family: Edward Savage / Wikimedia Commons; Washington with slaves: Everett Historical / Shutterstock.com

112 Public Domain

113 Cook: Wikimedia Commons; Wedding: Everett Historical / Shutterstock.com

114 Weathervane: Steve Heap / Shutterstock.com; Inauguration: Everett Historical / Shutterstock.com

116 Everett Historical / Shutterstock.com

117 Candle: ronstik / Shutterstock.com; Parchment: photolinc / Shutterstock.com; Adams: Everett Historical / Shutterstock.com

118 Federal Hall: Everett Historical / Shutterstock.com; Congress Hall: Everett Historical / Shutterstock.com; Banneker: neftali / Shutterstock.com; L'Enfant: Architect of the Capitol / Flickr / CC BY 2.0

119 Plan: Public Domain; Poster: N. C. Wyeth; Stamp: Brendan Howard / Shutterstock.com

120 Drawing: Maryland Historical Society; Portraits: National Gallery of Art

122 Irina Mos / Shutterstock.com

123 Birthplace: Mark Goebel / Flickr / CC BY 2.0; Fort: New York Public Library; Cow: Darya Fisun / Shutterstock.com

124 Wikimedia Commons

125 Escape: Everett Historical / Shutterstock.com; Settlers: Carol M. Highsmith Archive, Library of Congress

126 Portrait: Cliff / Flickr / CC BY 2.0; Drawing: Everett Historical / Shutterstock.com

128 Unit 6 Photo 2

129 neftali / Shutterstock.com 100681024

130 Wikimedia Commons

131 Fireplace: glenda / Shutterstock.com; Spinning wheel: David Ros / Shutterstock.com

132 Charlene Notgrass

133 Library of Congress

134 Cane Ridge: Library of Congress; Stone: Abilene Christian University Library; Cartwright: Wikimedia Commons

136 Ace Diamond / Shutterstock.com

137 Medal: Everett Historical / Shutterstock.com; Lewis: Everett Historical / Shutterstock.com; Clark: Everett Historical / Shutterstock.com; Signing: New York Public Library

138 Map: Everett Historical / Shutterstock.com; Council: Everett Historical / Shutterstock.com; Statue: Architect of the Capitol

139 Everett Historical / Shutterstock.com

142 Painting: Everett Historical / Shutterstock.com; Fort: Nagel Photography / Shutterstock.com; Bunks: Michael Warwick / Shutterstock.com; Pompy's Tower: Zack Frank / Shutterstock.com

144 Everett Historical / Shutterstock.com

145 Birthplace: Library of Congress; Other photos: Shutterstock.com (Brown and green bottles: Glevalex; Mercury: dcwcreations; Paint: Arthur Linnik

146 West Family: Everett Historical / Shutterstock.com; Fulton: Carol M. Highsmith Archive, Library of Congress

147 Portrait: Everett Historical / Shutterstock.com; Drawings: Library of Congress

148 New York Public Library

151 Everett Historical / Shutterstock.com

152 All a Shutter / Shutterstock.com

153 Tecumseh: Wikimedia Commons; Shawnee: Everett Historical / Shutterstock.com

154 Tecumseh: Library of Congress; Plantation: The Miriam and Ira D. Wallach Division of Art, New York Public Library

155 Harrison: Wikimedia Commons; Grouseland: Library of Congress; Leaves: NATURE FOOD / Shutterstock.com

156 Kuz & Allison / Library of Congress

158 KudzuVine / Wikimedia Commons

159 Needle: You Touch Pix of EuToch / Shutterstock.com; Fort: Fort McHenry social media team /

National Park Service; Drummers: National Park Service

160 Washington: James Cundee / Library of Congress; Key: Wikimedia Commons

161 John Bower / Library of Congress

162 Flag: Armed Forces History Division, National Museum of American History, Smithsonian Institution; Fort: Jon Bilous / Shutterstock.com

163 Everett Historical / Shutterstock.com

164 Art and Picture Collection, New York Public Library

165 Hat: Ysbrand Cosijn / Shutterstock.com; "ALICE": Mev McCurdy

166 Daderot / Wikimedia Commons

167 Gallaudet: John Chester Buttre / Wikimedia Commons; Clerc: Charles Willson Peale; School: Public Domain

168 Monroe: Wikimedia Commons; Stained glass: Nick Allen / Wikimedia Commons / CC BY-SA 3.0; School: Public Domain.

170 Star: Lyusaren / Shutterstock.com

171 New Echota: Jeffrey M. Frank / Shutterstock.com

172 Anna Pekk / Shutterstock.com

173 Charleston: Everett Historical / Shutterstock.com; Martin Station on Wilderness Road: Virginia State Parks / Flickr / CC BY 2.0; Fort Nashborough: Boston Public Library

174 Cabin: Zack Frank / Shutterstock.com; Hermitage: Everett Historical / Shutterstock.com

175 All from Shutterstock.com / Spinner: Dan Thornberg; Carriage: Zhukova Valentyna; Hog Feeder: Aby Angel Simon; Cattle Feeder: 3DMI; Seamstress: Vladimir Zhupanenko (thimbles, needle), MIGUEL GARCIA SAAVEDRA (scissors); Weaver: arogant; Blacksmith: FotograFFF; milker: ConstantinosZ; Washer: Jalisko (soap), 4Max (brush), washtub (Svetlana Mahovskaya); Fiddler: Baishev; Horse Groomer: 4Max; Carpenter: visivastudio; Cooks: Joanna Dorota (churn), SipaPhoto (grinder and plates); Gardener: lantapix (hoe), Ints Vikmanis (watering can), ; Waggoner: pandapaw; Children's Nurse: eurobanks (shoes), val lawless (block); Field Hands: MAKSYM SUKHENKO

176 Battle: The George F. Landegger Collection of District of Columbia Photographs in Carol M. Highsmith's America, Library of Congress; Jackson: Everett Historical / Shutterstock.com; Meeting: Everett Historical / Shutterstock.com; Cathedral: gary718 / Shutterstock.com

177 All from Shutterstock.com / Rachel Jackson: Everett Historical ; Tomb: Zack Frank; Supporters: Everett Historical; White House: Everett Historical

178 Jackson: Everett Historical / Shutterstock.com; Church: Joseph Sohm / Shutterstock.com; Dining Room: Joseph Sohm / Shutterstock.com; Front Hall: Library of Congress

180 Ross: Library of Congress; Blowgun: John Wollwerth / Shutterstock.com

181 Chief: Library of Congress; Fort: Charlene Notgrass

182 Ryan Maum / Shutterstock.com

184 Sequoyah: Library of Congress; Newspaper: Everett Historical / Shutterstock.com

185 meunierd / Shutterstock.com

186 Colin D. Young / Shutterstock.com

187 Top: Everett Historical / Shutterstock.com; Bottom: Edward Lamson Henry

188 Top: Erie Canal Museum; Bottom: William Rickerby Miller

189 Accordion: sbarabu / Shutterstock.com; Horn: Marahwan / Shutterstock.com; Lock Gate: Joseph Sohm / Shutterstock.com; Painting: Library of Congress; Lock: J. L. Levy / Shutterstock.com

190 Cash register: Charlene Notgrass; Potatoes: Roland IJdema / Shutterstock.com; Eggs: P Maxwell Photography / Shutterstock.com; Apples: Photoexpert / Shutterstock.com

191 Internet Archive Book Image / Flickr / CC BY 2.0; Jacks: Patrick Jennings / Shutterstock.com; Dominoes: osigurach / Shutterstock.com; Learning: Erie Canal Museum

192 mama_mia / Shutterstock.com

195 Carol M. Highsmith Archive, Library of Congress

196 Wilfred Marissen / Shutterstock.com

197 Top: Cucumber Images / Shutterstock.com; Bottom: David ODell / Shutterstock.com

198 Fotoluminate LLC / Shutterstock.com

199 Corn: TrotzOlga / Shutterstock.com; Austin: The Lyda Hill Texas Collection of Photographs in Carol M. Highsmith's America Project, Library of Congress; Alamo: Richard A McMillin / Shutterstock.com

200 Hundley Photography / Shutterstock.com

202 edella / Shutterstock.com

203 Loom: Ginae McDonald / Shutterstock.com; Cotton in field: Natalia Bratslavsky / Shutterstock.com; Cotton in hands: Jennifer White Maxwell / Shutterstock.com; Cotton in basket: Ken Shuffield / Shutterstock.com; Wheel: Andreas Meyer / Shutterstock.com

204 Canal: Jeffrey M. Frank / Shutterstock.com; Machine: travelview / Shutterstock.com

205 All from Shutterstock.com / Machine #1: travelview; Spools: Jeffrey M. Frank; Machine #2: travelview; Painting: Everett Art

206 Boarding house: National Park Service; Town: Library of Congress

208 RPBaiao / Shutterstock.com

209 Stamp: Wikimedia Commons; Stavanger: Bayard Taylor / Library of Congress

210 Skates: Charlene Notgrass / Vesterheim; Harbor: Everett Historical / Shutterstock.com

211 Charlene Notgrass / Vesterheim

212 Charlene Notgrass / Vesterheim

213 Charlene Notgrass / Vesterheim

215 robert cicchetti / Shutterstock.com

216 PDurham / Shutterstock.com

217 Applegate Family: Oregon Historical Society; Bull: Potapov Alexander / Shutterstock.com; Wagon Train: Library of Congress

218 Wagon Train: Theo. R. Davis / Library of Congress; Wheel: Paihom234 / Shutterstock.com

219 RuthChoi / Shutterstock.com

220 Chief Halo: Oregon Historical Society; House: Library of Congress; Band: Joe / Flickr / CC BY 2.0

221 Rita Robinson / Shutterstock.com

222 N8Allen / Shutterstock.com

223 Washington: W. J. Bennett / Library of Congress; Philadelphia: Rease & Schell / Library of Congress

224 Zaruba Ondrej / Shutterstock.com

225 Havana: Edouard Willmann / Library of Congress; Polk: Bogardus / Library of Congress; Trist: Library of Congress

226 Daniel Powers Whiting / Library of Congress

228 Library of Congress

229 Sutter: A. Morhart / Library of Congress; Gold: Albert Russ / Shutterstock.com

230 Monkey: LeonP / Shutterstock.com; Jungle: Rafal Cichawa / Shutterstock.com

231 Camp: Currier & Ives / Library of Congress; Panning: Everett Historical / Shutterstock.com

232 Laurens Hoddenbagh / Shutterstock.com

233 B Holmes / Shutterstock.com

235 TommyBrison / Shutterstock.com

236 Robert Havell / Library of Congress

237 Booklet: Everett Historical / Shutterstock.com; Handcuffs: David Whitemyer / Shutterstock.com

238 John Andrews / Library of Congress

239 TommyBrison / Shutterstock.com

240 State Street: Schomburg Center for Research in Black Culture, Manuscripts, Archives and Rare Books Division, The New York Public Library; Lawrence: Library of Congress; Border Ruffians: Blackall / Library of Congress

241 Jeff Zehnder / Shutterstock.com

242 Andrew Angelov / Shutterstock.com

243 sNike / Shutterstock.com 226348489

244 Pitchfork: Kaspars Grinvalds / Shutterstock.com; Whip: Moises Fernandez Acosta / Shutterstock.com

245 Hands: Dgrilla / Shutterstock.com; Mother and child: Schomburg Center for Research in Black Culture, Photographs and Prints Division, The New York Public Library; Fence: anthony heflin / Shutterstock.com

246 Farm: Olga Bogatyrenko / Shutterstock.com; Truth: Library of Congress

247 Schomburg Center for Research in Black Culture, Photographs and Prints Division, The New York Public Library

248 Kristi Blokhin / Shutterstock.com

249 Tinca Photography / Shutterstock.com

250 DnDavis / Shutterstock.com

252 Man: Ephraim Bouve / Library of Congress; House: Rdikeman at the English language Wikipedia / CC BY-SA 3.0

253 Drawing: Library of Congress; Window: Kevin Myers / Wikimedia Commons / CC BY-SA 3.0

257 37 emancipation / Library of Congress

258 National Park Service

259 Charlene Notgrass

260 Statue: Carol M. Highsmith Archive, Library of Congress; Painting: Everett Historical / Shutterstock.com

261 All from Shutterstock.com / Capitol: Nagel Photography; Portraits: Everett Historical; Statues: Pamela Brick / Shutterstock.com

262 Everett Historical / Shutterstock.com

263 Everett Historical / Shutterstock.com

266 Bulloch Hall: Michchap / Flickr / CC BY-ND 2.0; Trees: Upnexxdigital / Shutterstock.com

267 Roosevelt: Dickinson State Roosevelt Center; Parlor: National Park Service photo

268 Sr. and Bamie: Public Domain; Jr.: Theodore Roosevelt Collection, Houghton Library, Harvard University; Elliott and Corinne: Dickinson State Roosevelt Center; Mittie: Public Domain; Nursery: National Park Service

269 Library: National Park Service; Newsboys: New York Public Library

270 Photos and Letter: Dickinson State Roosevelt Center; White House: Library of Congress

271 photolinc / Shutterstock.com 519987763

272 Everett Historical / Shutterstock.com

273 Top and Bottom: Everett Historical / Shutterstock.com; Lincoln: Dickinson State Roosevelt Center

274 Mansion: alans1948 / Flickr / CC BY 2.0; Hill: Library of Congress; Sherman: Everett Historical / Shutterstock.com

275 Cotton: Library of Congress; Marching: Everett Historical / Shutterstock.com

276 Surrender: Everett Historical / Shutterstock.com; Funeral #1: Dickinson State Roosevelt Center; Funeral #2: Everett Historical / Shutterstock.com

277 Andrei Medvedev / Shutterstock.com

279 Frances Benjamin Johnston / Library of Congress

280 Alfred R. Waud / Library of Congress

281 Cotton: Tim UR / Shutterstock.com;

281 Tobacco: suthas ongsiri / Shutterstock.com; Hardtack: Library of Congress

282 Board: windu / Shutterstock.com; Dried whortleberries: Kateryna Bibro / Shutterstock.com; Gourd: Moolkum / Shutterstock.com

283 Richmond: Andrew J Russell / Library of Congress; Hiding: Everett Historical / Shutterstock.com

284 Carpetbag: Balefire / Shutterstock.com; School: Everett Historical / Shutterstock.com

286 Orhan Cam / Shutterstock.com

287 Letter: National Archives and Records Administration; Bible: Bjoern Wylezich / Shutterstock.com; Soldier: Library of Congress

288 Library of Congress

289 Capitol: Ben May Charitable Trust Collection of Mississippi Photographs in the Carol M. Highsmith Archive, Library of Congress; Revels: Everett Historical / Shutterstock.com

290 Top: Everett Historical / Shutterstock.com; Bottom: Library of Congress

291 Schomburg Center for Research in Black Culture, Photographs and Prints Division, The New York Public Library

292 Maridav / Shutterstock.com

293 Newspaper: Library of Congress; Polar bears: Jeff Stamer / Shutterstock.com

294 Miners: Library of Congress; Totem pole: Terri Butler Photography / Shutterstock.com

295 Inupash: John Driggs; Baskets: Library of Congress

296 Charlene Notgrass

301 Everett Historical / Shutterstock.com

302 Daderot / Wikimedia Commons

303 Library of Congress

304 Photo: OLBN Architects for U. S. General Services Administration; Letters: National Museum of Civil War Medicine

305 Barton: National Archives; Sign: U. S. General Services Administration

306 Top: National Archives; Bottom: National Park Service

308 Detroit Photographic Co / Library of Congress

309 South Dakota: The Miriam and Ira D. Wallach Division of Art, Prints and Photographs, Photography Collection, The New York Public Library; Interior: B. G. Grondal / Library of Congress; Homesteaders: Art and Picture Collection, The New York Public Library

310 Solomon Butcher / Library of Congress

311 Solomon Butcher / Library of Congress

312 Solomon Butcher / Library of Congress

313 Solomon Butcher / Library of Congress

314 National Postal Museum, Curatorial Photographic Collection

315 Owney: National Postal Museum; Newspaper: Library of Congress; Train: Swain & Lewis / Library of Congress

316 Everett Historical / Shutterstock.com

317 Photo: Everett Historical / Shutterstock.com; Advertisement: Strobridge & Co. Lith. / Library of Congress

318 Top: Currier & Ives / Library of Congress; Bottom: Underawesternsky / Shutterstock.com

319 Top: Library of Congress; Middle: Darryl Brooks / Shutterstock.com; Bottom: National Postal Museum

320 National Postal Museum

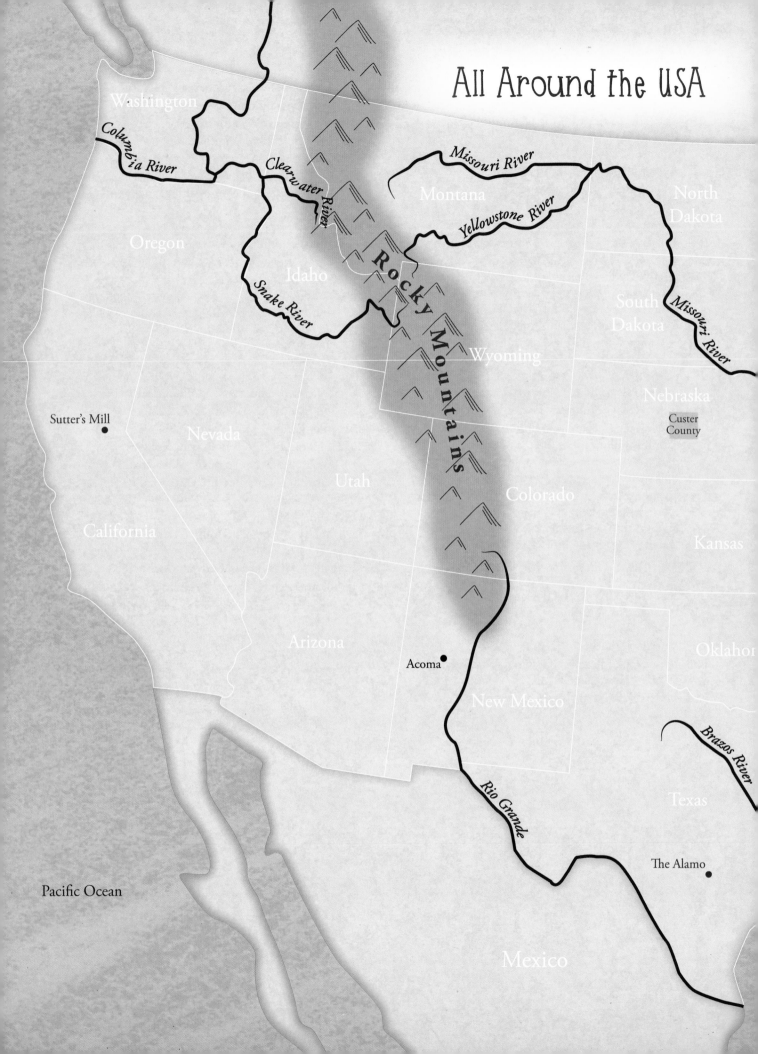

Washington

Columbia River

Clearwater River

Missouri River

Montana

Yellowstone River

North Dakota

Oregon

Idaho

Snake River

Rocky Mountains

Wyoming

South Dakota

Missouri River

Nebraska

Sutter's Mill

Nevada

Custer County

Utah

Colorado

California

Kansas

Arizona

Acoma

Oklahor

New Mexico

Brazos River

Rio Grande

Texas

The Alamo

Pacific Ocean

Mexico

Canada

Minnesota

Lake Superior

Mississippi River

Wisconsin

Lake Michigan

Lake Huron

Michigan

Milwaukee

Iowa

Chicago

Toledo

Illinois

Indiana

New Salem

Tippecanoe

Ohio

Springfield

Independence

Vincennes

Ripley

Ohio River

lawrence

St. Louis

Louisville

Little
Pigeon Creek

Boonesborough

Missouri

Hodgen's Mill

Cane Ridge

West
Virginia

Wilderness Road

Kentucky

Nashville

Tahlequah

Tennessee

Arkansas

Tennessee River

Jonesborough

Ross' Landing

New Echota

Bulloch Hall

Atlanta

Madison

Mississippi

Mississippi River

Alabama

Georgia

Louisiana

San Jacinto

New Orleans

Gulf of Mexico

Florida

Lake Ontario

Rochester

Erie

Buffalo

Iroquois Confederacy

Onondaga

Adirondack
Mountains

Vermont

Maine

Concord

New Hampshire

Lowell

Lexington

Albany

Massachusetts

Natick

Boston

Plymouth

New York

Hudson River

Hartford

Rhode Island

Connecticut

Manhattan Island

New York City

Pennsylvania

Berks
County

Exeter
Township

Lancaster

Philadelphia

Gettysburg

Potomac River

Baltimore

New Jersey

Delaware

Mt. Vernon

Montpelier

Washington, D.C.

Maryland

Chesapeake Bay

Monticello

Richmond

Virginia

Appomattox
Court House

Yorktown

Jamestown

Lexington

North Carolina

Waxhaw

South
Carolina

Charleston

Fort Sumter

Savannah

Atlantic Ocean

*Schoharie
Valley*

Mountains

Appalachian

Lake Erie

For more great homeschool curriculum and resources,
visit notgrass.com or call 1-800-211-8793.